D1156819

For Gillian Tett

Here is hoping we all help
build a better and stronger
asset management for the Good.

Best Wishes

29 7 14

ESSAYS IN POSITIVE INVESTMENT MANAGEMENT

Also by Pascal Blanqué
at the same Publisher

Money, Memory and Asset Prices, 2010.
The Social Economy of Freedom, 2011.
Philosophy in Economics, 2012.

Pascal BLANQUÉ

ESSAYS IN POSITIVE INVESTMENT MANAGEMENT

ECONOMICA
49, rue Héricart, 75015 Paris

First published 2014
Printed in France
Essays in Positive Investment Management
ISBN 978-2-7178-6700-8

This book would not have seen the light
without numerous exchanges of views
with Amundi's Asset Management teams.
I would like to take this opportunity to thank them.

We are grateful to Mrs Melanie Lanoë for the translation

For Delphine and Guilhem,
who have made the effort to go in search of finance.
May this work help show them the way.

Foreword

In this book, we argue that the investment world contains many elements of a fairytale or a story for children. It is inhabited by rational individuals who are pursuing clear objectives. Returns can be expected and the economy predicted. Diversification is easy and profitable. And the higher the risk, the higher the return.

This is, of course, far from the truth. We show that a mere confrontation with reality leaves its mark on the impressive procession of theoretical, sacred cows, of established beliefs and truths. As does the confrontation with crises, which have the ability to make any masks fall away. The risk-free asset, liquidity or the long-term horizon, among other matters announced by theory, do not exist in real life or at best only constitute a specific, individual case.

One might find this amusing, if it did not encourage a certain obscurantism, when faced with the presumed irrationality of the markets and an abandonment of investment activity. And yet there has never been such a need for sound management and allocation of global savings: this abundant amount of wealth has to deal with massive, unsatisfied investment requirements. We need new ways to rechannel investment management for the good. We need more investment science not less.

We make a claim for positive investment. We assign it the task of understanding what is happening in today's world. The essays included in this volume accordingly include an objective assessment of the discipline's sacred cows, the effective dynamic of the financial markets concerning value, liquidity and momentum, the possibility of expecting the return on financial assets and the reality of long-term investment. We revisit active and passive management and show that there are only active exposures – whether conscious or not –, the rest is (passive) implementation. We demonstrate the importance of a better understanding of the psychological referential of the Subject and of those individuals who interact within this universe of expectation and imagination, and also that of institutions and their governance. We describe the role of time, duration, memory and forgetfulness. These essays explore a number of ways to renew the traditional approaches (allocation, indices, inefficiencies which can be exploited...).

We consider that a normative temptation inhabits the investment discipline more than any other, since its activity depends on value and on the definition and measure thereof. Ultimately, the only way to avoid fanciful illusions seems to be the implementation of positive content. This is no doubt the price to be paid for a healthy, confident relationship with the long-term.

PART I

BEYOND THE SACRED COWS. ALLOCATING TO THE LONG RUN

Essay 1

SACRED COWS

Setting the scene

If it's just a question of repackaging the old stuff, selling the Holy Grail and capturing risk premia on hidden fat tails, it will end in tears again. No doubt the innovative devil never dies, whatever sweet little name is given to it: Diversified Growth Fund, target management or outcome-driven investment (ODI).

Much will boil down to managing expectations. We have to acknowledge significant changes to the macro-financial regime – the growth/inflation pairing is less readable and predictable, central banking policies are in uncharted territories and faced with a credibility paradox as the world is counting on them just when their DNA is about to change, and equilibrium levels of most asset classes are faced with a considerable degree of uncertainty.

End clients know investment returns are set to remain low. Yet they are still looking for some yield enhancement. Higher yield is the objective, capital preservation is a constraint, negative real returns are a distinct possibility and a risk. They are prepared to embrace the reality of asymmetrical returns, willing to give up some gains in order to obtain some downside protection. They are ready to pay a price for something which can help reduce losses.

Trends at work include various shifts from national/regional- to global-oriented investment universes; from benchmarks to total and absolute return, to smart beta and all related strategies which are exiting the classic cap-weighted indexes – risk biases and "time-traps" as indexes are a representation of the past; from information ratio to Sharpe ratio; from relative risk to total risk; from product push to outcome-driven investment.

The management of fat tails, risks, drawdowns and benchmark traps will remain in demand. Given the context of low yields and therefore the temptation to pile up risk premia on hidden fat tails, strategies like mean variance, smart beta, anti-benchmark have become fashionable, for some good reasons. Focussing on volatility contribution, risk contribution, or, even better, on volatility-weighted risk contribution (called maximum diversification), there are some promising ways to improve the risk/return ratio. Another way to proceed is to take an exposure to volatility as an asset class (directional, arbitrage). Any asset can be broken into at least two pieces, the underlying pure asset and its volatility. With equity volatility abnormally low (due to central banking accommodative policies), investors should prepare for a spike in volatility at some point, a mere normalisation in a macro-financial regime which is likely to see higher asset price volatility rather than lower. Liquidity forms part of this set of dimensions which should be carefully monitored.

The role of government bonds in portfolio construction has turned a corner in the crisis and has to be reconsidered. We were living in a very comfortable world during the last thirty years or so. The classic allocation framework included a (significant) government bond pocket which provided a cushion for the exposure to risky assets, based on a relatively stable correlation between bond yields and equity prices. This rosy period came to an end with the eurozone debt crisis. Since there is no reason to think that the process of repricing public debt in the West will stop at the eurozone border (UK, US, Japan – there are various candidates), one should beware. Bottom line, the efficient frontier and the utility function of (Western) government bonds have changed and they are oversized when compared with their main utility function (liquidity; a pocket of US treasuries is enough). This sets the scene for revisiting the bond side of the portfolio, for exploring "full cycle" global bond portfolios, which are truly agnostic when arriving in the alpha generation (searching for value wherever it lies), this in the belief that the broader the universe the better.

The simple truth is that most investors were not as diversified as they thought they were. Diversification does not work when you need it. They spent the last thirty years or so trading equities versus bonds in the classic 60/40 allocation framework. They were only able to count up to two, equities and bonds, notwithstanding the dreadful third category of so-called alternatives – basically the rest – not an asset class (more a marketing package), a bunch of multiple micro-exposures to the classic established asset classes.

Diversification is not dead. The question is what should be diversified. Asset classes are a simplistic approach and from this standpoint one can argue that the investment discipline is still in its infancy. Factor allocation is more effective than asset allocation and there are plenty of factors to be diversified. Risk, momentum, term and size are certainly some of them. Macro proxies for some factors or investment themes are a promising area of investigation, particularly when trying to hedge against macro exposure. Again, the discipline still relies on simplistic approaches (government bonds for inflation, equities for growth, commodities for inflation).

With strategic betas weaker in the new macro-financial regime, allocation processes and portfolio management will have to be active rather than static. The fact that betas are structurally weaker means that value relies on alpha allocation.

Advisory is a key component of the revisited equation. This ranges from portfolio diagnosis and the segmentation of the new portfolio, to implementation (there are many ways to implement a positive view on US equities, long only or long/short for example; FX exposure may help to build an exposure or to put in place a hedge based on macro fundamental analysis) and execution. The advisory function provides a form of consultancy discussion.

This should result in a better alignment of interests and more client proximity. There is also the need to explore new areas of research, such as risk factors, and for a better understanding it will become increasingly obvious that investing in understanding is critical. Diversification and allocation are powerful concepts. They just need to be revisited and rejuvenated with pragmatism and flexibility – diversification, for example, is not the ultimate recipe for everything, as there are times when concentration is a better strategy, i.e. when the portfolio is hit by a single factor.

Governance of investment beliefs. Alpha and beta policies

Alpha and beta policies are an area of confusion. The emergence of smart beta strategies adds to the confusion. In most cases, alpha and beta territories are poorly defined, the time framework is ambiguous and governance is not aligned. The very idea of implementing a systematic policy – or at least trying to clarify one – may seem strange to many. The fact is that despite significant pressure from consultants towards process-driven investment policies – and investment policies have become more formalised – obvious areas such as alpha and beta are not properly designed and defined.

Behind this confusion, there are doubts regarding the ability of asset managers to create value, doubts regarding value itself as a concept – after all, many in the investment community have come to the conclusion that animal spirits, volatility and distortions are too big to fight, like a form of self-fulfilling prophecy -, cost considerations, even sometimes conviction in the efficiency of markets, short-termism in the evaluation of alpha. This consequently results in a shift from active to passive strategies – often for negative rather than positive reasons, as moving to passive strategies is an easy hedge, psychologically easy to live with and report, a comfort zone - from public to private markets as the noise attached to the volatility of public markets in a regime in which bubbles do exist and eventually burst comes at a cost, with a simple truth: being in charge of a (supposedly) long-term strategy effectively assessed at the end of the calendar year is not an easy job when, in addition, it is obvious that public prices incorporate, at least in the short run, a reasonably large risk premium for something that is not directly linked to the underlying fundamentals of the asset. From that standpoint, private markets may look very appealing, possibly even too appealing as investors may think that volatility can be eliminated. All in all, there is a general feeling that the approach to these matters is random.

Alpha is a matter of belief; i.e. there are undervalued assets that can be identified, they tend to follow a mean-reverting pattern in the long run and investors will benefit when the gap is closed and the risk premium is captured. Alpha is a matter of conviction that there are inefficiencies to be exploited in the financial markets. It seems that there are, like in the Japanese equity market after nearly three decades of deflationary pressures and a severe lack of research coverage; like in the carbon sector, where significant mispricing offers some investment opportunities; like the development of loan funds, as a consequence of the deleveraging of banks in Europe. In addition, the very development of classic passive strategies brings inefficiencies that will eventually be exploited and corrected by the next generation of smart betas, mean variance or maximum diversification approaches. The very reason for the emergence of these strategies is the need to correct inefficiencies, which one might call an invisible hand. Once these opportunities have been exploited, those strategies will arguably lose favour and will be replaced by newcomers, just like in a Darwinian game.

Alpha is a matter of time framework. Alpha is a long-term concept, namely what is left when risks have materialised. In the meantime, risk premia collected on hidden (future) fat tails may and will expose a wise investor to severe underperformance that may last years. This is where the rubber meets the road, in an investment world where the longest definition of long-term is on average three years, the average period for which asset managers are under review by their clients; in an investment world where misalignment of incentive structures may persist despite research efforts to develop a culture of loyalty shares (L-shares) and more generally a new practice of time. Time matters. Time is a matter of culture, practice and policy. In all the alpha-related matters just described, governance and policy leadership can make a difference.

In the same way that they need to clarify their alpha and beta policies, investors must avoid fake alpha traps. What the investment community called "alpha" over the last twenty years or so was simply fake alpha – capturing risk premia on hidden fat tails – and the most popular investment strategies consisted in piling up supposedly attractive risk premia just waiting for their mean reversion to a so-called fundamental equilibrium level that never came or materialised. Fake value investment hit many portfolios. In an environment of low yields and potentially negative real returns, the management of risk, volatility, benchmark traps and drawdowns matters, as stated above. The (active) management of variance matrices matters as well.

We stated that factor allocation was more effective than asset allocation. Alpha, beta and smart beta strategies have to be defined within a factor allocation framework. The optimal combination of alpha, beta and smart beta is one of the next frontiers. They all matter and contribute to value creation. From a total risk standpoint, they are all in the same boat. Classic passive strategies may look less risky. This is not true, since their classic risk biases may prove significant. Defining an investment strategy as active or passive is not an easy task. There is indeed an official definition; i.e. a publicly well-recognised index and systematic replication for passive management; i.e. deviation from the reference index resulting from investment decisions for active management. Still, things are a bit more complicated. They all include exposure to one or more factors and, as mentioned above, classic passive management is not risk-neutral (from a total risk standpoint, they all contribute). Investors should wonder how mean variance or smart beta fit into the traditional active/passive distinction. *A priori* they are systematic strategies but mean variance, for example, should include active elements like active correction sectors or country biases or the quality of stocks. Alternative betas can also be reconsidered as active, since alternative beta indexes are real investment strategies.

All in all, the lack of clarification is a powerful source of misalignment. Investors need to define a policy. They certainly need to avoid fakes and traps. One should, above all, think of alpha, beta, smart or alternative beta as various contributors to total risk. The popular distinctions between them are, to a large extent, a producer's view. Seen from the client solution standpoint, there are obvious convergences at work, since the real question is their optimal combination. These strategies (call them factors) also involve some structural cyclicity and volatility. Ultimately, alpha, beta and alternative betas can be seen as exposures to factors across the full economic and liquidity cycle, i.e. driven by macro and financial factors, which range from real variables to interest rates.

A review of sacred cows

It is legitimate to wonder whether and how the crises have changed what was considered to be the normality. Slaughtering the sacred cows is part of the classic post-crisis cathartic exercise. Some of the cows are dead, most of them have to go through a process of reshaping, transformation and redefinition. Since many relate to what are fundamentally critical concepts, it would be unwise to sacrifice all of them, as the biggest challenge by far is to think hard about what they could and should mean today.

Starting in 2007, we have gone from one crisis to another through a long and painful process. 2007 involved a US crisis with subprime mortgages, the housing sector and credit forming the powerful ingredients. 2008 saw an enlargement of the scope and a worldwide financial crisis involving banks and credit. 2009 ushered in a new phase as an economic crisis hit, with recession in most advanced countries, deflationary forces and fears of a depression. It was not over. In 2010-2012, a debt crisis erupted in Europe, a mixture of institutional and market failure, all reverberating on a weak global landscape, with growth struggling against the deleveraging cycle, a recession in Europe – austerity plans, deleveraging – and in the United Kingdom – deleveraging, again -, subpar growth in the US and fears of recession in some "emerging economies". Exiting this crisis equation back to some "normality" has become the biggest challenge. But defining "new normality" is not easy when most central banks have entered uncharted territories and when the equilibrium values of key variables such as interest rates, bond yields and spreads are lost in transition waiting to be defined. Regarding central banks, we have to some extent entered a credibility paradox. The world and the financial markets are relying heavily on central banks at a time when they arguably look lost in transition and uncharted waters, under pressure to deliver too much of everything that sound monetary policies cannot deliver without unintended consequences. What is presented as a transitory phase may prove an ongoing change in the DNA and the regime of most Western central banks. The change is not yet formalised and the theory will follow as usual. Volcker's period has come to an end. Whether you think central banks are trapped in an asymmetrical position with no way back and are forced from bubble to bubble; whether you think the very model of Western central banking was flawed and needs a fix or a change; whether you think that long-lasting unconventional policies may eventually become conventional; ultimately, some Darwinian evolution is at work. One consequence for an investor is that normalisation, as it is presented, may prove to be a trap.

Some of the holy cows were already being questioned before this crisis, i.e. market efficiency hypotheses, CAPM, the Gaussian law applied to financial data and "normal" distribution of returns and risk, the rationality of agents, the homogeneity of traders/investors..... The crisis has killed some of them – but not definitively. We will now examine some of the holy cows. This is not intended to be an exhaustive list – but just a selection of those which we consider to be the most relevant, moving forward.

Risk-free asset

The first one states – "government bonds are safe enough to be considered risk-free assets". This immediately boils down to the seminal question: "what is a risk-free asset?" It might be said that any so-called risk-free asset should exhibit at least two features; one, effective decorrelation with risky assets and, two, perfect convergence (equality) between expected return and effective return. In theory, T-bills should therefore be considered a risk-free asset, assuming there is no confusion between solvency and liquidity – and there is some confusion, since T-bills are favoured in most cases for liquidity purposes, especially since the efficient frontier of Western government bonds has changed and their utility function has been refocused on liquidity objectives. So, assuming no confusion and a theoretical case for T-bills as a proxy for the risk-free asset, government bonds were in practice taken as acceptable proxies for risk-free assets or at least as safe as T-bills – they were not – this with a higher yield, an attractive carry and so on. The apparent lack of trade-off between the properties of a risk-free asset and the benefits of a riskier asset (return, carry ...) – no price to pay for holding the risk-free asset - was not taken seriously as the warning sign of an impossibility. In real life, solvency and liquidity account for the major risks for which yield curves give a price – the steeper the curve, the higher the price for risk. From confusion to confusion and complacency, the concept of risk-free assets has eventually been lost in translation in the same way that the risk-free asset should be seen as the appropriate vehicle to convey (literally) into the portfolio some key considerations of solvency and liquidity (mainly on the asset side) but, also, key elements of the liability equation - the definition of the risk-free asset should be provided by the specific features of the individual liabilities of any portfolio or investor, and more generally, the question of risk-free assets should be considered within an asset and liability framework.

Government bonds and portfolio construction

In the same family, akin to a relative or cousin, the second cow concerns the role of bonds and portfolio construction and, more specifically, the role played by (Western) government bonds in shaping the portfolio. We have already discussed this hot topic. We will briefly reiterate that, in theory, government bonds were considered to be risk-free assets, or at least safe assets, or at least as safe as some form of fluctuating proxy, or at least liquid assets (with a confusing tendency to encapsulate the liquidity concept into the safety concept, indeed to subordinate it): this cascade of proxies, approximation and "*à peu près*" sound like a series of intellectual defeats and a lack of precision. It is therefore unsurprising that government bonds were supposed to be non-correlated with the risky component of the portfolio – longer and longer maturities of government bonds were taken as proxies for the risk-free asset. This flawed and so-called theoretical framework contained a line of reasoning and a conclusion: since government bonds – whatever the duration, the solvency and liquidity features of the underlying – were acceptable proxy candidates for the safe pillar of the portfolio in the portfolio construction process; it was logical to think that risk was being taken elsewhere. In practice, this reasoning proved to be nonsense. One aspect has much to do with the challenging pattern of correlations – correlation is not reason. Correlations are characterised by their volatility, their discontinuity (they are sometimes very weak but, in times of crisis, correlations tend to one – a peculiar feature of the pattern of asset prices, where the time function shows accelerations and sudden expansions/extensions of the time-space, in the same way as a psychological referential where memory, forgetfulness and other forces shape the time-space matter). Correlations should be seen in the context of *regimes* driven by macro-financial characteristics but also, we would argue, by some peculiarities of a time-space function and, therefore, a time-space referential driving various factors like expectations.

In practice, correlations come as a surprise. It became clear that some government bond prices were incorporating a risk of default (Greece, Portugal, Spain). The crisis has also shown that sovereign bonds may bear abnormal levels of interest rates or yields – abnormal compared with what would be indicated by a fundamental analysis of the individual sovereign bonds – on both an absolute and a relative basis (say France vs. Germany vs. the Netherlands vs. Portugal in the midst of the crisis – deteriorating debt/growth fundamentals in the Netherlands and in Portugal did not translate into comparable risk premia, while France retained a sort of safe haven status despite an unfavourable gap analysis with Germany). From an investor standpoint, this involves an asymmetrical risk in the portfolio. While it may be tempting to treat the asymmetries as rather irrational and therefore temporary inefficiencies, it is worth keeping in mind that solid explanations may be found for most of these apparent anomalies, in the context of a psychological time-space referential, where good or bad memories of the commitment of individual sovereigns to sound fundamental policies can make a difference. It is not entirely fortuitous that, when eurozone debt crisis erupted and threatened to lead to a break-up of the zone, memories drove the eurozone bond yield spreads back to what they had been just prior to the launch of the Euro.

A government bond and a risk-free asset (we make a distinction between the two) may eventually prove – sometimes, it depends – to be pure relative concepts and not absolute. Once again, it is all about asymmetries, namely national biases inherited from the institutional sovereign structure, which will include effects of memory and idiosyncrasies; i.e. the fact that Spanish government bonds are viewed differently by Spanish investors and German investors, particularly in the context of a fragmented European bond market (the asymmetries due to national biases may possibly add to the fragmentation). Again, asymmetries do not necessarily mean irrational inefficiencies, as they can be explained and integrated as such in the portfolio construction process.

Diversification and concentration

The third holy cow states that "diversification adds returns, concentration adds risk". In theory, the statement seems to be true, if one assumes that the concept of diversification itself is properly defined. As stated above, the problem is not with diversification *per se* but with what should be diversified – and, by what should be diversified, we mean what should bring effective diversification as opposed to a flawed collection of redundant bets or themes. It is clear that the way diversification has been considered and implemented in the last thirty years has rarely been consistent with the objective of adding return – to some extent, erratic or even apparently consistent, positive returns were the mere results of a random process involving significant contributions of hazard, chance and luck.

That being said, real life portfolios have shown that, in certain particular circumstances, concentration is the most appropriate strategy to apply, when the portfolio is hit by a single factor. As evidenced by the crisis, it then makes sense to go for some concentration on low default risk or low bankruptcy risk – despite the fact that this conclusion may seem counterintuitive. The European debt crisis in 2011 provides a compelling example, when all markets and asset classes were down but some issuers were still profitable and/or safe (i.e. banks/corporates and emerging economies at that point). This can be seen as evidence that, although asset diversification is a poor means of diversification and factor allocation is more effective, factor diversification may reach a cut-off point, where one single factor takes all. Diversifying the one single factor syndrome is the ultimate new frontier.

Hierarchy of risk premia

Cow number four relates to the sovereign family: "sovereign bonds are safer than corporate bonds and emerging debt". We have already touched upon the new paradigm in the government bond space. However this goes further, embracing a broader topic, i.e. the stability of the hierarchy of risk premia. While it is still true that, in some cases, sovereigns rank first, it would be misleading to conclude that (i) they are all in that enviable situation; (ii) always; and (iii) that this has been the case for a long time without some cyclicity, some reversal or ups and downs. The hierarchy of risk premia forms part of a *regime* which is determined by macro-financial forces and a time-space referential which expresses preferences and expectations (as discussed in other works and books, there is a mix of duration, memory and forgetfulness at work in the referential). The regime provides some temporary stability, experiencing fluctuations within the parameters of the referential/regime. The accumulation of imbalances will precipitate, sooner or later, a change in the regime. The hierarchy of risk premia is first defined and presented within an individual regime/referential, accepting fluctuations around some kind of mean (i.e. the hierarchy). There is then a second level of definition of the hierarchy of risk premia, across the various regimes, a second degree of cyclicity as regimes are born, live and die. While the amplitude of risk premia – not the hierarchy – is likely to fluctuate at the regime level, the hierarchy itself may be turned upside down at the general cycle level (for all regimes). While it is always difficult to make an immediate distinction between the two levels (if one looks at the hierarchy of spreads in 2011-2012 – sovereigns vs. bonds vs. corporates and at the CDS, there was clearly a relevant indication but it was inconclusive). It is hard for the investor to determine whether a structural change is looming or not. With the jury still out for some time, as the crisis matures, the investor should analyse the concept of safety in greater detail, e.g. by considering the size of the debt; considering debt metrics (tax receipts/debt servicing, exports/debt ...), debt dynamics (fiscal deficits, GDP growth ...) and debt financing (capacity/ability to attract foreign investors and/or to absorb debt). Although it is a simple truth that most advanced countries are faced with a task of managing significant debt problems, it is difficult (impossible) to state *ex ante* that a reversal will take place together with a structural shift in the regime, whether or not this is accompanied by an actual solvency issue, such issue being more or less pronounced. There are no systematic thresholds or magic numbers which are clearly associated with points of no return since, as we stressed, there are always two dimensions at work: first, the macro-financial component or pillar of the regime – which is by far the most discussed, with a specific, fetichistic focus on some magic numbers for the level of debt -; second, the time-space psychological referential of preferences and expectations. What actually occurs is the result of the interaction of these two dimensions. These are challenging times for the investor, faced with various sources of asymmetrical risks and a reasonably low level of confidence in any scenario, from the usual central case to the most surprising risk scenarios. Collecting data in the first dimension in order to form a judgement with some degree of probability is key but it is not enough. Investigating the forces at work in the time-space referential of preferences and expectations will prove even more important. Until a higher degree of probability and an acceptable coefficient of confidence in any scenario emerge, the best insurance policy is to stay on the sidelines.

Correlations

Another cow – number 5 – states that asset classes are not highly correlated. While we would first point out that this is not an appropriate assessment of diversification – asset class correlation is less effective than factor correlation, and the same applies to diversification and allocation – the implied assumption that correlations are high enough (and stable) lies behind most investment approaches. We have already discussed the question of the stability and cyclicity of risk premia – and their hierarchy – within an individual macro-financial regime and "psychological" time-space referential and across various individual regimes and referentials. The same remarks hold true for correlations, since they should be viewed as one of the features of the regime and the referential, as defined.

Still, most investors tend (i) to focus too heavily on an *ex ante* ahistoric vision of correlations (a correlation is a time function) and (ii) to overestimate the absolute level of correlation and therefore the benefits. In fact, most correlations have risen in the last thirty years, partly reflecting some kind of self-fulfilling prophecy, where the stronger the belief in the benefits of diversification, the larger the amount of money at work playing classic (historical) correlation matrices, the lower the level of correlations within the matrix, partly reflecting a bumpier market environment, as crises intensified and proved more numerous. Both played a role. The former is arguably challenging for investors – the statement that, since *ex ante* correlations form part of any framework of expectations, from the portfolio to the market as a whole, their explanatory power can only diminish over time. Again, a lot will depend on the interacting forces between the two pillars: (i) the macro-financial regime, including the full set of historical data that provides the bulk of the "objective" infrastructure of financial markets and investment practices from the manufacturing of indexes to risk and correlation matrices and (ii) the referential that shapes and drives preferences and expectations.

With actual correlations higher and increasing compared with the last thirty years, investors find themselves in a context which is difficult to escape from and unable to protect portfolios from tough market conditions – and it may prove even more difficult to implement macro-hedging policies. Diversification – as defined – does not work when you need it. Rethinking diversification (see above) cannot provide all the solutions but should improve the situation.

Risk, return, liquidity and transparency

Next come three cows in one, since numbers 6, 7 and 8 stand for the same premise and can thus be merged: "asset allocation boils down to a trade-off between risk and return, and risk measures are appropriate. In addition, there is a positive relationship between risk and return." As stated above, when discussing classic asset allocation – we only managed to count to two, equities and bonds – it can also be said that the approach to investment as a general concept (objectives, qualities, features and characteristics) has remained simplistic – we have simply counted to two once again, risk and return. Things have become more complex with concepts like liquidity and transparency, in addition to the classic risk and return. In the same way that an examination of the universe of factors offers a promising area of research, these magic notions will require more rigorous work (risk, return, liquidity, transparency ...), if they are to be defined and ordered. To a (large) extent, they are factors which apply to various underlying assets – but it is unclear whether liquidity is of the same nature as size or momentum. Moreover, the additional list (i.e. in addition to risk and return) has not been stabilised (4, 5, 6, more? less?) and it needs to be, on clear consensual grounds, since general investment management should be expressed as a function of key variables/characteristics using the following formula:

$$Ivtg = f(x_1, x_2, ..., xn)$$

Where Ivtg = general investment management. We use the term "general" to mean the ability of any dimension/factor noted x to be relevant for as many "assets" as possible within the classic definition or the portfolio features.

x = variable, factor.

On the basis of what has been debated and to an extent concluded from the crisis, the function has shifted from f (R, r) to f (R, r, l, t), where

R = risk

r = return

l = liquidity

t = transparency

It is clear that we are left with at least two questions: (i) the degree of generality of these key factors or variables and (ii) the optimal number of these variables, since the ultimate objective should be to express a general investment function and work on its properties.

The trade-off has shifted to more numerous variables which are likely to explain more clearly what the classic risk and return failed to explain and some business models are/have been revisited, moving in sympathy (hedge funds, alternative investments, structured products ...). At the same time, within the risk component itself, traditional risk measures have come under intense questioning – tail risks not only exist but matter and stress tests are necessary; tracking errors or VAR (Value at Risk) measures are highly imperfect indicators, to say the least. Again, a lot boils down to a static, historical version of risk (see above, regarding risk premia and correlations) which is not *per se* a nonsense – the past is the time matter of investment – but the classic approaches lack the dynamics of the referential of preferences and expectations, where duration, memory and forgetfulness play a significant role. Here lies a fundamental area of research. Invest in understanding.

The biggest surprise came from the relationship between risk and return. One of the most entrenched beliefs in investment management is that the higher the risk, the greater the return and, in theory, it seems reasonably well-established that there is an additional unit of return for any additional unit of risk. Real life has proved to be different with, in practice, low risk stocks tending to outperform over time. The most successful positions have associated low volatility stocks and low leverage – a possible interpretation of Buffet's approach. This adds to the case in favour of "next generation" equities, including mean variance portfolios, for example. The bumpy structural environment of financial markets – no trend, no friend – was one of the reasons behind the positive case. A stronger case may emerge from the fact that, due to the overwhelming presence of classic cap-weighted indexes, inefficiencies have developed in the financial markets. Low-risk portfolios proved the best way to exploit them. Moving forward, this may imply that there is not an infinite amount of space for this approach, as inefficiencies will eventually disappear over time. Generally speaking, the classic [equities/bonds/ cap-weighted benchmarks] framework has generated significant inefficiencies, setting the scene for factor-type approaches – the mean variance portfolio has to be seen as a factor strategy which is overexposed to one factor, mean variance; while the specific factor exposure *per se* can deliver attractive returns, investors should bear in mind that (i) they are exposed to concentration in a single factor; (ii) the alpha attached to the factor is arguably to a large extent a beta factor, nurtured by the inefficient structure of cap-weighted indexes, and the beta factor will fade; and (iii) in that context, factor diversification out of the variance factor will be required, since overexposure to variance will, in mechanical terms, bring some imbalances and non-optimal exposures to other factors (momentum, value...). The specific case of mean variance – the focus was intentional, as a leading example of low-risk strategies – can and should be expanded to all factors. If one assumes that the significant bias of investment management over the last thirty years towards asset allocation (rather than factor allocation) and cap-weighted benchmarks (versus nothing or anti-benchmarks) has resulted in an alpha ocean of inefficiencies, research and investment positioning should be steered towards (i) setting a general factor allocation framework, and (ii) identifying specific factors that are associated with the biggest inefficiencies.

Long-term returns[1]

Two cows (9, 10) are chasing long-term returns. Their belief is a simple one: "long-term returns are all about adding spread elements or equities and, in the long run, equities outperform all other asset classes". Whatever the good or bad reasons behind the move, there are first some barriers at the entry, which are erected by the general regulatory framework, ranging from solvency II for insurance companies to financial repression, whatever its definition. Assuming that the move makes sense, there is a discrepancy between what, in theory, a portfolio could be invested in and real life. When one adds up the regulatory constraints, internal rules, ratings and benchmark limitations, all within a long-term investment horizon that proves in fact to be the sum of calendar years, then real life ultimately looks very different from what is written down on paper. This is why positive investment management matters more than normative approaches (the same applies to long-term versus short-term horizons – see below).

In theory, once again, equities bear short-term risk but higher long-term returns, outperforming inflation. The same theory states that, while government bonds offer some short-term protection (they should be less risky), this is compensated/balanced by lower long-term returns. However, in reality, the past decades have diverged from the theoretical case. One simple explanation is that growth (i.e. long-term growth prospects and expectations) has been disappointing, since the long-term returns on equities are a direct function of the capacity of the global economy (with national and regional discrepancies which must be

---

[1] See also Essay 2 – The Long-Term.

accounted for) to deliver growth consistently – as the fate of Western civilisation has developed with the emergence and then the ascendancy of the growth factor, from the first industrial revolution to the most recent wave of new technological advances, and as the so-called emerging economies eventually emerged as an increasing contribution to global growth, the reasoning goes like this - as long as growth (potential) is present in the global economy, equities will post not necessarily stellar but superior returns as an asset class. True, the apparent failure of the general rule in the last few decades has masked sharp contrasts (Japan versus emergings, to take one striking gap) in so-called advanced economies and between advanced and emerging economies. To a large extent, the gaps have reflected macro-structures (deflation in Japan, booms and bust in the US from dot.com to subprime mortgages, in a sort of creative destruction process), and some cyclicities were related to these macro-structures (global growth has, after all, proved rather weak and, above all, desynchronised most of the time, which has added to the contrasts). Micro-structures also played a role and there are various examples – structure of international investment portfolios and capital flows with some strong geographical biases that have accentuated the appetite or aversion for risk; structure of financial markets (depth, liquidity, role of end holdings by domestic players versus non-residents) and benchmarks in a static (in fact *ex post*) world of cap-weighted approaches which necessarily produce some inertia. Assuming there was a unified global equity market and a unified global (government) bond market, returns posted by global equities should have proved less disappointing than they were, with at least a zero-sum game resulting from the structural shifts of growth across the global economy. This was not the case and global bonds outperformed. Part of the explanation lies on the equity side, with benchmarks and portfolio structures imperfectly reflecting the reality and the amplitude of the growth factor that shifted from West to East, and part on the bond side, where the size effect of Western bond markets – coupled with some regulatory frameworks which make government bond demand captive – compared to emerging bond markets, which are still in their infancy, introduced a strong structural bias in favour of global bonds versus global equities. Some characteristics of the macro-financial regime may provide more additional information, i.e. bubbles and imbalances fuelled by *ex fiat* money creation, leverage and credit: part of the growth pattern – and growth numbers – has arguably been overestimated, since growth was artificially generated from credit excesses and did not reflect an increase in growth potential; this unsustainable component of "flawed" growth disappeared when bubbles burst and never really existed at all. One way to account for this phenomenon is to admit that inflation (properly measured as a global variable, including the price of goods and services and the price of asset prices; i.e. the actual general level of prices in a contemporary market economy) was (much) higher than many people thought, including central banks.

Equity long-term returns are shaped (*ex post*) by some form of multiple which interconnects growth and earnings (7% average earnings growth in the US 1870-2000) and a multiple which interconnects earnings and stock prices, with both relationships showing a short-term and a long-term cyclicity. In practice, any cyclical deviation of earnings growth (versus economic growth), of equity price variations (versus earnings growth) has been ultimately corrected by a move in the opposite direction. Two factors may have played a role: various phenomena of asset price inflation in a regime of bubbles may have accentuated the cyclicities mentioned; and the progressive emergence of a global growth factor (the exposure and reliance of any individual, national stock to/on global growth dynamics).

If global government bonds outperformed, they ultimately owe their outperformance (versus equities) to the simple fact that, contrary to theory, government bonds were not as safe as had been thought; that, as already pointed out, it was wrong to take government bonds, irrespective of their duration and their underlying fundamentals, as a proxy for a risk-free asset. In that case, higher long-term returns came with the materialisation of risk – alpha is what was left after risks materialised. Another observation is that the long-term volatility of bonds has proved to be higher and not lower than the volatility of equities. Memory and forgetfulness, once again. Long-term history shows that, most often, states will default or restructure (transfers and repayments are more rare). What was encapsulated in the long-term observations regarding bonds and reflected in the *ex post* risk premia had simply been forgotten. The long-term efficient frontier for government bonds is fundamentally different from the one we worked with during the last thirty years.

Short-term and long-term[2]

Number eleven can be said to be one of the most famously sacred, for a holy cow: "short-term investors and long-term investors are two different worlds". Any wise investor will pay attention to short-term considerations – as a matter of survival. This could be framed as the survival paradox of the long-term investor. There are, however, many aspects to this classic question. The question is often raised through the topic of short-termism. A mixture of, first, institutional and/or regulatory frameworks and, second, human nature and/or animal spirits – lead to the problem of (fiscal, governance, financial) incentives. As pointed out earlier, there is a considerable gap between what is (officially and unofficially) stated to be an objective (long-term investment) and real life. There are many reasons behind this fact of life; some of them presented (with some legitimacy) as external factors (regulatory constraints), others analysed as the product of a lack of incentive structure, although driven by some characteristics of human nature – various aspects of the definition, management, evaluation and governance of the so-called long-term policies of many institutions, i.e. their absence or at best their ambiguities.

Why is it so important that long-term policies are pursued? To what extent are the objectives, which are set for the institution's policies, consistent with an appropriate long-term framework? As already discussed, with regard to "alpha policy", there is a long way to go down a path which is crowded with contradictions and inconsistencies – since it is critical that the underlying, fundamental concepts behind the structure of most policies, e.g. delivering alpha or delivering alpha after taking account of SRI considerations, are simply aligned with what could or should be a long-term agenda. This is not the case with alpha, since the general structure of governance and evaluation is much shorter (on average, 3 years) than is necessary, if one wants to produce alpha which is in line not only with the long-term stated objective but with the very nature of the concept of alpha.

It is important for appropriate and efficient incentives to be designed to drive and direct the appetite for long-term investment. One of the most compelling reasons behind this is that the shift to long-term could prove less natural, spontaneous or rational than is commonly

[2] See also Essay 2 – The Long-Term.

believed. While there is a broad acknowledgement of the need to channel the pool of savings and reserves at world level out of unproductive static instruments and into long-term projects – we would call it a macro-truth – there may, however, very often be a different vision at the individual institution level where (i) long-term, as a time concept, has not been given a dedicated definition apart from a simple addition of short terms; and (ii) the risk attached to long-term positioning is contrary to the need not only to deliver wise returns but simply to survive. The question of incentives goes together with safety nets – and it is not clear that it should be managed at the individual institution level; it is more a matter of global macro policy. Translating the long-term ambition into every objective and feature of the investment policies which are supposed to embrace this long-term ambition is another important step forward. Strengthening the structure of incentives is an additional step, distinguishing between pure financial/fiscal drivers and elements which aim to modify the functioning of financial markets, e.g. loyalty shares (L-shares), rewarding actual long-term investors for their patient commitment.

The general view is that while short-termism may be bad in the long-term, we will also be dead in the long-term. The asymmetrical focus of most comments and analysis (on dangers of the short-term versus benefits of the long-term) is the opposite in real life, as there is a perceived asymmetry which is unfavourable to long-term. This is where positive (what is observed) approaches matter more than normative (what should be/happen) ones. The short-term/long-term debate is one illustration of potential conflicts between positive and normative investment management approaches. We should start with the positive assessment of the situation and then move on to show why long-term matters and what long-term is about. More people than commonly thought doubt the benefits of long-term investment; many do not know about the key features of asset class or investment items which take a really long-term horizon – they may differ significantly from their behaviour within a short-term horizon. Time is a matter of education.

Benchmarks[3]

According to holy cow number 12, "benchmarks are comfortable". We have already noted how old-fashioned the classic

[3] See also Essay 4 – Revisiting the concepts of active and passive management.

benchmarks were. We should add that they are a danger – a benchmark trap. They became very popular as a result of some intellectual defeat or retreat by investors and/or their governance; while alpha is the product of an active investment decision relating to a benchmark, the generalisation of benchmarks did not herald the rise of active management but rather the blitzkrieg victory of passive management. Their popularity also has a lot to do with their simplicity – it is easy to report losses and performances, especially losses when a decision has been made to shift the exposure to passive management, once again a retreat. There is, no doubt, a significant degree of comfort attached to benchmarks.

However, trapped in their comfort zones, few investors saw the storm coming, since the crisis provided evidence of some unpleasant biases shown by benchmarks generally and by classic references specifically. A benchmark is a representation of what has happened, a proxy for the world, based on average past observations and the assumption that past observations are an acceptable proxy for expectations that move slowly and adapt progressively with some inertia. This adaptive mechanism is not appropriate when there are sudden structural changes, when the very definition of Europe dramatically changes for a debt investor (the Greek storm). Notwithstanding the fact that classic benchmarks are not risk-neutral, many investors thought they were and still think they are – once again, this represents a comfort zone, which allows it to be argued that passive management, or even so-called active (very low tracking error) management, is a cautious stance, which is simply incorrect. Presenting passive and/or benchmarked active management as a cautious way to reduce and manage risk is one of the biggest lies in investment management – the actual confusion between simplicity, or even transparency, caused by benchmarks and risk neutrality proved to be an intellectual mistake and was evidence of complacency on the part of most governance bodies, since it ended in tears. Benchmarks provided the wrong map, when investors needed to find their way into new territories.

Still, it remains to be seen to what extent (whether) investors can (really) get rid of benchmarks, whatever their definition. This is arguably the second mistake by investors, i.e. intellectual arrogance, making them think that they can really move away from reference points or frameworks or, following the new fashionable trend, that so-called intelligent benchmarks can do everything (they can certainly help but, as was stressed earlier, they should be seen as an element of a general factor allocation policy; what is intelligent in "intelligent benchmarks" is to have identified the inefficiency attached to a specific factor, on the basis of which the new benchmark is designed). In reality, it is impossible to eliminate the idea of reference, while it is easy to eliminate the word benchmark. Most so-called absolute return portfolios are prisoners of some past framework or reference. By reference, we mean the underlying structure of the asset side of the portfolio; we made the point that it should be seen as a DNA structure of factors on a static basis, the dynamics of which are created by forces at work within a specific time-space psychological referential. The aim of investment management is to match this DNA structure of factors with the characteristics of the liability side. Translating these characteristics into the language of the DNA structure of factors is the objective and, during the exercise, it should become apparent that (i) any investment or portfolio cannot fly or walk properly without any DNA structure; and (ii) the most appropriate definition of the required and relevant DNA structure (benchmark) is the one provided by the characteristics of liabilities.

The questioning of the so-called "classic" benchmarks, principally due to their systematic risk bias (consequently, the passive replication strategies can be considered risk-neutral) cannot fail to take account of (i) the recent nature of the emergence and dissemination of such benchmarks (at the end of the 1990's, once the biases appeared clearly to destroy value in the Internet bubble; demonstrating at their extremes the idea and the fact that financial assets are distinguished by a positive correlation between the price of such assets and the demand for such assets, the existence of benchmarks making this proposition self-validating by accentuating the phenomenon); (ii) the backward and static nature of such "classic" benchmarks which are a fixed representation of the past (benchmark traps), although they are accompanied by a gradual rebalancing dynamic which can give the appearance of a process of imperfect adaptive expectations, and all of this occurs as if the long-term vision were taken into account in the current "short-term" prices (which is partly true, since the price of any stock will incorporate to a greater or lesser extent the long-term prospects of the company or the State which is affected by the stock) and as if the passive inertia of the benchmark was only gradually called into question, once a piece of news or event proved sufficiently important to call into question the long-term value of the asset, all other pieces of news or events being described as cyclical noise or variables which are cancelled out over the full cycle and therefore of little relevance from the long-term point of view; (iii) the *apparent* lack of consideration of the long-term dynamic and the expectations which contain it (*apparent* since, as stated above, instantaneous prices are supposed to incorporate a long-term vision and, second, the future (long-term) expectations are defined by a time-matter stemming from the past with a gradual review coefficient. (The long-term is a direct function of the short-term with a corrective coefficient of past time-matter as the temporal convergence process moves towards fair-value: LT = f (CT, M/f), where M = memory and f = forgetfulness).

Consequently, one can understand that the concepts of active and passive management are, themselves, subject to considerable ambiguities and misunderstandings. The concept of passive (which can best be defined as the replication of something, that something not being neutral with regard to risk or the factors, which means that active factors are at work in that which is replicated) is the replication of an envelope of a certain number of active items; the concept of active (which can best be defined as a voluntary deviation from a reference index, which is combined with the overall appraisal of the active factors which are already present in the benchmark) cannot accordingly imply that the sole active dimension is found in the deviation from the benchmark which results from the manager's investment decision (the said manager is often credited, as a result of his unique talent, with what is actively at work within the benchmark and which far outweighs the impact of the deviation from the benchmark which is, *in fact*, directly dependent on him – the opposite being true during periods of market downturn).

The sudden emergence of a new generation of benchmarks (alternative beta equity/bond investments) does not help clarify a situation which is already very unclear. One can see that the definition of an investment strategy as active or passive is, *in general*, not an easy task, other than at the extreme points (it would be difficult not to distinguish as active or passive the position of Warren Buffet's Berkshire Hathaway fund or that of an ETF on a major stock index).

Active and passive are recognised at the extreme points, although it is still not easy to define them.

Real life is made up of intermediate situations which are much more complex, where different levels of intensity are at play within the active or passive nature of the investment strategy. Consequently, it is at the extreme points and after a certain degree of reduction and simplification that money defines the concept of passive as an investment strategy which permits the unambiguous identification of a systematic replication of a well-known and transparent index. The concept of passive is therefore based on a technical pillar (replication) and a more psychological pillar of belief (a recognised and transparent index), since the passive is a communications vector towards a market which is by definition broad. Accordingly, the characteristics of the benchmark must be recognised and widely accepted and therefore transparent (the passive is the vector for entering into consensual communication with others, the passive derives its legitimacy from the perception and the approval of others). Systematic replication is a more technical matter (the passive is the market, the vector for the creation of a belief concerning what the market is – in this instance, the benchmark). At the same time, the concept of active can be defined at the extreme points by the *manifest* deviations (both in terms of holdings and in terms of returns) from a reference index.

Although the alternative beta strategies seem closer to an ETF than Warren Buffet, they are not, however, purely passive in the sense used above and, among the different strategies which make up the spectrum of alternative beta strategies, various degrees of passive intensity coexist (risk parity is a quasi-ETF strategy; minimum variance may prove more active).

Since the reason for the existence of the alternative beta strategies is the inefficiencies of the classic benchmarks, the "classic" benchmarks (market cap index) should not be used as a reference for the alternative beta strategies. Consequently, this implies that the TEs (tracking-errors) of such strategies by comparison with the market cap reference indexes, which are often high, are not sufficient for such strategies to be described as active.

That said, whilst the market weighted indexes provide systematic access to their composition, to the rules for the inclusion or exclusion of companies from the index – geographical affiliation, sector classification and size – together with the rules for index weighting – all of this in a continuous stream of public information -, the alternative indexes (e.g. a minimum variance benchmark like the MSCI minimum volatility index or a maximum Sharpe ratio benchmark such as the EDHEC risk efficient index) are not based on objective metrics which can easily be calculated (whilst investors can directly calculate the composition of a classic benchmark, using the construction rules and publicly available information). Alternative beta strategies do indeed assume at the very least an estimation of the risk measure (the variance/covariance matrix of stocks, which is both data and matter which can form the subject of assumptions and active bets – there is no prohibition against making a dynamic projection of such a matrix, if someone believes they have the capacity to do so) and the objective function which is being maximised (portfolio variance is minimised or the Sharpe ratio is maximised, subject to some constraints – minimum stock threshold, stocks' upper bounds, sector concentration constraints…). Finally, an optimizer is required (and its numerical algorithms). All of this is very provider specific (risk model, optimizer) and discretionary (set of constraints), and ultimately resembles something which leads to the drawing-up of an investment strategy rather than the construction of a "classic" benchmark.

This is important. By clearly distancing oneself from the methods for drawing-up standard indexes, the alternative beta benchmarks are more similar to the *real ex ante* investment strategies. Such indexes seem to have an active character, which is, as it were, innate.

If one examines the case of the minimum variance strategy (portfolios and benchmarks), it is clearly necessary to estimate the whole of the variance/covariance matrix, which precludes a simple approach using historical data and requires one to use statistical and synthetic methods (principal component analysis, fundamental factor models). This is the cost of managing the variance/covariance matrix, which may include millions of parameters. Consequently, it can be understood that the minimum variance portfolio is influenced by a relatively complex risk model and a numerical algorithm of the optimizer. In general, one sees a better homogeneity of risk forecasts which come from different risk models rather than from portfolios optimised using different optimizers (small discrepancies in the estimate of risk will determine significant discrepancies in the optimal stock weightings and the differences of numerical algorithms will accentuate the distortions in the portfolio construction). The choice of normalisation (risk model, optimizer) alone will enable one to satisfy the criterion of recognition and transparency which the alternative beta index must comply with.

The concept of minimum variance is therefore "*constructed*". One is all the more convinced of this, when, as part of an *active* gesture, one has to correct the natural biases of the mean variance. These are factors with which any index, whether or not classic, is endowed or provided, since mean variance, as such, is at the same time a factor – the general portfolio and/or its allocation must be aware that a certain weighting of the MV factor is taken (which must possibly be corrected by applying a counterbalance to other factors elsewhere in the portfolio). Such biases are known: excessive concentration on only a few sectors or on a few and sometimes illiquid stocks, involuntary exposure to styles such as small cap or momentum. The portfolio manager will therefore introduce some constraints such as x% minimum holding threshold; y% general upper bound on each stock; z% of the daily average volume times w days of trading for the limit of holdings in each stock; limit for sector and country holdings (the corresponding MSCI Index weight cannot be exceeded by more than x% and y% respectively); calibrated prudent exposure on style factors.

Such rules, because they are discretionary, lead to calibrations by the investor or are specific to the investor and therefore make the benchmark (i.e. the investment strategy determined *ex ante*) specific to the investor. Accordingly, we are far removed from the criteria of universality and recognition (broad consensus and information); and therefore from the established criteria of the classic benchmark and consequently from the conditions for the admission of the concept of "passive". It is, however, probable that this framework of criteria will cease to apply due to the rise in strength of "specific" customisation processes which reflect more fundamentally the unique nature of the investment solution for a given investor. The individualisation of benchmarks will then bring the concept of a benchmark (or an *ex ante* investment strategy) back to the function, which is by definition unique, of the expression of the equation and of the issue of liabilities, irrespective of whether the investor is an institutional or an individual.

The question of knowing whether all the constraints (a few examples of which were noted above) should be considered as integrated and integral characteristics of the benchmark rather than as characteristics of portfolio management – which would be our inclination – is not decided. This bears witness to the considerable ambiguities which persist with regard to the concepts of the benchmark and therefore of active or passive management. It all seems as if the forces at work were causing the concept of a benchmark to explode. The dual movement of (i) the individualisation of the benchmark (literally sticking to the individual Subject, whether collective – institutional – or a private person), as compared to the past, when the benchmark represented the world – the benchmark is a representation of the world – and was therefore essential, in a slightly external fashion, for the majority, which explains the criteria of recognition (widely recognised) and (ii) the weakening of the link between benchmark and asset class, which results in a weakening of the link between benchmark and beta (the asset class at least obeying the criterion that a beta exists).

To return to our discussion of the example of minimum variance, we conclude that the satisfaction of the criterion of transparency and the normalisation of market solutions (risk models, optimizers) does not manage to make us forget the many heterogeneous and specific constraints which, in practice, prevent the benchmark from satisfying the criteria of universal representativeness and recognition. The normative yields to the pressure of the positive practice which in return pushes towards new normative territories. The benchmark is literally impossible to locate, at least in this example, although there are many others.

(Il)liquidity and return

Number 13 states that "the higher the liquidity risk, the greater the additional return". Adding illiquid assets to portfolios is certainly a way to capture (il)liquidity premia – but how much is too much? While many investors realised during the crisis that liquidity is a key dimension of any asset and can suddenly dry up and evaporate – liquidity is a risk – it is generally admitted that exposure to illiquidity is consistent with the nature of long-term investment (investors). Liquidity has to be defined and managed as an additional source of risk and return. It is not certain that effective risk premia appropriately and fully reflect the nature and the amplitude of risks – and associated returns – attached to the liquidity factor. At the same time, investors have not yet (adequately) dedicated the resources and research required in order to better understand and monitor the liquidity factor itself. Capturing liquidity risk premia makes sense for long-term investors – investors who are not subject to a potential asset/liability mismatch – assuming that there are risk premia to pick. One aspect, and a lesson from the crisis, is that there was arguably some mispricing of the liquidity risk – risk premia were too low; the crisis can be seen, in part, as a repricing of the liquidity risk (and not only of the credit risk) and we should, in the future, see higher equilibrium levels for long-term liquidity risk premia as investors seek better remuneration for the liquidity risk.

More fundamentally, investors need to improve their understanding of the nature of liquidity as a separate factor from the classic factors of value or momentum. Liquidity can be defined by its infinite and amazing capacity to vanish and appear, by its discontinuity and the changing nature of its life and death regime. Unlike other financial or economic concepts, liquidity needs the other to come into existence and one has to be able to count to two in order to understand that liquidity as liquidity is fundamentally that which reflects the link or relationship (whatever its nature, from exchange to conflict) and brings it into being and also a *regime* of links and relationships, this between at least two persons, for example the economic subject and what we would call the other. This interpersonal link involves various key notions such as confidence – since confidence is the other name for liquidity, just like there are two sides to a coin. Liquidity is always liquidity for someone, in someone's view, under someone's consideration (or lack of consideration). Any financial asset is liquid for some kind of interpersonal and collective game or framework. And liquidity comes to a stop when this link experiences discontinuities or comes under stress. The regime of liquidity is alternative (on/off). Any asset is made liquid for someone, meaning that liquidity describes the existence of conditions for an appropriate functioning of the exchange, whatever its format (market, donation …). Since anything liquid can become illiquid (there are no limits to the assumption that, under certain conditions, all forms of exchange may come to a stop), investors are faced with an asymmetrical risk when assessing (il)liquidity. At some point, investors have to rely on a lender of last resort, to restore, guarantee or make the liquidity, in the same way that a "social" contract is signed (again). This is why liquidity premia involve some risk of moral hazard, since the task of maintaining some liquidity may ultimately be transferred to a central bank.

There are considerable ambiguities regarding definitions and the accepted understanding of what is and is not liquidity. As mentioned above, liquidity is the capacity of any asset to enter into an interpersonal link with the other through various forms of exchange. In order to "attract" attention from the other and create the link, other qualities such as value are required. While value, return or risk can be seen as absolute notions, i.e. fully attached to an individual asset, liquidity is fundamentally relative (to the existence of the other) and gives form to a relationship which is above and beyond materiality (of an object, of goods, of a service, of an asset).

While many investors are aware that there is something specific about liquidity, most analyses are confronted with various sources of confusion. Liquidity is often defined in the conceptual framework as a stock and at the same time as a flow, i.e. as a proxy for portfolio flows or, more generally, for capital flows. On the one hand, there is a degree of confusion between money and liquidity, with liquidity taken as a given pool of money, an external variable driving developments in the financial and real spheres (the bigger the stock of money, the higher the inflationary impact, a simplistic reading of the quantitative theory of money, an equation where money drives all variables rather than an identity where $MV = PT$). On the other hand, we can find various measures of *variations* in certain ratios, where the stock of money is put to work in the real economy (M/Y, where Y is a proxy for production) or in the financial sphere (M/T, where T is a proxy for financial transactions) – where M is the stock of money or some segment or counterpart of it. Liquidity is used here as a concept of velocity – the amount of production or financial transactions per unit of the money stock. What is liquid is what circulates in the real and financial spheres and the general theoretical framework behind it is a vision of the cycle driven by money as an external factor, an active non-neutral factor explaining price movements. What we would call the monetary interpretation of liquidity is the first of three pillars at work in the financial markets.

The second pillar is closer to Keynes' concept of preference for liquidity, where the focus is on the nature and duration of assets included in the money stock, typically short-term/cash-type instruments versus long-term assets. In this case, ratios of M to M1 or base money will be seen as a proxy for the liquidity or the liquefaction (read derivative, liquidity as a variation).

The third pillar is based on the balance of payments, (total or partial) measures and elements, often on a variation basis (an approach based on flows rather than stocks). Basic balance, current account, trade balance, the balance of long-term capital and its breakdown and so on: these elements are used to explain the evolution or the determinants of financial variables (interest rates, foreign exchange movements, equity prices). An absolute analysis of one country is accompanied by a relative analysis of the evolutions of various countries or regions or even the central role of the US balance of payments across the global economy. The balance of payments, together specifically with some of the elements like the current account or the basic balance, are considered as highly relevant elements of what we would call "macro-liquidity", because they can be seen as proxies for (net) savings – typically the current account and the nature of the financing of any deficit in the current account (current account and balance of long-term capital, i.e. basic balance).

Our objective here is not to effect an exhaustive analysis of liquidity (we will come back to this topic later in this work) but to show that many holy cows are not easy to define (like liquidity) but are easy to recognise (when the crisis hits); above all, that *positive* analysis is required, i.e. an analysis of what people tend to understand and use in the market economy. Liquidity provides a perfect example. Positive analysis of investment will focus on how liquidity is understood, how it is defined, measured, typically what sort of indicators of liquidity are used and how by the market players – we have identified "macro-liquidity" indicators based on a measure extracted from the balance of payments or one of the elements thereof, "micro-liquidity" indicators based on a ratio between a measure of real or financial transactions and the stock of money, and "micro" indicators" based on a measure of the stock of money or, more often, the relative movements of two more or less liquid sections of the stock of money. Positive analysis matters because every set of indicators contains a definition of liquidity;

because, in real life, the action of market players is based on the sum of sometimes contradictory definitions, imperfect indicators and grey areas. However, this is the way it is, in reality, beyond any more theoretical approaches. The same applies to the concept of value as it is actually used in the financial markets – including various biases – rather than those concepts which may be more satisfactory on an intellectual basis but which provide little information as to how representations, actions and (asset) prices form in the global financial marketplace.

Imperfect normality

Positive analysis matters because the much-debated concept of normality (what is "normal", the new "normal" …) is *in fine* based on an imperfect set of indicators, just like the ones described above relating to liquidity and just as imperfect as the representation of the world they symbolise. The positive analysis of these imperfect norms and anchors applies to monetary policies and the art of central banking. Holy cow number 14 states that "everything is under control in the art of central banking". Still, there are changes at work: conventional versus unconventional monetary policies; questions relating to quantitative easing (efficiency, medium- and long-term impact on growth and inflation, exit strategies, the credibility of central banks and their mistakes).

Essay 2

THE LONG-TERM

In search of a positive concept of long-term

Long-term investment is akin to an illusion or the dodo. Considerable ambiguities distinguish the concept of the long-term – which is clearly not a series of short-term sequences. The long-term is not a sum (of sub-periods, of factors ...) but rather a culmination (a value of equilibrium is then attained) or, which is not exclusive, a process leading to the said point of equilibrium, a process of trial-and-error and apprenticeship. The long-term is that which cannot be precisely standardised in and by time, since it is more a status, a state (in the same way one speaks of the state of a gas) than a given point of temporality. The long-term is normative and unobservable – to such an extent that one may wonder whether it is an artefact, the necessary product of a reasoning which establishes value as a substance and postulates (a-temporal) equilibrium. Moreover, a certain number of people are increasingly beginning to doubt the existence of a fundamental value within a reality which is made up of animal spirits and rationality which is, at the least, limited.

In order for there to be something which we can call "long-term savings", there must be a long-term investor and therefore someone who believes or thinks that there exists a fundamental value towards which (process, culmination) the financial asset might be directed after possibly distancing itself from it. These connected premises form a self-validating proposition. The opposite is also true: if one does not believe or think that the fundamental value exists, then the lack of an investor and of long-term savings validates the lack of a point of equilibrium. The short-term is, on the contrary, positive and observable.

A certain number of observed behaviours are frequently cited in order to "explain" the difficulties of the concept of long-term. The same is true of the reduction in the average holding periods of assets – which is, strictly speaking, short – of the dictatorship of the calendar framework, of fears, ultimately of short-termism. It is not strictly speaking an explanation of what might act as a brake but rather the observation that, in real life, the behaviours do not seem to be incorporated in the concept of long-term. And to try and explain the difficulties of long-term by the existence of a "short-termism" clearly shows the ambiguity. The interplay of constraints and incentives, the frameworks of rules and regulations may in turn seem to provide a reason – that the concept of long-term is constrained by an inadequate institutional interaction which should be modified – but the argument does not appear to be definitive. In any event, the long-term remains hidden, concealed (by short-termism, by the observed action of the individual Subject, by institutional factors). The long-term should and could be revealed by a voluntary turnaround or imposed by individual behaviours and institutions. The theory which can be described as "realistic" would suggest that no substance (value) or point on the horizon (equilibrium) exists since they are so well concealed, masked, unobservable and outside temporality (this may be recalled by the phrase "we will all be dead in the long-term") and suspected of having been invented by speech and language. According to this theory, there is only what we call short-term within a framework of action by individuals and institutions which is consistent with "reality", i.e. that which is observed. In this context, the affirmation of the long-term implies a combat in defence of substance and equilibrium (the point of value of the long-term) and the "belief" in the possibility of modifying (normative) that which is observed.

The concept of long-term therefore joins the weakened family of unobservable concepts (real, natural variables, equilibrium, and fundamental value) which can therefore be described as premises.

Without assessing the difficulties posed by the concept of long-term, one finds oneself in a process of analysis which is both normative (that which should be – we make the assumption that the existence of such a concept is a good thing) and positive (that which is, the starting point in the observation). One axis is the interaction of the various players with regard to the long-term – one can note a general heterogeneity where one has to differentiate between external constraints and factors which are experienced and the mere lack of desire to incorporate the long-term or even to accept the principle thereof. A second axis, which is classic and normative, involves stating the negative effects of an inadequate consideration of the long-term. Accordingly, the issue was to reduce non-productive savings, a store of pseudo-value. The existence of surpluses (savings, foreign exchange reserves) which have been inadequately remunerated (generally packed into government securities which are deemed to be safe) against the backdrop of significant investment requirements, under-employment and low global demand carries a cost and results in a crowding-out to the detriment of research and development, the consideration of ESG criteria and particularly the funding of SMEs.

Such a global mismatch creates a paradox. There is no lack of savings (or monetary creation *ex nihilo*, which is placed in the same category as savings) but they have not been sufficiently attracted to the most productive channels. There is a geographical imbalance between pools of savings and dissavings, as well as a structural imbalance. Accordingly, although there is an abundance of savings, the financial savings structure of all the economic agents is, generally, of short maturity, directed towards state securities and very little towards the funding of the economy. The state sphere has produced a *crowding-out* effect in the context of a high and increasing level of debt where the recycling channels are more or less restricted or more probably prompted. These crowding-out phenomena, which reflect a biased structure of state or national preferences, lead to pro-cyclical investment behaviours. The new phase of the crisis which commenced with effect from 2008 added to these features (change of volatility regime, both higher and more volatile; multiple confusions between risk-free assets and liquid assets, between savings and money...) and created a paradox: although the crisis resulted in a sudden break with the relationship with time, there had never been so many references to the "long-term". Although, at a macro level (e.g. large worldwide equilibria of savings and investment), the inefficiencies and "maladjustments" are visible and convincing, at a more micro-economic and financial level of individual and institutional attitudes and rationalities, one notes, however, a certain number of principles which lead the players to behave as they do within a framework which is ultimately fairly deterministic. This is true of the principles behind the national fragmentation of the eurozone bond markets with intentional recycling behaviours on the closed national circuit of domestic savings (a possible similarity can be seen with the phenomenon of forced savings in a crisis, in the same way that, during the preceding euphoria, the aggressive use of credit to fund growth left the level of savings at an artificially high level, particularly financial savings, which means that the savings available for financial assets were both artificial - that portion of growth which was excessively funded by debt – and forced). The principle behind forced savings in government debt instruments, which therefore has a crowding-out effect on "productive" savings, coexists in an impressive manner with a discourse and injunctions in favour of funding growth over a "long-term" perspective. The concept of long-term naturally resides within the normative, which in turn operates alongside the positive, where observations provide evidence without there being any possible hesitation regarding other attitudes and rationalities.

Saving the concept of long-term

One can, consequently, understand the doubt that crosses certain minds. What if, quite simply, the long-term were a normative arrangement, a necessary construction at a certain moment in the drawing-up of the economic discourse but which does not, therefore, remain relevant for ever or for long?

This may, for some, lead to the conviction that this concept of the long-term must be saved by demonstrating that it is possible to make it appear by stretching the practices and the institutional framework. For others, one has to conceive at the outset of a framework which no longer contains the long-term as a normative point of equilibrium and thus create new determinants and equilibria for it.

Practices, incentives and institutions

The regime of constraints and incentives which had to be modified includes *inter alia* aspects of communication and education – ranging from the understanding of the phenomena of mean reversion, which form the basis of the long-term structure of the temporal horizons, to the teaching of some counterintuitive facts, e.g. the fact that the long-term volatility of bonds is greater than that of shares, which might in part explain the surprisingly higher returns on investment noted over long periods and up to the networking of the potential long-term investors, since what may link reflections and practices seems to be involved in a possible change of regime of practices and expectations, a form of apprenticeship which is partly self-validating by means of example (the mobilisation on the network of sovereign funds is one example thereof).

The regime of incentives has not been left behind. The principal themes concern the legibility and the structure of the fiscal framework – horizons, risk – with the fairly consensual and practical idea within the restricted economic context that one needs to restructure taxation within an unchanged global framework. The incentives to hold securities for longer, remunerating loyalty in the form of Loyalty shares or to invest in a "contrary" manner – which enables mispricings to be corrected and also enables the phenomena of mean reversion to be validated – in the form of Capital Access Bonds, represent a second pillar of incentives; the structures of governance and supervision (boards, tenure) are also included in this task. Finally, Asset Managers are expected to design more transparent products which provide adequate matched funding for liquidity and implement remuneration structures which are compatible with the long-term incentives desired; and, for their part, the producers of norms – solvency, risk, performance – are expected to try and find consistency and the most homogenous framework.

The use of incentives leads one to assume, rather too rapidly, (i) that there is a neutrality or indifference between the concepts of short- and long-term; (ii) that "short-termism" is essentially the product of a certain incentives structure; and (iii) that consequently it is relatively easy to redirect the whole system of savings and investment. The discourse is a normative one and obstructs only the incentives, precluding the possibility that the positive description of the attitudes and behaviours of the economic Subject is fundamentally that of a "short-termist" decision-making system. Although the framework for the incentives and the institutional constraints can indeed be modified, nothing is said about the positive (vs. normative) behaviour of the players. Unless it incorporates this realistic dimension, the task of promoting the long-term runs the risk of defending a normative, transcendental zone, which is out of reach and possibly moralistic, forming part of determinations other than those which are *actually* those of the Subject and which guide his actions and in any event offers a zone of tensions and contradictions. The concept of the long-term must be tied to a theory of the Subject, of action and time and must be linked to a vision of the dynamics of the institutions and therefore of the norms.

On a more immediate and more technical level – but which still forms part of the same considerations discussed above – it can be argued that norms and constraints which define the investment universes for the allocation of savings and investors' decisions (premises and practices of diversification, benchmarks, multiple norms of external or internal ratings and limits) have an adverse effect on the long-term's emergence into reality. It will once again involve, in a normative approach, the substitution of new norms for the former inappropriate norms. The distinction between short and long-term will essentially be a question of norms and these concepts will be normative. We are proposing a positive approach, starting first from the Subject and second from the institutions *as they are*. It is, however, undeniable that such factors play a role but are undoubtedly the symptoms of a serious difficulty in defining and establishing the concept of the long-term and its utility function in a manner which is consistent with a realistic theory of the Subject's action in time rather than the primary cause of the difficulty.

Similarly, at the product level, the technical approach to the problem of the "long-term" highlights the extent to which the design and dissemination of products by the players in the worlds of savings and investments hinder the disclosure of the "long-term" (once again the idea of an unobservable substance which is removed from reality by reality itself, i.e. the positive practices which are at work there). Existing channels and products, new formulations and supports, a whole significant trend develops around what is often presented as a reform. It is fairly accepted that the broadening of the field of investments available to small- and medium-sized businesses, to take one example, forms part of a move to allocate savings to the economy, on a long-term basis, when it accepts, although with some difficulty, the reality of the illiquidity which distinguishes and defines it – this represents a difficulty, since the requirement of liquidity for the asset seems to characterise the general expectation of the players, or at least the link between (il)liquidity and "long-term" does not appear to be explained!

One finds, in the link between illiquidity and "long-term" – the premise which states that a long-term investor must be able to extricate himself from the total requirement that the asset be liquid, in order to obtain, which is the price to be paid, the price of long-term equilibrium which justifies his investment. These are the substantial features of the concept of long-term, separated from "traditional" temporality and inhabiting a different ontological zone (a zone of that which *is* of itself and not that which is in a state of not yet being, which is the territory of the shorter-term). Accordingly, the liquidity which indeed appears within the relationship with the other (something is liquid, if it makes itself liquid *for others*), becomes weaker within the ontological horizon of the concept of long-term, which is an arid zone where to some extent the other, and thus the exchange, are less present or indeed absent.

One can also see, at the level of incentives, the structure of the constitution of savings which, if left to its sole spontaneous determinants and the decisions of the players, would prove to be insufficiently "long-term", thus justifying corrective action, i.e. to save earlier in order to stick to the life-cycle, since product solutions may accompany this new technical variation to the incentives (target-maturity funds).

The funding role of the long-term investor

There can be no long-term investment without a long-term investor and no long-term investor without a self-fulfilling belief in mean reversion within the regimes of individual means which are more or less stable (and therefore in the fluctuations and deviations by comparison with the said mean, i.e. mispricing). The question of the long-term is that of the (long-term) funding of the economy. From this point of view, the start of the century, given the context of successive crises and the weakening of a certain number of banking players who were forced to deleverage, has witnessed the confirmation of the asset managers' essential role in recycling and routing savings (savings is used in the wide sense here, to include foreign exchange reserves and all counterparties of the monetary base, and therefore to include monetary creation *ex nihilo*), and has witnessed the emergence of an increasingly direct funding of the economy; with disintermediation and deleveraging sustaining the trend. Accordingly, one sees loan funds (midcaps, infrastructure, real estate ...) originated from multiple sources by the investment banks, analysed and put together by the asset managers (the investment banks retain part of the risk) and, even further down the direct link with the asset manager, bond funds issued for example by small businesses, *especially* in the context of the creation of a pool of end-investors organised by the asset manager. Thus emerges a model with a new approach which starts with the investors and then moves on to origination.

The internalisation by the asset manager of the role of primary equity market manager, faced with the cost generated by transactions on the primary equity market, is one of the examples of this transformation – the durability of which remains to be seen, once the banks' situation is restored. It means accessing new sources of information, e.g. by deciphering the composition of an order book in order best to gauge purchasers' potential and the evolution of the stock price after the IPO or the accelerated book building. It also means facilitating access to new sources of liquidity, thus by arranging for a reverse inquiry or by selling through accelerated book buildings for a guaranteed price in the event of significant and/or not very liquid positions. It means improving the asset manager's information (about the primary equity market) – e.g. by advising the company manager and the negotiating table to postpone an investment in order to wait for a liquidity event which will be executed with a discount. It also means placing pressure on the broker from a centralised primary equity market position which will allow the best allocations to be obtained. Finally, it means helping to improve the asset manager's image as a responsible long-term investor – since image and practice are merged. Accordingly, a regular dialogue will be developed with the management of listed companies at a *very early stage* of the IPO or by underwriting the capital increases and also with the clients, e.g. by participating in market debates regarding good practice for the primary equity market.

The funding role – which is more or less direct – and the role of recycling and routing of savings thus contribute to the corporate and social responsibility role of the asset manager. The concept of routing refers to that of the (optimal) allocation of the capital (savings) and the proper running of the market. The concept of recycling refers in turn to that of the necessary transformation of savings within the structure of its underlying assets and/or its geographical destinations and objects. The two concepts are located well beyond that of the role of collection, which is most commonly used to define the action of the asset manager, a role which he retains moreover.

Mispricings

Another illustration of the concept of long-term at work can be found at the intersection between the asset manager's corporate responsibility role and market inefficiency. One example is the mispricing of carbon (state subsidies versus taxes) in the context of global warming. The environment is complex (technologies which are not very stable, state interventions in pricing, the politicisation of the academic debate...) and the long-term horizon does not seem very propitious for investments. Added to this is a certain number of incidents with clients, such as frequent losses recorded for "carbon investments", including frequent references to the case of CalPERS. Moreover, there is a debate surrounding the social responsibility objectives which may come into conflict with the objectives and responsibilities of strict economic performance – other than for clients which belong to the sovereign segment. The fact that the expertise is confined within a niche and that the field of activity is not standardised – with a multiplication of solutions – does not help. The use of generalised benchmarking for all the investments and the shortening of the investment horizons referred to above will often act as a deterrent.

However, faced with this problem, which is as much a financial one – the operation of the market, in this instance, market failure – as a social one – global warming leads to an issue of political economics – certain players (asset managers acting on behalf of institutional clients, pension funds or sovereign structures such as central banks or sovereign funds) have explored certain solutions. These include a low-weighted index with low tracking error, the principle of which involves selecting a reference index, removing polluting companies according to the criterion selected for the emission of carbon gas and reducing the tracking error. Such a solution enables a view to be taken regarding a possible change in the valuation of companies resulting from the repricing of carbon, while also buying time for only a nominal price due to the low tracking error. The advantage of such an approach is that it reduces the complexity of the subject to a series of simple propositions which mobilise different skills (carbon filter, reduction of the tracking error) and creates a standard.

An additional example (and a very visible one, given the public debate arising from it) is the ESG criteria (the SRI approach incorporating the environmental, social and governance dimensions).

There has been a long running debate regarding over-performance which is (or not) linked to such criteria – the lack of hindsight and the still recent, modest and heterogeneous dissemination of the criteria within practices urge caution in a sector where the players are concerned (at the least) about the neutral impact of the criterion on the return. Once again one is dealing with a field which is not standardised – dominated by the multiple practices (or lack thereof) linked to historical, geographical and cultural differences. However, the field of communication needs to be structured by norms. There is a "normative" bias in favour of financial criteria and multiple cultural biases which make it difficult to define and expand a norm. In addition, there is the issue of the conflict of objectives, a tension between social responsibility and pure economic performance. Although the ESG approach is undoubtedly tied to the question of the long-term, it is not surprising, at this early stage of the emergence of the subject and approaches, that the issue is peripheral and generally requires niche skills. As with carbon, investment solutions may seek to combine the selection of a relevant index (high sustainable index) and the reduction of the tracking error. Once again, a greater normative homogeneity can be sought with regard to the communication of the ESG criteria. The emergence of integrated reporting lends support to the movement.

As we stated, proving the existence of a short-termism does not necessarily lead to the existence of a concept of long-term. It is, however, factually true that such short-termism is increasing on the financial markets (the period for which investments are held and high frequency trading, in particular). It can be deduced, as a strong central assumption, that businesses or institutions which manage savings can be diverted away from long-term investments. In particular, the disincentive to produce research and analysis – the utility function of which seems correlated to the temporal horizon – is both a factor which penalises certain players (asset managers, financial institutions which carry/manage savings) and also an element which makes the proposition that "short-termism kills or prevents the long-term from emerging" self-validating. The polarization of the debate on the rise of short-termism (which exists and is visible) tends to mask or appraise the necessary definition of the long-term (which may not exist and is not visible). This means that the concept of the long-term must be understood as such and for itself, if only in order to deal with its appearance as an undiscovered factor, which causes the market players to harbour doubts.

Although we remain in an approach which uses the short-term to structure the concept of the long-term – with serious risks (the long-term, a series of short terms; the long-term, a short term which has been rectified) – some practices have emerged. These include in particular the idea of generalising fidelity rewards with the extension to L-shares, a simple principle of rewarding loyalty over the long-term through the allocation of preference shares. (The idea once again that the long-term must be supported by incentives, which may imply that, without such support, the concept of the long-term, left as it were to its own devices, cannot *spontaneously* maintain itself). The alignment of the remuneration structures over the long-term (fees policy) also forms part of the same approach. The educational challenge of explaining and communicating goes together with the challenge of dissemination through campaigns which bring together the greatest number of issuers (bargaining power) and practical initiatives with certain clients (proposal to calculate the fees over a long period). The asset manager, by mobilising his bargaining power, by proposing a better performance than that offered by the classical indexes and by basing the calculation of fees over the long-term, may also seek to align the component parts of his offer – fundamental analysis, financial solutions and tools for over-performance and fee structure. Ultimately, it is a question of giving financial significance to the long-term, which does not spontaneously seem to have one and of managing to monetise this long-term horizon. Other fields exist – insurance principles which are naturally consistent with the long-term and liquidity principles, the dynamics of which can be organised by the asset manager over the long-term, since liquidity and time seem to have a negative correlation.

The long-term as duration and a process

The general and fairly consensual idea is that to move from a short-term investment horizon to a long-term structure may create a winning situation for all the players (businesses, investors, society). Before considering the possible determinants of such a movement (incentives), it should be noted that the short-term framework and the long-term framework are rarely defined, which results in a considerable degree of ambiguity; it seems established that a translation or substitution would not only be desirable but also possible through modification of the preferences or arbitrages (incentives); it is implied that there is an equivalence between value and the value allocated to time – which seems fair – and that the preference for the long-term is desirable – which is possible in normative terms but comes up against the positive observation of a certain preference for the short-term; the sequencing of time and of horizons (between short-term and long-term) stems from a spatial theory of time, whilst the time of economics and finance is more a *continuum* of non-linear duration containing contractions and dilations and is closely linked to a psychological time referential of the acting Subject; in this regard, the spatial classification of time within the categories of the past, present and future is incorrect and therefore the distinction between short-term and long-term is artificial or at least a source of confusion – as is the idea that the short-term *precedes* the long-term, whilst in fact the temporal levels coincide and are superimposed.

That said, one can distinguish the possible resulting gains for businesses from the active existence of long-term investors – essentially two, financial over-performance due to the incorporation of ESG-type criteria, more generally criteria which reflect the structure of the long-term (it is not easy to determine such a structure, i.e. to describe the concept of the long-term or, more prosaically, to identify the elements which are actually relevant for a long-term horizon); and the expected reduction in the cost of capital. For the good society, the incorporation of the long-term (e.g. the ESG criteria, but this is only one of the possible structures for the concept of the long-term) is expected to produce positive externalities and contribute to sustainability (a normative element of the definition of long-term which is largely self-validating – the long-term is that which lasts – which nonetheless has the advantage of establishing the long-term as a process; *the long-term as duration and a process*; we will come back to this). It is assumed that greater sustainability is achieved by means of improved macro-economic stability and a modification of the structure of the economy resulting from targeted investment incentives in certain sectors or initiatives (green infrastructure, for example). Finally, for investors, the principal gain lies in the prospect of producing additional returns by means of the monetisation of the long-term. Counter-cyclical investment lies at the heart of this assumption, its performance being presumed to be greater than that of a mere momentum strategy. Behind this assumption lies the strong premise of the existence of a concept of value defined by a substance which unifies the temporal fields and sequences and which we have located next to duration, as a substance of economics, which overlooks and determines the cycle from a dynamic convergence point (dynamic, because duration is in motion) which is specifically the long-term insofar as the concept of long-term is not viewed as a temporal point but as a substance. It should be noted, finally, that the existence of a long-term horizon is expected to enable investors better to estimate the future value of their investments, and therefore to make a better quality allocation and generate greater profitability than that of short-term investors. (The introduction of L-shares may consolidate this point). The concept of the long-term and that of expectations can thus be seen to be two sides of the same coin. It involves both the organisation of a favourable framework for a more stable production of expectations and a method of directing the formation of expectations (incentives). At the end of the day, the existence of a concept of long-term entails a theory of expectations with which it merges, an analysis of the relationship between the Subject and time, and therefore an analysis of value as value rightly allocated to time, value which structures the processes of mean reversion and which justifies the counter-cyclicity of investment strategies.

The natural long-term investor

Accordingly, the framework for the analysis is an ecosystem which contains businesses, investors and society, driven by short-term forces and which is confronted with a certain number of difficulties, once it decides to move towards a long-term horizon. Such challenges include *inter alia* governance, remunerations, the benchmarks which enable a long-term performance to be valued, risk metrics and institutional and regulatory constraints. Such difficulties exist at different levels of the ecosystem. At government level, the long-term incentives are limited (e.g. the tax system on capital rarely exceeds the calendar year). At the regulatory level, deregulation and the rise in power of a regime of patrimonial growth based on the dynamics of credit, where the prices of the financial assets play a key role, have led to bubbles and financial crises. At the behavioural level, it is established that short-term attitudes increase during phases of agitation – preference for the present, phenomena of forgetfulness, exponential increase of risk in the vicinity of certainty. At the shareholder level, changes to the structure of the holdings can be noted, a withdrawal of the retail investor base in favour of institutionals as well, it would seem, as a preference for momentum strategies to the detriment of strategies in favour of a return to fair value over the long-term. Finally, with regard to governance, the structure of the Boards of Directors (shorter tenure) and earnings guidance from the shareholders (quarterly) add to the phenomenon of short-termism.

From the State's point of view, the ability to play or to continue to play a long-term financing role has been weakened and limited in the economic and budgetary context resulting from the crisis. Since the financial markets have shown serious difficulties (market failures) in providing (in certain circumstances, although incentives and corrective steps may be introduced), the long-term financing of the economy, it can be deduced that the long-term investors (a heterogeneous category) might or should replace the States and the investors who have failed in their role. The concept of the *natural* long-term investor supports this theory. A certain category of investors is granted an ontological status, a sign of the difficulty in identifying, standardising and marking the concept of the long-term (the concept emerges by default, through the victories of the short-term, which are the only ones to be recorded and observable). This concept of being natural, which is part of substance rather than that which is observable, assigns to the concept of the long-term a status which is not temporal (a series of short-terms, a longer short-term ...) but instead ontological: the long-term is the place of substance and therefore of value defined by substance.

From the business' point of view, the long-term horizon is supposed to create value through the incorporation of the ESG criteria, which should also benefit society. The long-term is that which enables value to be revealed. These expressions are ambiguous, since, strictly speaking, the long-term does not create value as the long-term is in fact value. Equally, it is the incorporation of the ESG criteria which creates the long-term horizon. The spatialisation of time within language (one speaks of the long-term *horizon*) prevents one fully grasping the substantive nature of the concept of long-term.

From the investors' point of view, such natural long-term investors are essentially expected to help reduce financial instability through their strategies for the identification of fair value which take precedence over the momentum strategies.

As can be seen, many assumptions, premises and ambiguities exist. It can be noted tangentially that the long-term is *desired* but that it is rare or absent in reality; that a concept of a *natural* long-term investor corresponds to the objective of long-term value (which forms part of substance and equilibrium, fair value where a process converges) but the natural long-term investor is rare and, even if identified, is not spontaneously directed towards such an approach without adequate structures and incentive policies; that, accordingly, the concept of the long-term, unless described as impossible to locate like the dodo in Mauritius or the Yeti, would, in order to become real, require the will of a certain number of players (a non-spontaneous will; investors, States, businesses), together with a certain institutional framework and a process of convergence within time, a path of apprenticeship; that, consequently, the long-term could be confused with this process over time, the point of arrival (equilibrium, where value and substance merge), which is the point of equilibrium, cannot be preserved, a point of suspension of time which is therefore struck by impossibility within the temporal framework; that, all in all, the concept of the long-term must perhaps be considered as showing two faces with different ontological natures but which form one whole: as a substance of itself, the point of aim of equilibrium, where time is suspended and as an apprenticeship process, within the referential framework of the action of the Subject (who may be an individual or more often a collective body or an institution) and within that of the institutions and incentives where the action of the individuals and collective bodies occurs.

Consequently, if one is willing to admit that there a concept of the long-term does exist (which is admittedly unobservable in reality) – and which is not therefore impossible to locate, that it is not the product of fantasies (reality is arguably deprived of such a concept, left alone with the animal spirits and other determinations and volatilities, which is shown by observation), then two types of action present themselves: (i) to give body and meaning to the arrival point; and (ii) to structure the process (path of apprenticeship). Effort is required to give body to the arrival point in order to make the estimation of fair value and the value of equilibrium as comprehensible and objective as possible – the concept of the long-term is weakened by the ambiguities and hesitations regarding the definition and the norm of value and its valuation, short-termism prospering within the grey area where multiple indicators of "valuation" proliferate, which are not consensual enough to avoid being, rightly, criticised as short-term indicators; short-termism is also and above all a certain inability to standardise long-term indicators; the practices being languages, the language of the indicators of (long-term) value represents a vital issue. Moreover, the structuring of the process which must lead towards the (unattainable) point of equilibrium passes through disciplines, norms once more and incentives which ensure, for a certain number of leading players within the process, that there is an adequate alignment and constraint in order to continue to steer the process beyond the short-term. All these remarks can be reduced to two propositions: the provision of standardised estimates of long-term value and the construction of incentives and long-term governance. The concept of the long-term is then presented as a structure which includes these two pillars. One is of a fundamental nature and the other of an institutional nature.

This approach must enable one to step over and move beyond the agreed interaction of constraints which are often advanced in order to explain/justify the difficulty in establishing a long-term direction – although the majority are fair and legitimate, none contain the question raised and fail to offer anything to structure a long-term revelation process. They are unwillingly used as a pretext to do nothing or at least a failure to try to consider the concept of the long-term other than by default. One must therefore leave behind the rhetoric of those constraints which are usually put forward. These include operating constraints (short-term benchmark constraints) and more theoretical constraints (the belief that long-term strategy is equivalent to the sequence of short-term strategies). They include financial constraints (volatility has increased in the financial markets and the correlations of asset classes have limited the risk-reduction benefits of diversification; low interest rates and longer longevity contributed to underfunding, as reductions in the discount rate increase the value of future liabilities), political constraints (unpredictable withdrawals by governments experiencing financial pressures), legal constraints (fiduciary duty – and ERISA, for those governed by US law – prevent some ESG screening factors), further operating constraints (poor quality of corporate disclosure, governance and resources issues within investment institutions), financial constraints (shortage of investable opportunities and management teams in some areas with high societal impact, public sector crowding out private investments in others); and regulatory constraints (new regulatory rules – Solvency II, Basel III etc...). All these points are valid but present a self-validating barrier to any solution because they talk less about the concept of the long-term than about what prevents it, in the short-term, from emerging. The concept of the long-term is therefore discussed indirectly and by default, while ultimately (unintentionally) legitimising short-termism through the force of the constraints which are in fact exerted in the short-term. The discourse on the long-term is full of considerations regarding the short-term.

One notes, however, a very small minority of initiatives which are intended to shake up the prognosis and result in positive and normative proposals. This is true from a theoretical and fundamental perspective (clear understanding of the distinction between momentum and fair value strategies and consequences for policy practitioners). It is true from an operational perspective (integration of fair value strategy in the mandate to balance short-term benchmarks). Finally, it is true from a financial perspective (financial rewards to long-term investors). It is true of state policies (government action to internalise externalities, clarify fiduciary duty, require corporate disclosure) and also from an operational viewpoint (investment beliefs, governance, process and incentives with long-termism). Economic policy may evolve for its part (clear long-term mandates from the governments to allow long-term investments). Others add, for their part, with regard to operating matters (cooperation: platforms for co-investments; need for a level playing field for long-term investors; new investment fields: infrastructures, agricultural land, mining, technology industry, etc...). And finally, there are the directions of economic policy (clear rules to avoid protectionism; realignment between developed and developing countries).

All in all, the normative approach overrides the positive aspects. It is difficult for the concept of the long-term to shake off the impression that it is impossible to locate and unobservable, since the principal feature of the long-term, and its major risk, is that it does not seem to exist.

Essay 3

ALLOCATION

We have seen a blow being struck to the classic asset allocation framework. The positive effects of classic diversification (asset classes) have diminished (correlation) and asset behaviour has been increasingly polarised (safe haven versus risky assets). In the traditional world, the idea is to allocate to asset classes, under the influence of macro-financial elements on which forecasts are based. In the new approach, asset classes are taken as representatives of macro-economic variables, liquidity or stress indicators. Portfolio construction is consistent with macro factors/scenarii (taken as proxies, hedges or both) and takes account of the sensitivity of asset classes to macro factors.

The concept of risk and, therefore, the management of risk were dramatically shaken up by the crisis, principally imposing changes in three directions: risk measurement, drawdown and fat-tail management, the definition of the risk-free asset. The crisis showed in fact (i) the trend and temptation, as the rising financial cycle matures to capture risk premia on (future) hidden fat-tails, (ii) the overreliance on a single measure of risk – volatility – i.e. a *symmetrical* and *procyclical* measure, where reality is asymmetrical and the natural position of long-term investors should be *contrarian* and mean-reverting. What matters most is *downside volatility* (*ex post* and *ex ante* maximum drawdown parameters). Investors should not rely on a single measure of risk and should broaden the scope (stress tests, multiple scenarii ...), (iii) the false nature of the definition of the risk-free asset (it should be an asset for which the expected return = the effective return and it should reflect to some extent, when feasible, the liability equation for the portfolio – in reality, long-term maturities were taken as acceptable proxies for the risk-free asset with a reduced or non-existing link to liabilities, this coming with considerable confusion between safety and liquidity) and the relative nature of the concept (as compared with liabilities, as compared with the investor's nationality) consequently pose a serious problem: the measure of performance (Sharpe ratio), which has an absolute design, is faced with confusion and relativity.

Much comes down to procyclicalities. Risk measures are procyclical. (Classic) benchmarks are procyclical. Regulation is procyclical. Human nature is procyclical. Building effective counter forces from investment to governance is the battlefield.

Beyond the classic asset allocation framework

The classic asset allocation framework based on modern portfolio theory (maximisation of return for a given level of risk) has been challenged by the crisis. For example, the hierarchy of returns in real life proved somewhat different from what was forecasted and expected by most investors. From 1999 to 2009, US equities underperformed US 10-year Treasury Bonds. The idea that, *in the long-term*, investors should and will be rewarded for their patience has been denied by reality and the idea that the higher the risk, the higher the return was also defeated by simple facts – the lower the volatility of a stock, the better the return. In addition, increasing correlations between classic asset classes in times of crisis (due to higher volatility) have diminished the positive impact of what was expected from classic diversification. In fact, diversification proved to be much more limited than expected and the risks much higher. Performance was disappointing. As a matter of fact, most asset classes have shown a "polarization phenomenon" with, for example, two clear poles consisting of (so-called) safe havens and risky assets. Analysis (principal component) confirmed that the risk spectrum included many more axes of risks to explain the behaviour of asset classes than was generally thought to be the case.

The traditional approach of asset allocation is based on *asset classes* (equities, bonds, cash and the rest, the rest being often a greyish area or a black box whose risk is not properly allocated) and the idea that *asset classes are driven by macro-economic and financial elements that can be predicted*. An alternative approach lies in the idea that *risk factors are driven and polarized by macro-economic and financial variables, for which traditional asset classes may provide a proxy or a hedge*. In other words, asset classes can be seen as representatives of macro-economic and financial variables, as well as indicators of liquidity or stress. For example, inflation proves to be one of the macro variables with the strongest power of polarization over asset classes, often occurring at the same time as worsening economic conditions. This means that (i) any portfolio incorporates a given sensitivity to a set of macro variables and/or liquidity/stress factors or to a set of scenarios; (ii) those sensitivities are in most cases unknown or underestimated; (iii) there is an implicit risk structure in the portfolio, resulting from the *ex ante* sensitivity of certain asset classes to a set of macro variables or scenarios – and this, even before taking any particular view.

Another area of challenge lies with measures based on Sharpe ratio methodology. In order to estimate the Sharpe ratio, a measure of the risk-free rate is required (the non-risky asset). Although the best proxy for the risk-free rate should be the shortest maturity of the government bond yield curve, we have seen a complacent shift in the last thirty years to much longer maturities as a proxy for this rate. And, assuming that the short-term government bond definition is effectively adopted for the risk-free rate, we are still left with embarrassing questions – are government bonds an acceptable proxy for risk-free assets when debt-fuelled countries come under severe pressure? In the eurozone, does it make a difference whether Germany or Spain is selected as a reference for the purpose of expected returns? Should we go for a common average figure or maintain separate approaches?

Unrealistic assumptions are also made regarding the so-called normality of asset classes when estimating expected returns for strategic asset allocation. Real life is about asymmetrical distributions of returns or fat tailed patterns. Volatility itself as a symmetrical risk concept does not correspond to reality and downside volatility is more appropriate, with a focus on maximum drawdown, i.e. an *ex post* measure of volatility. *Ex ante* risk criteria and *ex post* measures are therefore needed in order to assess the real life of asymmetrical distribution of returns.

This involves a necessary shift from the traditional investment-product-oriented approach to advisory work, taking account of the various elements of the client equation – starting with the feature of liabilities – in order to build the strategic allocation framework, together with more tactical views on asset allocation. Research capabilities are critical to achieving this program in both benchmarked and absolute return types of environment.

Turning to solutions in the absolute return space, if one gets rid of forecasts or assumptions on expected returns, then new territories of research are opened up. Mean variance, risk parity or maximum diversification are some well-known examples in that field. In particular, the risk parity approach to allocation allows one to make selections based on a risk model for asset classes, providing risk diversification while being independent from a macro input (scenario) or elements of valuation. However, these approaches face limits and challenges when the financial market environment takes a turn for the worst – the introduction of some element of robustness/resilience to the crisis is therefore required.

Finally, flexibility is necessary in a world of traditionally static allocations. The ability to cut risk exposure – significantly – when required by deteriorating/adverse market conditions makes a difference. For example, starting in 2008, the crisis regime led to a dual pattern in the markets (risk on/risk off): a flexible allocation was *expected* to be in a position – given the appropriate signals – to detect changes in this dual pattern of financial sequences. The ability to switch between risk-on and risk-off modes provided a higher benefit than traditional asset diversification in terms of effective risk reduction. This evolution was accompanied by an enhancement of the concept of risk, moving away from the unique measure of volatility to a wider set of definitions and objectives – scenario analysis, stress tests, drawdown analysis. Risk has become a multiple concept, applying to many sub-segments of the portfolio structure, such as liquidity or credit. Traditional risk measures are not dead, new ones are added in an incremental process.

The crisis has made investors aware of the difficulty in predicting risk and returns, thus fuelling interest in pure risk strategies or allocation by risk factors. Moreover, a low interest rate environment leads long-term investors to consider introducing new asset classes or new currencies in their investment universe. Some central banks have set an example, trying to decorrelate the risks attached to the management of their FX reserves from the consequences of their monetary policy on their balance sheet.

Allocation by risk factors instead of asset classes is on the rise and "polarization" approaches, i.e. sensitivity of an asset class, a market segment or any portfolio to a set of macro factors (e.g. growth, inflation) and financial factors (liquidity, stress) are promising. This at least enables a better understanding of the biases of any portfolio and a possible adjustment of those biases.

Asset and (macro) factor polarisation for diversification[4]

Correlations across assets depend on asset polarisation: those that are close in the "polarisation cloud" should be positive, stable and weakly affected by the dynamics of factors; those concerning dual assets should be negative, stable and weakly affected by changes in factors; those that are characterised by non-dual, different polarisations are not stable – they are expected to move in sympathy with the relevant macro-economic factors. Investigating the *distance* among assets (polarisation) is therefore key to the approach. This can be extended to the analysis of equity sectors and styles clustering.

The recent crisis has shown a loss of confidence in the effectiveness of diversification to meet the objective of drawdown reduction ("diversification does not work when you need it most" was the motto of many investors). Nevertheless, recent portfolio construction schemes – like risk parity or maximum diversification – have made diversification the kernel of asset allocation. One key element of progress is to question not diversification *per se* but what should be diversified (most approaches diversify by asset classes), and then to move to factor diversification. What has been briefly described above is one way to think differently (relative to the classic asset allocation), i.e. diversifying across fundamental factors – with a strong assumption behind this approach that those factors are the main drivers of the dynamics of asset prices. This shift involves rephrasing the investment decision process (rephrasing means that language and thought – two sides of the same coin – have to change): distance and polarisation are key to the analysis of assets; macro factors and stress are powerful drivers of distance and polarization; these factors do not need to forecast returns, contrary to most other approaches (typically standard mean variance optimisation).

Screening the investment universe, searching for polarization with some fundamental macro factors is one of the possible ways forward. And it is a promising one. Without trying to be exhaustive, some examples are particularly compelling. For instance, with asset classes mostly located in the corners of the "macro-map" (inflation and

[4] See also Essay 4 – Revisiting the concepts of active and passive management.

growth factors), it is clear that they polarize to the macro-economic dynamics of the selected factors. Unsurprisingly there are (very) few situations of rising inflation/weakening growth (limited polarization). Analysis shows that two types of equity sectors can be identified: equity-like sectors polarize towards falling inflation/rising growth macro factors, while commodity-like sectors polarize towards rising inflation *and* rising growth. Despite some apparent heterogeneity, credit markets are close to the behaviour of commodities, with a polarization towards rising growth and rising inflation factors (the heterogeneity disappears when the interest rate contribution is removed from credit indexes).

There are many examples of polarization. For example, in the US, nominal bonds are a good hedge against falling inflation, falling growth and rising stress. Linkers are – unsurprisingly – a good hedge against rising inflation, while the link with falling growth and market stress is weaker. Corporate IG tracks the behaviour of nominal bonds on inflation and growth but not on market stress. Corporate HY is independent of inflation, while (weakly) related to rising growth and market stress scenarios (strongly to falling stress). Emerging market debt tracks the pattern of commodities (local currency), while the hard currency component is more independent of growth and inflation. The zero-duration credit market tracks the behaviour of commodities. Equities are a very good hedge against rising growth and falling market stress types of scenario (falling inflation also, to a lesser extent). Commodities (CRB index) show a strong polarization to rising inflation and growth and falling market stress (note that gold shows the same kind of pattern, while agricultural commodities are less polarized to growth and stress factors). Interestingly, most FX rates show polarization to macro scenarios including rising growth, rising inflation and falling stress. Hedge funds – though not an asset class and rather a heterogeneous universe – do not, in general, provide any hedge against rising market stress and behave overall like commodities (macro systematic strategies are an exception). Last but not least, volatility behaves like nominal bonds. The list is obviously not exhaustive and our purpose is above all to suggest that the nature and behaviour of financial assets are different with some strong, clear patterns of polarization to macro factors like growth or inflation (the most simple macro factors – there are potentially many others); that asset classes can be seen as a universe of substitutability and/or opposition (+ and – polarization) with duos positively or negatively polarized to macro-fundamental factors. Some exhibit the same behaviour and they can be substituted for each other – for example, building an exposure to a given macro scenario can be implemented through an exposure to different asset classes, and this gives a wider range of possibilities than the traditional usual suspects – others show orthogonal behaviour and can provide hedges.

Analysing the nature and behaviour of asset classes gives a better understanding of the universe. For instance, it is firmly established that commodity stocks are more commodity-like; that high-yield bonds behave like equities rather than bonds with a positive polarization towards growth factors and a negative one to market stress.

The idea is to deviate from the efficient frontier (entropy-based diversification) and to allocate part of a sub-optimality (relative to the efficient frontier) in terms of expected returns to the portfolio, in order to obtain a more diversified and stronger allocation. This allows allocation decisions to be monitored on the basis of diversification of risk and of a process of optimisation through polarization towards macro factors (to some extent, risk diversification and macro-polarization are equivalent propositions within the framework discussed above); to run impact analysis before introducing new asset classes or market segments into the portfolio; to simulate and recommend additional diversification into new currencies. Above all, it must be remembered that, in this approach, the definition and the role of an individual asset class is much more diverse than the classic definition, since the asset class is defined by a utility function across other asset classes ("duos") rather than *per se* (the collective meaning of the asset class is more relevant than the individual), as the most relevant question for the portfolio is "what can this asset class be used for?" with a very strong emphasis on the word used for (to replace, protect etc....). The asset is defined by what it can contribute *to the other* assets.

The analysis of diversification is equivalent to the polarization analysis (i.e. polarization coefficient of asset classes in the client's universe). Maximum polarization of the asset class for a given macro factor is associated with a 100% coefficient – coefficients below -90% and above +90% are considered significant. Bearing in mind the fact that coefficients identified at a given portfolio level are not a linear combination of polarization coefficients for underlying asset classes, one can envisage enhancing/optimising the sensitivity of a portfolio to a given (macro) factor – i.e. making the investor aware of a possible hidden sensitivity, some unconscious biases *and* providing him with new tools to run practical combinations enhancing the portfolio profile. Typically, the polarization/diversification analysis will show that dynamic and balanced portfolios are equity-like while those which are bond-like are more stable.

Identifying or defining *macro-financial regimes* is critical to allocation management (and more generally to investment management) both on a static and, even more importantly, a dynamic basis (shifts in regimes). This applies to growth or inflation macro factors and also to market stress, since there are some reasons why the resilience or the resistance of a given asset in times of crisis is a powerfully distinctive feature.

Market stress and risk regimes

Market stress can be measured by an index which includes various stress indicators (liquidity, implied volatility, high yield spreads …) and this approach (principal components analysis) can be applied to every individual asset class or market segment. An assessment can be obtained of the probability of being in a given regime of market stress (which is more or less pronounced). Volatility spikes and market stress unsurprisingly go hand in hand. On that basis, the idea is to define a risk regime which has some special features of stress intensity and "normality" – the concept of normal is highly relative to a given regime. The regime is temporal and will be replaced at some point by a new one. Incorporating several regimes into the analysis is valuable when trying to distinguish between "normal" and stressed markets (i.e. *relative to* some measure of intensity and normality). Being able to identify the features of a risk regime and the early signs of a change in regime are challenging perspectives. Assuming that the investor can identify some "normality" – or at least what will be called normal *ex ante* – then the main objective will be to optimise diversification, for example by an equal contribution of volatility to the total risk of the portfolio (volatility contribution and not the amount of capital). It is not surprising that some normality is required – otherwise unstable correlations and volatilities would invalidate the approach. This also helps provide a better definition of normality as the temporal sequence of stable (the measure can vary) volatility/correlations, stability being itself relative to some instability within the regime (regime can apply to a full cycle including more or less stable sequences or to an individual sequence of stability or instability within a broader full cycle regime).

Juts as "normality" involves some investment strategy (optimal diversification, because diversification is expected to work), stress (or abnormal conditions) leads to strategies of drawdown management (correlations increase in times of crisis). Resilience is embedded in the portfolio and the investor will try to minimise the volatility gap between "normal" times and stress. Since it is hard to predict a crisis, this approach will help switch from one regime to another.

Combining optimal diversification in normal times and robustness in times of crisis, without having to predict crisis or to rebalance the portfolio in the crisis seems to be a financial version of the Holy Grail. A lot will depend on the ability to define and quantify some measure of normality and of stress. Past experience will provide the basis of the analysis for all the relevant market segments or assets included in the investment universe. Some coefficient of memory and forgetfulness can be added to take account of the fact that normality and stress are memorised concepts with some progressive erosion and, sometimes, a brutal non-linear spike of memory bringing back some historical regularities.

The contribution to volatility by all classes and segments – in normal times and times of stress – will be calibrated and robustness will also be calibrated by a measure of the normal gap between volatility in normal times and volatility in periods of stress.

Smart solutions, no free lunch, execution is key

In the equity world, risk parity approaches have been categorised as smart beta concepts – i.e. a systematic management of the portfolio using optimisation techniques and historical covariance matrices. In the multi-asset world, risk-parity means allocating on the basis of risk modelling for asset classes. This approach often tends to give too much weight to low-risk assets, leveraging them in order to enhance the risk across the portfolio whilst equalising the various risk contributions of asset classes. Robustness, independence from macro-scenario assumptions and market valuations are much appreciated. As mentioned above, the combination of risk parity and what we would call *resilience* (some ability to resist market stress or a shortage of liquidity) is a promising area of research. This framework allows risk distribution to be checked across the various asset classes included in the portfolio, in at least two situations of market stress (risk on/risk off). Risk allocation will vary depending on the market stress regime. Simulating a maximum drawdown in adverse market conditions is also a possibility.

With interest rates expected to remain low (as *a regime* – despite more cyclical adjustments ranging from tapering to some normalisation of leading interest rates, although we have some doubts as to what normal could mean in a profoundly changed environment), diversifying into new currencies or asset classes is a legitimate plan for some long-term investors, such as certain central banks which have invested heavily in US Treasuries and which face the prospects of rising US interest rates. Not all central banks share the same analysis, since for some the generation of returns is not the primary goal, liquidity management being a priority (a simple basket of a very limited number of safe/liquid currencies). The generation of returns is then the role of another institutional body – a sovereign wealth fund, if there is one, or some entity linked with the Ministry of Finance.

Having said that, there is room to diversify into new currencies when feasible. This includes currencies which have long-term potential for appreciation (undervaluation, attractive long-term fundamental prospects for the underlying economic environment). There are many opportunities in the emerging sphere – assuming that the concept of "emergings" is not considered to be a unique category and that one distinguishes along critical fundamental lines and maps this large universe: quality and structure of growth, exposure to and dependence on the commodity cycle, total financing needs (including external "hard currency" debt), structure of financing (including the nature of capital flows, direct investment versus the rest) and the ratio of the total financing needs to FX reserves, total credit dynamics, under/over-valuation of currency and key asset classes, FX policy ... In particular, the RMB has attracted interest following its internationalisation. Still, there is no such thing as a unique situation for emerging currencies. Since fundamentals can differ considerably across the universe, proper analysis and diversification are warranted.

Diversifying into currencies also includes currencies that can offer some properties of portfolio diversification, either because the given currency can provide a more liquid substitute for a macro theme and/or a hedge against some macro scenario or because it can behave like a safe haven. Regarding the former, commodity-linked currencies, such as the AUD or the CAD can be taken as examples – these currencies provide an exposure to the commodity cycle without the impediments of being directly invested in less liquid and politically more sensitive underlying instruments, while traditionally performing well in contexts of rising inflation (we have here an example of the polarization effect of an asset class – commodities – to a macro factor – inflation – and of another asset class or market segment – currencies here – that can provide a substitute and/or a hedge). The CHF is a good example of the latter, in an environment of rising stress.

Some central banks have started first to broaden their fixed income universe, typically adding mortgage-backed securities and/or TiPS (inflation-linked bonds) to their portfolios. While TiPS have not always matched expectations in an environment where deflationary pressures are a bigger threat than inflation, they do in general provide some of the hedging properties of diversifying assets, while also seeking higher yields and accepting a higher risk of default in the portfolio.

Some central banks have stepped into the equity space and some have publicised this move – such as the Swiss National Bank. While the Swiss announcement of a 15% target exposure to equities may be linked to currency management on the back of a reasonably low (and even negative) correlation between equities and fixed income instruments, others, as already mentioned, have tried to decorrelate the risks attached to the management of their reserves from the impact of their monetary policy on the balance sheet – typically central banks with ballooning FX reserves which are massively invested in one or two types of fixed income instruments; and/or to find some decorrelation and protection from a scenario of (future) rising inflation. It is a challenge to obtain acceptance (at board level) of the underlying risk regime in times of crisis. In particular, the management of the global portfolio of a central bank or sovereign wealth fund (which can be asked to fund or support government bodies in times of crisis) has to take account of the nature of equities in order to avoid liquidation of the positions at a bad time.

Real estate, private equity and infrastructure assets are natural candidates for the diversification of the portfolio of long-term investors – bringing returns and decorrelation across asset classes, geographic and instrument segmentations – although limited by illiquidity and specific risk, when compared with what their theoretical presence could and should be. It should be noted that the time unit and the general time frame are specific – long – since building exposure is a long learning process (acquisition of knowledge for the long-term investor and of confidence in the asset manager). Hedge funds are not included in that approach, as they are not an asset class *per se* and should instead be considered in the context of specific asset classes (M&A with equities, credit arbitrage with credit).

Dynamic and flexible allocation is important, once the strategic framework is defined. A set of rebalancing rules – when significant deviations from the strategic allocation occur – will improve the risk/return profile of the portfolio. Risk parity rather than asset weightings will provide a robust approach to rebalancing (combined with *ex ante* risk management). Rebalancing rules do not necessarily have to be dynamic. Some evolution of the strategic allocation following significant shifts or changes in the executed/assumed risk and returns in the portfolio is also a legitimate definition of *dynamic allocation*. Significantly reducing the exposure to Western government bonds – because the efficient frontier of bonds has changed *and* they are massively overvalued – is one example of action by a sovereign wealth fund, retaining a small amount of USD bonds for liquidity purposes only.

Tactical active management can lead some long-term investors to externalise Tactical Asset Allocation mandates – especially when faced with some limitations regarding the use of derivatives or resources to run the overlay. Externalised allocation can also replicate the total portfolio in order to benchmark internal teams on the learning curve.

Implementation and execution are very important in a world where 1bp is one bp. In order to minimise market impact when implementing allocation changes due to the large size of some long-term investors, implementation issues are critical. When implemented passively, the investor will make sure of a cost-efficient execution (bargaining power of the manager), the lowest Tracking Error and high quality index rebalancing. Calibrating the implementation (passive or active, with or without derivatives, with or without Exchange Traded Funds ...) in order to optimise costs and returns is a crucial component of the investment process. Having established a clear α/β active versus passive policy, its governance, well-aligned with the Board and the appropriate time horizon will prove a definitive plus for a long-term institution. The emergence of "smart beta" approaches, because it can add to the confusion between α and β (or active vs. passive) requires clarification, at a time when classic borders are blurred and the combination rather than the opposition of these "styles" (α, β, smart beta) is the next frontier.

Diversifying into currencies

Currencies constitute a unique class of assets and, for this reason, may and must be given a special place in the management of a portfolio. A currency is cost-efficient, liquid, will not default as such and offers diversifying properties. A currency (or, more accurately, a "pair", since a currency only has meaning when compared with another currency or basket of currencies) is both an asset class in its own right, which has to be distinguished and "unwrapped" from the underlying asset with which it is often incorrectly confused, and a proxy of a certain number of macro-economic or other factors, which allow one to use the currency as a proxy/hedge within the scenarii. The currency question should not be confused with that of the underlying asset: they are two distinct types of decision, one sole management talent may suffice but this will be unlikely and rare. A more serious and more important issue is not being aware of this and thus destroying value, either by not managing the currency question (do I have a special talent, in order to take active decisions on this subject? If not, what is my natural position, hedged or not?) or by handling it badly (a manager of rates or shares may dilute its time and value by becoming lost in this universe). Furthermore, the management of currencies presents several interwoven layers: (i) a currency is both an absolute concept (e.g. one talks about a currency in real, effective terms) in view of identifying an intrinsic value, which is itself absolute and a relative concept (in real life, the management decision will be made through a cross, a pair or several) and (ii) a currency maintains a relationship with both the short-term (specific categories of participants for sometimes daily or even quasi-immediate purposes consolidate this temporal structure) and the long-term (once again, specific categories of participants may explain this in part). Finally, although the general feeling, supported by studies, is that this universe follows a random walk which exposes active management to many disappointments, a few observed successes may, however, imply that this is not the case, if (i) the deepest and widest possible use is made of the investment universe, (ii) the currencies are considered and used over and beyond their direct fundamentals, i.e. as active elements expressing the portfolio positions which might be expressed through other asset classes (an investment theme which is traditionally expressed by shares may instead be expressed by currencies) or themes which are not immediately investable (many macro-financial topics, risks which have no "natural" asset classes or even a proxy.) The important idea here is that the traditional *causality of reasoning must be reversed*: the usual studies move from an analysis of the (assumed) *direct* determinants of currencies (and also of variables of balance of payments, activity and price for the country affected by the said currency) (in passing, this analysis is most often effected in absolute terms, i.e. without taking relative situations and dynamics into account, since the decision concerning a currency always concerns another currency or basket of other currencies). A more interesting approach starts with the currencies themselves, in order to include any revelations from observation of their evolutions and without worrying too much, at least on first approach, about any associated predictions; it thus starts with the currencies themselves and moves towards the portfolio and its themes (typically macro-economic factors, or simply factors in general). If I wish to introduce a theme of either exposure to and/or protection from a deflation scenario, observation will inform me of certain currencies which are characterised by a regular, historic polarisation with regard to this theme (since this stability is not guaranteed, such relationships should be challenged and stress placed on them, in order to identify possible switches of regime.)

This is one of our principal propositions and convictions: (i) our view of *all* the asset classes may and must be reversed. The portfolio is not the result of a series of decisions relating to each asset class, including currencies, such decisions are themselves the result of an analysis of direct determinants, which are most often absolute (see above) (within this traditional context, currencies are very frequently not even identified as an asset class). On the contrary, through its themes, the portfolio *precedes* the asset classes, with regard to the representation, proxy and hedge properties of such themes. Such a reversal naturally has considerable implications for the organisation, allocation and governance of the resources which are devoted to portfolio management. An asset class, and in particular currencies which have special properties, is not primarily the subject of a prediction but a historic observation of regularities and properties for constituting an *element of language of the story which the portfolio intends to recount* (the prediction dimension or stress test applies to the regime, which is identified through observation, which causes, for example, some or other currency to maintain a high level of polarisation with some or other macro-economic theme – this may evolve or change), (ii) this first proposition (the portfolio precedes the asset class; the principal merit of the asset class is its capacity to act as an analogy, proxy, hedge or representation of themes, and therefore not what it directly displays but rather what cannot be seen of it, i.e. its capacity for the purposes of equivalences/analogies), this first proposition is therefore connected to another important proposition, which has already been discussed: the immediately available information concerning *the whole* of the variables and themes of the portfolio and asset classes is of little relevance, other than to modify the referential of memory, duration and forgetfulness which, in turn, dictates the essential part. Once again, the organisation, allocation and governance of considerable resources, which are focussed on the immediate moment, must result in a reversal. The only thing which really matters is that which, from deep time, may make itself present.

Currency returns

Let us return to currencies. The extremely broad universe of daily transactions will certainly allow for certain costs to be reduced, including the transaction cost. Of the various asset classes, currencies offer among the best market access. This does not mean that other costs do not exist, such as the cost of hedging, the cost of execution or the opportunity cost. In addition, currencies are very liquid, they involve no risk of duration or issuer risk (although one can theoretically conceive of the disappearance of a State and, less theoretically, a default, which will then affect the whole of the investment's underlying financial and real assets). The potential for diversification in other asset classes and within the class of currencies itself completes the comparative advantages of currencies. The heterogeneity of the participants in the currency market, which we discussed above (from central banks and sovereign funds to intra-day traders), of the temporal investment horizons and the styles of investment in the currency universe (the style provides all the more momentum, overall, the closer one comes to the immediate moment in time but there is still a dispersion of styles, even over the short-term; one can, in general, argue that, relatively speaking, these styles are not very consistent with the macro-economic directions which characterise the long-term asset class universes), such heterogeneity therefore helps facilitate the establishment of a diversification framework. In particular, the determinants in the analysis and decisions of those participants who work with currencies are sufficiently different (i) from those which characterise shares, bonds or real assets, and (ii) as between themselves, in order to justify a clear separation of the underlying asset from the currency issue.

A certain number of FX crosses (pairs) offer a weak or negative correlation with the universe of risky assets, which may allow for increased diversification of the portfolio. By way of example, hedging a global equity portfolio may prove problematic and may increase the total risk, if there is a high level of correlation between the USD/JPY cross and the relative performance of Japanese shares: being long in Japanese shares or short in yen amounts in both cases to a position on the reflation of the Japanese economy. The currency position here does not divide the risk and instead increases it. This is due, in part, to the fact that, from the point of view of the portfolio theme (exit from deflation, action for reflation) the currency is instrumental (and an action variable in the case of the yen, through the central bank's quantitative easing).

Currency returns can be analysed in terms of factors of style which have (i) a certain intra-factor diversification, (ii) a relatively low level of correlation with the determinants of the long-term assets and portfolio themes (macro-factors). These styles are usually associated with the temporal investment horizons: the value over the long-term, the carry over the medium-term, the momentum and volatility over the short-term. Such associations are fragile but remind us how important the value given to time is for the purposes of economics and finance, and therefore for the investor (value is the value given to time) and the extent to which the management "styles" or style factors (value, momentum etc...) correspond to or even represent a structure of value given to time. The momentum or volatility style is therefore both *a choice* of temporal referential by the investor and an actual structure of the market, which exists because a sufficient number of participants practise such a management style (which explains the self-validating nature of the choice of some or other style or factor). Consequently, the search for an active allocation of style factors, because it is a diversification of the typologies of intervention which structure the currency market and a diversification at the same time of the various values given to time, may give the portfolio a sturdier or indeed a more profitable foundation.

Consequently, active management of the universe of currencies within a portfolio may help increase the *expected* return of the asset classes which make it up, without increasing the total portfolio risk and therefore the expected portfolio return as a whole. The universe of currencies may help (i) diversify this asset class because the currency has a low level of correlation with the asset class or one of such topics, (ii) replicate the class (proxy) or one of these topics, (iii) protect it or (iv) provide the portfolio with the diversifying effect of a matrix of style factors which have a low level of correlation among themselves and which is specific to this universe of currencies.

Much depends, for the purposes of the active management of currencies, *on where one is coming from* (base currency). The points of view of a Chinese investor or of a portfolio manager from a Latin American country or Japan are not the same. The underlying exchange risks are specific, as is the volatility regime of the base currency, by comparison with other currencies, or at least certain of them, or exposure to the macro-economic factors. Furthermore, each investor, as a base currency, constitutes a particular view of the world for the purposes of the definition which each will provide of the risk-free asset, and which will be closer to its national/sovereign equations and also its liabilities. Each investor is subject to its *own* home biases: to which will be added those of the expert opinions of external managers which the investor has selected. The global portfolio allocation must not only be aware of this but take active account of it.

Currency factor allocation. Currencies as proxies or hedges

In a traditional approach, currency allocation is a function, among others, of macro-economic trends, expectations of monetary policy, valuations, elements of flows (net purchases of funds...) and factors of technical market analysis (patterns of development of trends or signs of their reversal.) In this approach, (i) one finds to a greater or lesser extent *value, liquidity* (macro-liquidity, in the sense of variables of balance of payments or monetary policies), *momentum* indicators, (ii) one is very often tempted to predict these indicators, certain of their components or the relationship between the indicator and the market variable. We have stated earlier in this work (i) the radical limits, not of value as a concept, but of the indicators which are commonly used – since they are "stuck" to the immediate information, have no predictive power and do not provide a relevant signal, until they incorporate richer and deeper space-time referentials of duration, memory and forgetfulness, (ii) the considerable confusion which surrounds the concept of liquidity: crude approaches based on monetary variables or dynamic ratios of real activity/money (proxy or element of the monetary base of the balance of payments); i.e. elements of the excess liquidity which is available for the financial markets; zero predictive force; the failure to take into account in the concept of liquidity the expression of choice, a preference of the individual (a preference for liquidity) in a social context where the other is important (the exchange, the liquidity crisis), and therefore a psychological space-time referential (memory, duration, forgetfulness); there is no discussion of the so-called micro-liquidity approaches (flows of purchases and sales of assets), although their pro-cyclical nature (strong, directional correlation with the underlying asset classes) provides hope for relevant signs of a recovery at the extreme points (which validates in passing how one expects in the same way that one remembers), (iii) the self-validating, at best, and non-predictive nature, in the vast majority of cases, of the technical patterns (momentum), even at the extreme points in contrarian mode.

All these elements contribute something, even if only their limits and the questions which they give rise to: (i) they may, for the most part, be improved by including in the method the referentials of memory and forgetfulness, which will remove the need *inter alia* to make predictions regarding the variables – whether objective or intermediary, (ii) the approach remains that of a causality which moves from an analysis of the supposedly direct determinants of the asset class to a prediction of a return per asset class and, finally, to the portfolio structure (in a more interesting version, *indicators*, which are supposed to provide signals at the extreme points, being normalised, incorporate the asset class itself into the relevant value and liquidity variable(s), an attempt to describe a price *from the viewpoint of* the liquidity conditions and/or the value considerations.)

Taking the traditional approach once again, i.e. within an *asset* allocation (equities, bonds, currencies), the universe of currencies will be segmented (i) between major currency blocks (USD, EUR, JPY) and (ii) within the currency blocks: USD B (USD/TWD); EUR B (GBP, CHF, NOK etc...); ASIA B (SGD, KRW ...); COMMODITY B (AUD, NZD, CAD).

A segmentation into the widest possible universe of currencies is sufficiently rare for one not to remember it, since this approach, as such, contributes value (the most frequent approaches are those which are limited to a few big FX crosses). On this basis, if this is the case, the essential part of the work often involves predicting various elements of the matrix of currency (de)correlations, based on an analysis of value, liquidity or momentum which lead, within the portfolio, to two principal types of strategy, which represent the short-term and long-term temporal horizons, and to FX management styles which are themselves distinct. Ultimately, the portfolio is the result of such predictions. The reverse causality, which we have discussed, starts with the portfolio and its topics and then goes on to select, from within the widest universe of currencies, clones, avatars, proxies and hedges of themes and/or asset classes; currencies for which there are no predictions but whose utility function is the rich, thematic history which is formed and sustained by the variables, themes, clusters of variables and topics borne by memory and a certain factor of forgetfulness. A currency is, at first, memory rather than the subject of a prediction.

Rather than trying to predict some or other asset class or market segment on the basis of macro-economic variables and *then* turning to the portfolio which is to be created (traditional approach), it is possible to start with the portfolio and the sensitivity of the asset classes or market segments to a certain number of macro-factors or macro-scenarii. Such an approach may be adopted for currencies, in which their *function* will be to *represent* macro-factors or scenarii (e.g. growth and inflation or stress-scenarii for the scenarii; this universe may be expanded). The currencies will be treated like other asset classes for the purposes of mapping the sensitivity and polarisation of such factors. By doing so, the portfolio construction commences straight away, *upfront*.

Currencies have significant power to represent macro-scenarii. Taking merely a few of the simplest examples, it can be seen that certain currencies (USD, CHF) constitute (or constituted – the stability and changes of regime must be analysed and tested within a dynamic approach) an interesting hedge, when there is an increase in global risk aversion. Similarly, it is not always easy to achieve exposure to the macro-factor inflation directly (and direct investment in commodities is not always authorised): certain commodity currencies permit this (AUD, CAD ...). Finally, certain currencies provide exposure to the theme of the global economic cycle. Consequently, an area of research and identification of factors which form the principal structure of a scenario and, simultaneously, of equivalents/clones within the asset classes, opens up for the investor. This approach offers solutions for the implementation of macro themes or scenarii. Such macro themes may be passive (identification of all the existing themes, including in contradiction with each other, i.e. inflation and deflation, since the portfolio construction must incorporate exposure to/protection against both, within a diversification process, since these two risks exist; no prediction or choice of particular scenario is required) or active (choice of a particular scenario, prediction concerning a variable – although loss of diversification constitutes a weakness here; an agnostic approach with regard to the scenarii and a non-prediction of variables seem more robust). For all these reasons, it seems sensible to include currencies within the general definition of the allocation framework.

Unsurprisingly, movements in the currency market tend to polarise and form clusters around a common set of factors, themes and risks (factor analysis of FX rates vs. composite basket), capturing both behavioural and fundamental drivers. One undoubtedly notes a dispersion (mean block dispersion; segmented currency universe vs. dispersion of unsegmented currency universe) according to time (time-varying FX dispersion) and market movements but also to effects of persistence and the regularity of certain effects over sufficiently long periods to characterise a *regime*. This allows for a targeted/segmented approach to the themes and currencies.

Such an approach facilitates the identification of directional/systematic risk factors, with risk premia which can be exploited and viable relative-value trades, whilst limiting exposure to potential systemic crises (the situation of the eurozone crisis in 2011 is a good example thereof).

In addition to greater consistency in the investment process, the investor should benefit from effective risk-budgeting. Accordingly, once an idiosyncratic view has been formulated, the question of its implementation arises (as against which currency?). However, each cross (pair) is dominated, within a *regime*, by macro-factors, as we have seen, and, *therefore*, if one adopts the same logic, by other *crosses/pairs* (within a polarisation cluster around macro-factors or scenarii). Thus, by way of example, an idiosyncratic view of CNY will lead to identifying those currencies which form the most relevant cross (CNY/USD? CNY/EUR? etc...) and then, once one has, for example, identified CNY/JPY, to identifying the dominant crosses (USD/JPY in this instance).

Currency blocks (USD, USD-Asia, JPY, EUR, EUR-emerging, Commodity, Commodity-emerging) can be distinguished using four, strong, common factors which revolve around USD, EUR, Global growth, Asia, which are themselves divided as between emerging and non-emerging sub-groups. In short, the USD block unites the pegged or semi-pegged currencies (currencies which are principally managed by comparison with the USD anchor). The Asia block is linked to the USD block (guided management of the exchange rate with the USD is a factor for incorporation in the block), consolidation of intra-regional trade supports the block – although these characteristics are indeed those of the current regime, one will have to follow closely the process by which the dollar link is released, in proportion with the emergence of more independent internal demands and/or a higher risk premium required for dollar-denominated assets. The yen block is idiosyncratic, in the sense that the yen plays a fairly solitary role, within a context of limited cross-border flows, and is thus of particular interest for portfolio construction. The euro block is, in turn, more systematic, with the euro as a focal point, reflecting the commercial and financial structures – and the economic policies – which are incorporated or coordinated. The euro-emerging block reflects close commercial exchanges and a management of currencies by comparison with the euro. Finally, the commodity and commodity-emerging blocks can be seen as a global growth "beta" basket (of commodity producers, for the most part).

The identification of common factors provides room for strategies, which can be envisaged in the field of currencies, while also enabling the capture of common, systematic themes. A block approach provides the investor with flexible space to make active adjustments to the scenarii, *a fortiori* in a moving market context. The block may consequently be seen as a gateway for considering the implications of a scenario for a given FX cross. That said, block regimes and gateway processes are subject to a superimposition of cross-block/cross-asset themes, especially when one is dealing with a crisis situation (a crisis may be described, in the extreme, as a disappearance of block processes and as a strong correlation between blocks.) Two axes and processes therefore co-exist - a vertical one (the block process) and a horizontal one (cross-block/asset/themes process) - and must be dealt with.

Organisational aspects of FX investment

We have said that it is appropriate to incorporate currencies in the allocation policy. This leaves several options for organisational purposes. In a centralised approach, an FX overlay team steers the whole of the net FX exposure (FX expected return *and* the correlation factor between the FX and the asset class). In this specific context, the underlying managers must comply with the target currency exposure. Such a scheme seems particularly suited to the universe of equity management, where currency expertise is usually more limited. A more decentralised approach will place responsibility for steering the FX exposure with the underlying managers per asset class. Bond managers will consider this to be consistent and will view it as a management opportunity, since common macro factors, which have a strong impact on both fixed income and FX markets, will in fact make the bonds *and* currencies universe into a consistent universe. Expertise in the FX markets can, unsurprisingly, often be found in these teams. Consequently, a mixed model seems more appropriate: an FX overlay team establishes the FX exposure; with leeway granted to certain asset class managers. Or, in another version: a central research input and the core of the FX class management system placed in or close to the fixed income system; a range of controlled implementations in other asset class universes.

One of the issues concerns optimal currency hedging. Overlay currency management involves a decision whether to hedge or to keep the exposure to foreign assets unhedged. Optimal currency hedging will depend upon the structure of the portfolio allocation (as between asset classes; geographical blocks; the typologies of economies, which are more or less developed; and between factors, in general), upon the degree of risk aversion and also upon the currency block. Hedging may vary from 0% to 100%, depending on the investor's profile (it means minimising the *regret* associated with the advantages and disadvantages of whether or not to hedge). If the aim is to avoid increasing the total risk of the portfolio, then fixed income components, in particular, will be hedged, *a fortiori* if certain currencies have a weak or indeed negative correlation with the underlying equity market(s). Finally, the more the relevant currencies are characterised by regimes of high volatility, the more advantageous it will be to keep the exposures unhedged, in order to increase the diversification effects. This must all be decided upon individually by each investor. In any event, circumstances will dictate the manoeuvre to be adopted, which thus advocates an active position.

Currencies are elements which make a significant contribution to the structure and formation of returns within the bond universe (global fixed income), much more so than in the equity universe – the contribution is even more pronounced in the field of "developed" economies than in that of "emerging" economies. There is, accordingly, room for a differentiated approach between the equity and bond universes. The factors which determine both interest rates and currencies (most commonly, monetary policy or macro-economic trends) are mostly the same, whilst more specific factors, which are generally more micro-economic, are at work in the equity universe (sector-specific risk factors, dividend policy, Mergers & Acquisitions, earnings trends ...while recognising the relevance of the global macro trends). Finally, it is a well-observed fact, which may evolve, that equity managers with currency management talents are fairly rare (it is, therefore, appropriate to try to separate the two areas of management); conversely, one may consider that a search for talents which combine the ability to manage both dimensions simultaneously *or* the implementation of an organisation which enables (i) the equity manager to concentrate on the underlying shares, (ii) a team to be devoted to the management of currencies, should create a competitive edge allowing for an inefficiency in the equity market to be exploited.

Fully-centralised organisations – investment is a question of governance and execution – have the advantage of leaving any decisions on currencies to specialists, whilst the bonds and equity managers take advantage of their views, in order to form their strategies for the underlying assets. Centralisation means incurring exposure to a concentration of risk regarding the decisions of one, sole team, no matter how expert it is. Furthermore, by allowing, as is often the case, a certain degree of latitude in management to the management teams of the underlying assets (currency weights matching), operating costs and risks may be increased.

In the fully-decentralised model, the benefits of diversifying the currency risk within the various decision-making centres of the managers of the underlying asset (equities, bonds) are undeniable, even if uncertain (the total contribution may be low; the net benefit of the negative impacts on the quality of the pure management of the underlying may be disappointing). Such a decentralised approach seems more appropriate, when the view of the underlying asset and that of the currency are fairly closely linked. Such an approach leaves the currency view to non-specialists, which may constitute a weakness and requires a clear distinction to be made between the various sources of return, when analysing the performance attribution.

Mixed approaches may seem more pragmatic, since they avoid interference between the FX decision and the investment processes in respect of the pure underlyings (this is particularly true in the event of delegations to external managers). This may imply different views as between teams (the diversification benefit of which should be estimated) and generally higher transaction costs.

One may consider that it is preferable to incorporate central currency management into the overlay asset allocation, i.e. allocation of risks for all asset classes for the whole of the portfolio; supervision of the real positions by the teams of managers of underlyings; the possibility of implementing tactical currency management, in addition to target currency weights. This type of organisational model is based on a central definition of the investment strategy, which incorporates various inputs (macro-economic scenario and its impact on the asset classes, target asset allocation). It ensures that the equity and fixed income allocation is delegated to specialist teams, together with currency hedging targets (with the possible grant of leeways, in particular in fixed income, provided that a talent is established). Execution and risk-monitoring are carried out centrally, with attention paid to certain instruments (swaps) and liquidity management (impact of margin calls).

Irrespective of the model selected, a certain number of questions must be raised by the investor: the importance of currencies in the allocation framework, a question of investment philosophy; possible differences between the currency management philosophy and the investment philosophy, with regard to the pure underlying asset classes (e.g. macro-process for fixed income, bottom-up for equity and short-term momentum for currency); confidence/belief in the internal or external capacity to create over-performance through active currency management; the capacity of the tools to distinguish the origin of returns in the portfolio; the capacity to install an efficient, centralised platform for the execution of transactions.

The fact remains that currencies are a component of efficient portfolio allocation, which should be actively managed. Currencies are a source of risk diversification, which allow for exposure to macro-scenarii. The hedging policy must suit the allocation structure, the status of the currency and market circumstances. The segmentation of the analysis and decision framework is important (themes/factors) and must be dynamic within time. The need for currency specialists for the active management of the currency exposure, within the context of an asset allocation overlay, seems established, insofar as this is carried out with a transparent view of the positions taken by the underlying managers. Consequently, the managers of the underlyings may have to take currency positions in their portfolio, if this component is explicit and is linked to the investment process and properly (appropriately) monitored. In addition, issues such as tactical solutions for currency overlay management or macro-edge solutions to cope with extreme risks may be the subject of additional investigations.

Allocation for SWF

The question of the optimum allocation for a sovereign (wealth fund) is not, or no longer, a theoretical one and practical case studies are now analysed. The concept of sovereign is addressed in the widest possible sense (central bank, government budget entities, SWFs strictly speaking, pension funds and state entities which are dependent on the sovereign) and the whole of the sovereign assets and liabilities are incorporated within an Asset and Liability Management framework. Optimum allocation will depend upon the nature, size and uncertainty thereof. It is not an easy matter to value intangibles, such as human or natural capital, and the usual, macro-economic variables do not seem appropriate (flow variables rather than stock variables). Furthermore, the necessary link between the sovereign's wealth management and the core elements of fiscal policy, monetary policy and public debt management is influenced by relevant statistical aggregates[5].

The question of optimum allocation for the sovereign is very similar to that of the allocation of FX reserves, the latter constituting a large part of the sovereign portfolio. That said, the reasons and objectives for a central bank or SWF to hold the portfolio (limiting the risk of a sudden suspension for the central bank; maximising a utility function in relation to domestic objectives for the SWF; this argues in favour of a riskier allocation by the SWF) are various. Furthermore, SWFs may pursue a return objective or a tax-smoothing objective. We have seen that certain central banks have recently started to diversify assets, occasionally by referring to a return objective, in addition to the more traditional objectives (risk-free assets, liquidity) (possible conflict of objectives).

It seems to be accepted that a SWF should incorporate a hedging demand against commodity price variations. The starting point is an analysis of the sovereign's balance sheet (an estimation of all the state's assets and liabilities at market price; risks, macro shock sensitivity, volatility of the items). The sovereign balance sheet includes (i) (assets) foreign reserves, gold, Special Drawing Rights; pension fund assets; SWF; other public-sector assets (state-owned enterprises, real estate); present value of future taxes, fees seigniorage; (ii) (liabilities) base money; local currency debt; foreign currency debt; pension fund liabilities; contingent claims (implicit guarantees to banks ...); present value of expenditure on economic and social development, security, government administration, benefits to other sectors; present value of target wealth for future generations. Liabilities can be valued as contingent claims on sovereign assets and the value of the sovereign's assets and their volatility can be proxied as a function of the promised payments in foreign currencies, i.e. default barrier.

The optimum depends upon (i) fiscal assets, their nature and size and on unconditional liabilities and their uncertainty, (ii) a performance-seeking portfolio and a hedging demand portfolio which takes into account the variability of the fiscal surplus and external and domestic debt (risks linked to inflation, to fluctuations in the price of raw materials, linked more generally to the fiscal surplus and to

[5] Cf. Zvi Bodie, Marie Brière, "Sovereign Wealth and Risk Management", Working Paper Amundi, WP-011-2011, May 2011.

domestic and foreign liabilities). Finally, in practice, there is a need for institutional coordination of entities which hold assets and liabilities (at the very least the Ministry of Finance, Treasury, debt office, central bank, SWF). Supervision of the ALM might fall to the SWF, since the other entities are exposed to conflicts of objectives and/or conflicts of interest (monetary policy for the central bank). The fact that the MoF is often in charge of the SWF, of fiscal policy and debt issuance may facilitate this. Taking such an approach, the concept of a sovereign must be as broad as possible, including all those entities whose assets may be fungible in a state of crisis.

A stabilising assignment for a SWF represents an exposure to fluctuations in the price of raw materials which affect income, to uncertainties concerning the level and rate of production and extraction. The SWF performs a hedging function.

Essay 4

REVISITING THE CONCEPTS OF ACTIVE AND PASSIVE MANAGEMENT

From smart beta to factor allocation

Let us return to the categories of alpha, beta and smart beta. As producer and not from the point of view of the portfolio, in respect of which each strategy includes exposure to one or more factors; (ii) multi-factorial allocation is therefore the appropriate objective in order to optimise exposures; (iii) simultaneous clarification of the governance framework and of the investment beliefs (beta, alpha, smart beta: why, where, how?) completes the process.

Consequently, it can be understood that (i) a smart beta index cannot, strictly speaking, be considered to be passive exposure, since it includes a non-express/implied decision in favour of active exposure to one or more factors; we call it active when there is (un)conscious exposure to some factor; passive cannot mean no exposure, because there is always some exposure, but instead signifies a mode of implementation; everything is active, the rest is execution; (ii) a transparent clarification and full understanding of such factors are an absolute necessity since, from the point of view of the portfolio and the investor, knowledge (at the very least) or the direction/selection of factorial biases are requirements; (iii) accordingly, everything seems to take place as if the detailed analysis of the inefficiencies and risk biases of the cap-weighted indexes – which constituted the legitimate basis for their denunciation – was *not* accompanied by a similar effort with respect to the alternative indexes and strategies which were intended to replace them: this black box asymmetry has not helped answer the principal question, i.e. regarding the use in the portfolio of (classic) beta, alpha and smart beta; however, the answer lies in a general portfolio *diagnosis* based on an in-depth knowledge of the factors of each of the strategies; and then, the construction of their active allocation. Some or other smart beta (or alpha or classic beta) strategy has no meaning, as such, if its specific, factorial contribution to the overall portfolio cannot be explained, possibly corrected or directed. The factorial allocation for the whole of the portfolio is the ultimate benefit.

The universe of factors is very broad – extending well beyond those factors alone of value, low volatility and (small/medium) size which seem, however, to make a significant contribution to *all* smart beta strategies. The factor universe is infinite. It makes sense for the investor (i) to know that some or other factor is present in a given strategy (factorial composition), and (ii) to select/direct that factorial composition. Many investors, who are still at point (i) or an even earlier stage, are exposed to criticism that they, unknowingly, choose value and small-cap selection strategies, old wine in a new bottle (marketing joke). This criticism falls away, if the widest factorial world can be the subject of a decision to select and allocate *ex ante* and *ex post*, based on an exhaustive knowledge of the current situation. Similarly, even greater inefficiencies which are present in the classic market value bond indexes (concentration risk, weak response to change) open up a field for identifying more relevant factors (credit volatility ...).

The smart beta indexes contain (i) an *active* exposure to factors, whether conscious or unconscious, and therefore an (express or implied) decision; (ii) which acquires meaning in the context of a general allocation according to active strategies/factors (from this perspective); a smart beta index or an external alpha manager may have things in common in terms of factorial DNA (style, size ...); to allocate to one or the other may prove comparable in part; however, passive allocation to a classic cap-weighted beta also includes an implied/express decision regarding exposure to certain factors. Consequently, it is the very concepts of *active* management and *passive* management which must be reviewed: an established exposure to one or more factors, which are not neutral either for strategy or for the portfolio as a whole, forms part of an express or implied *decision*, the unconscious or involuntary nature of such a decision does not eliminate the active nature of the factors under consideration; (iii) if the implementation of a smart beta (or even classic beta) index-based strategy is *passive* with regard to a given strategy X, the selection of that strategy is not neutral from the point of view of the global, factorial, portfolio exposure and, therefore, the portfolio construction: it therefore forms part of an (express/implied) decision concerning active elements; (iv) the multi-factorial allocation must lead to a clarification of the investment beliefs for *each of the principal factors*, over and above the three categories of alpha, beta and smart beta alone.

Smart beta strategies provide a good example of the governance issues involved when adopting investment directions – *a fortiori* new ones. The task of explaining to the Board, the need to find the best way of benchmarking performance (smart beta is often compared to a traditional index, which is evidence of the extent to which classical indexes are used as benchmarks), the question of positioning the long-term strategy in order to be able to accept and withstand prolonged under-performance (by comparison with a classical index) are all challenges and obstacles which should be taken seriously.

Beyond active and passive investment

There are three issues of debate with regard to active versus passive management: whether active management can add value; implementation within a global portfolio; (in)efficiency of the benchmark, in the case of passive management.

Active management is beneficial for those who doubt that they can select a successful asset manager; for mature asset classes characterised by high liquidity and strong efficiency; for linear, non-volatile bull markets, where exposure to the asset class provides the entire performance; for the implementation of market-timing allocation decisions with no interference between asset allocation and active management decisions. Conversely, active management is a plus, when a manager's skill is established and most useful, i.e. in non-mature markets (emergings, small caps) and/or in trendless/unclear markets; when replication is costly (typically in less liquid markets), enhanced management, which is intended to limit costs, is better; when the investment universe is not totally or only partially investable, as in the case of SRI or Sharia investments; when there are doubts as to whether the usual benchmark is efficient enough (over-concentrations, style/size biases etc...).

Exhaustive academic work has been carried out, in order to challenge the usual, cap-weight of most mainstream benchmarks. It shows that many risk-based weighting schemes are more efficient (minimum variance, maximum diversification, risk parity). The added value is spread/shared between active asset managers (because they use these strategies as *active* strategies, including judgmental sequences and/or because they use smart beta indexes as an *active* exposure to some factors or as an exposure to some *active* factors) and index providers (because they manufacture), making the distinction between active and passive less clear (the classic cap-weighted index providers are also the providers of smart beta indexes). These strategies exhibit high TE (tracking errors) by comparison with cap-weighted schemes, even higher than classic, actively-managed investment processes. These supposedly more sophisticated strategies come at a higher cost, since index providers charge a licence fee on top of the classic fee charged for mainstream benchmarks. These indexes may prove more costly because they are difficult to replicate due to a reasonably high turnover and a size bias in favour of small caps.

Implementing this kind of risk-weighted strategy, which optimises the concentration risk, will favour the risk parity strategy. When concentration and turnover are high, as in the case of the minimum variance strategy, a filter is used before imposing the risk-weighted scheme, in order for stock-picking and turnover not to be blind. Finally, the low volatility anomaly (outperformance which is contrary to the "high risk, high return" theoretical prophecy) will have to be seriously questioned, if the trend toward alternative betas continues unabated (note that neither systematic nor total risks are associated with higher returns; and the higher the risk, the lower the stock return).

These strategies are arguably introducing a new frontier within the active management space between judgmental and rule-based (algorithmic/quantitative) management. Rule-based does not necessarily mean passive. Since it may prove costly to replicate, some enhanced management of a rule-based model portfolio may prove more cost-effective. In addition, the *judgmental* field may prove larger than expected (on top of the classic, discretionary choices): choice of the rules used, together with fundamental stock picking; market timing of the rules. Any new rule-based benchmark provides a means of clarifying the various steps in the active investment process.

There are only active exposures; the rest is (passive) implementation

Behind the sudden emergence of the "smart beta" strategies, which call into question the classical cap-weighted indexes, appear serious issues of portfolio construction and allocation, of execution, of governance and investment beliefs and, finally, of organisation. The revolution enters, as it were, through the back door of the integration of smart beta strategies. One notes that (i) the indispensable analysis of the risk structure of such strategies (total risk, systematic risk, specific risk), together with that of their exposure to factors (size, style, low volatility ...), that for low volatility (mean variance), risk parity or equal weight, e.g. maximum diversification, leads one to wonder about the construction of the combined, factorial exposure of such strategies; (ii) it leads one above all to wonder about the factorial exposure for the whole of the portfolio once, for example, the existence of a small-cap exposure in a mean variance strategy means that such exposure will be added to the already existing exposure, which is present in a strategy, such as for example, an active strategy delegated to an asset manager. Such exposures add up in terms of the total risk. And so on and so forth; (iii) this means that the investor cannot ignore this, that it is best for the investor to choose this exposure: in this way, the ensuing multi-factor exposure, even if passively implemented, is the result of a choice or action. This will also apply to the factorial components which are present in the classical indexes and which have been maintained in the portfolio. *The concept of an "active" asset transforms and expands.* There are only active exposures, whether known or not, whether chosen or not, but ideally both known and chosen. Only the implementation *may* be passive; (iv) This gives rise to questions of execution, organisation and governance: (a) if factor exposure is, in our view, *active* in the sense in which we have used the term *active* (conscious or unconscious choice), implementation is *passive*. The quality of execution will prove to be key, (b) if the smart beta approach leads, more generally, to an understanding of the factors for the whole of the portfolio and of the resulting implied or express choices, questions of organisation arise: does smart beta have to be managed by the indexed management department, or by the active equity department? However, since the subject is ultimately the correct, multi-factor allocation at the overall portfolio level, one realises more naturally that this comes within the jurisdiction of a "strategy" team which has a good overview and is, for example, able to arbitrate the simultaneous presence of a given factor within different pockets, which come under the control of distinct entities (classic passive, active, smart beta), thus placing the indexed department no less naturally in an implementation/execution role. More generally, this is an illustration of a reality: organisations adapt belatedly to the lessons learnt from crises and/or from new developments, (c) these questions of organisation are accompanied by the need to align the whole of the governance (including the Board) and, in this instance, by the learning exercise regarding how to explain and convince, according to the clearest and simplest terms and conditions of evaluation. One must, therefore, be persuasive with regard to the investment objectives within a smart beta strategy (e.g. by emphasising the expected reduction in volatility), while warning of the need to accept a duration of evaluation (it is clear that such a strategy may underperform a classic index for several years in a certain market environment), to agree upon the evaluation method (paradoxically, the strategies which aim to extricate themselves from classic cap-weighted indexes are often measured by comparison with such indexes), to note, accordingly, that a smart beta strategy, as compared to a classic index, will mechanically show a risk-taking (TE). Confidence, alignment, duration. This is a broader aspect of the subject of governance of investment, of investment beliefs and of the temporal horizon, when faced with a reality made up of human nature and reflexes and incentives based on the calendar year. A cultural challenge, since (new) investment culture has to be ingrained in both an appropriate and firm manner.

Challenging smart beta, playing the devil's advocate

"Just old snake oil in new bottles?"[6] "Smart beta=Dumb Beta + Smart Marketing"? The most detailed criticisms of smart beta rightly highlight the fact that the reason for the better performance of these strategies is due to a value and small-cap bias, which is known to generate over-performance over the long-term – at least until now - (and not to a better covariance matrix, contra trading against the cap-

[6] Cf. James Montier, "No Silver Bullets in Investing", GMO White Paper, December 2013.

weighted index, etc...). However, this finding does not invalidate the strategy. On the contrary, it confirms its original element, i.e. the (un)conscious, active, factorial selection. The factors are not limited only to elements of style (value) and size (small-cap). Of more relevance here is the question of the *price* at which, for example, the actual entry is made into the value and/or small-cap universe when the investment is systematic (blind). Finally, risk factors are presented as a transformation function of the assets, i.e. essentially long/short combinations (assets = long-only, constrained instruments). It would not be surprising if the risk factors, as defined, have a low correlation with the assets which they represent. "No risk factor is going to do well independent of its pricing". "Risk Factors = Assets + Leverage".

The question of leverage is important, since it comes at a price. This may be fatal for anyone who ignores short-term market fluctuations (you have to have a view on the market path, i.e. path dependency.)

That is not all. The measure of risk (volatility) in risk parity style approaches is criticised for its procyclical nature (the opposite of a value-driven instrument), i.e. an accentuation of exposures when historic volatility is (abnormally) low and a reduction thereof when it is (abnormally) high (2007, 2009).

(1) Pricing and valuation are the most important. (2) Is it good to be agnostic about expected returns? Let us consider (2) for a moment. Distrust of the capacity of *active* managers to deliver, over the long term, a satisfactory (over)performance, adjusted in order to take account of risk and costs, and strong doubts regarding the very possibility for an investor to predict (forecast) and expect returns and/or sources of return (relating both to human limitations and the "irrational" features of the financial markets), have led to a certain number of options, which are often questionable. The choice of a classic, market cap weighted, "passive" management is an example thereof but the *apparent neutralisation of the active decision* is misleading, since (i) opting for such an index with regard to a portfolio is a decision, (ii) the index itself is not risk-neutral or factor-neutral. The apparent, *impersonal* neutralisation of the decision conceals a lack of management accountability which raises serious problems from the point of view of investment and also governance (areas of confusion and misunderstandings, blurred responsibilities). A second example, of a different nature, can be found within the public/private equity arbitrage

with regard to investment in shares, which is favourable to private equity: equity would then supposedly escape the volatility and irrationality of the public markets, where a clear vision of a particular share's specific fundamentals may be polluted, or indeed nullified, by global, market factors; private equity would, in turn, provide a more solid vehicle for long-term investment which would also be closer to the specific fundamentals of the investment case. This apparent benefit is misleading, since it is not stated that (i) the apparent anaesthesia of volatility (as compared to that of the mark to market) does not eliminate risk, (ii) private equity is to a certain extent equivalent to public equity + leverage, (iii) illiquidity is a cost and a risk. Not the winning formula which is sometimes announced. It is, however, probable that this is to the advantage of a certain number of "decision-makers", in terms of tranquillity and time, which once again raises problems for both investment and governance.

However, one of the most fascinating manifestations of this trend of lack of accountability in respect of making investment management decisions (or the so-called neutralisation of the decision/forecast) is contained in the intention, claim or assertion not to make any prediction/expectation of returns or variable which may contribute to it. The optimisation of diversification systems which are systematically implemented could be a good replacement for it. Once again, the neutralisation and removal of the decision-making investor, who is transformed into the invisible man, cannot conceal (i) the presence of implied or express choices which are *effectively* in favour of some or other strategy or factor (accordingly, an analysis of a certain number of systematic strategies seeking to maximise or optimise diversification shows a low volatility component, whether or not paired with a low systematic risk-high specific risk barbell component (barbell exposure to low and high total risks), a size (small/medium) bias and a significant low-beta portfolio component; the minimum variance portfolio shows, in turn, a low systematic, specific and total risk component, (ii) the existence of a temporal dynamic of the elements or factors which form part of the strategy (they are not independent of the upward/downward market trends, whether more or less volatile, turbulent or correlated; their relevance and their performance may decrease, possibly linked to an inefficiency which is exploited by the strategy) calls for human action/decision, (iii) the price and valuation of a certain number of stocks, at the time they are included in the portfolio, cannot be neutral or of indifference, *a fortiori* when the strategy incorporates a significant value factor (moreover, a judgmental filter is seen to be added to the systematic portfolio construction in the case of the highest performing strategies, such as minimum variance).

Ultimately, we think that there are considerable areas of confusion regarding the concepts of investment *decision* and *active* investment, the consequences of which are felt in the quality of management, governance and assessment of responsibilities.

Exploiting inefficiencies

Observation seems to indicate, contrary to what is postulated by theory, that the least volatile shares outperformed, at least in the last thirty years, and outperform the most volatile shares (which therefore seems to contradict the assertion that the higher the risk, the higher the return). Although this factual observation may, in principle, represent a certain macro-financial environment at a certain point of time, namely the secular fall in interest rates, it invites reflection nonetheless.

Challenging the theory

Theory teaches us that a low-risk strategy should ultimately produce low returns and that, within a sufficiently broad portfolio, the volatility of the individual return on a stock is less important than its contribution to the overall volatility of the portfolio (which in turn depends upon the correlation between the return on a particular stock and the return on all the others). A certain number of approaches and experimentations have prospered on the basis of this challenge to theory by observation: inverse stock volatility weighting (reduction of risk); equal risk contribution weights (risk equalisation) of individual stocks or groups of stocks (clusters). Some optimisation refinements have been added: a construction of weightings in the so-called mean variance (inverse volatility) approach; a premise according to which there is a degree of proportionality between the expected return on individual stocks and their volatility (the more volatile a stock's return, the higher its average return), which forms the basis of the so-called maximum diversification approach (search for optimal weightings which maximise the Sharpe ratio); a premise according to which only a downside deviation from volatility has a proportional relationship with the expected return. And there are others.

What is striking at this stage, in addition to the shared characteristic that they do not comply with traditional theory (which is not, *a priori*, an adequate condition for dismissing them), is their heuristic nature based on premises (assumptions), which may seem arbitrary in the affirmation of a certain relationship between risk and expected return. There is much at stake in the very formulation of such premises. The propositions of the theory: "the lower (higher) the risk, the lower (higher) the return" and the premises of a certain number of experimental approaches (premises because they are not yet demonstrated, experimental because they result from a positive approach by trial and error: "the lower the risk, the better the Sharpe ratio" (mean variance), "the more equal the risk contributions, the better the Sharpe ratio" (equal risk weights), "the higher the risk or some component of the risk, the higher the expected return" or "the higher the volatility of an individual stock return, the higher the average return" (maximum diversification). It can be seen that, although they appear to be dealing with related concepts, these propositions and premises risk creating misunderstandings, if one is not careful: return/average return/*expected* return (if it can be demonstrated *ex post* that high volatilities have not produced high returns, this would still not invalidate the proposition that "the higher the risk, the higher the *expected* return" (role of expectations); the element of expectations also potentially applies to the risk component (*expected* risk); high/low asymmetries/dissymetries regarding the relevant concepts and variables (the great majority of the propositions and premises suggest a symmetry of forms as between highs and lows, of return and risk); return versus Sharpe ratio. In particular, we do not consider that all these approaches take adequate consideration of time, memory, forgetfulness and expectations (or at least fail to clarify their position), although such consideration seems critical (i) in the approaches which have to use series of (historical) returns and postulate some assumptions with regard to expected returns; (ii) and incorporate a human science dimension (this is a wide spectrum: behavioural, psychological, philosophical ...), given that such propositions and premises are advanced by an economic Subject in connection with its own specific referential. Accordingly, a theory of time and expectations is required, together with a theory of the economic Subject – the two being linked – in order to anchor all the approaches which may, otherwise, seem to float arbitrarily in the ether.

The few tests which have been effected in respect of the premises of each of the approaches, together with the behaviour of risk-adjusted performance (return, standard deviation, Sharpe ratio), on an average basis over the long-term (since at least the 1970's) and per ten-year sub-period, would tend to suggest that (i) the higher the volatility of the stock return, the lower the average return; (ii) all the approaches have a tendency to improve the risk-adjusted performance of the classic market cap index; (iii) the better performance of the market cap index over a few sub-periods seems to be linked to a strong upward directionality of the share price (and therefore the use of some or other approach seems to involve the expression of a view/expectation of the market and the stocks which comprise it); (iv) the Minimum Variance approach seems better and the most robust (drawdown); (v) the alternative approaches to the classic market cap weighted index derive a non-negligible part of their performance from exposure to a certain number of factors which differentiate them from the market cap weighted: size (small cap) and style (value, high price to book) constitute a pronounced bias; a more neutral momentum factor; the low exposure to big caps and to market risk (beta) explains the less favourable sub-periods.

All in the same (factor) boat

In the same way that the classic market cap weighted index is not risk-neutral but, on the contrary, interposes an exposure to a certain number of factors (in particular beta and big stocks), the alternative strategies also include pronounced exposures to certain factors, so that, from the point of view of the total portfolio risk, there is a greater or lesser diversification of factors (i.e. the optimal combination of classic and alternative strategies is equivalent to a factor allocation). These new approaches may be seen as a means of exposure to one or more diversifying factors, risk and/or macro factors, which provide an additional return by comparison with the market risk (beta factor) alone, which a merely passive exposure to the risk factor should allow us to capture. It is also probable that such strategies enable inefficiencies and therefore associated risk premia to be used (and ultimately reduced); such inefficiencies themselves resulting in part from the domination by the classic cap-weighted indexes. These strategies must be seen within a general approach to the arbitrage of market inefficiencies and as an injection of diversifying factors within an allocation framework which is governed by (risk) factors rather than by asset classes. Equally, it is probable that such strategies show a sensitivity or a polarisation towards certain macro-economic factors or scenarii, which might help explain the behaviour of such strategies during certain sub-periods which may have constituted a break in the macro-financial regime.

In general, all these approaches and strategies, which may appear somewhat scattered, must be understood, on a non-exhaustive basis, as an *awareness* of a broad field – much broader than the ultimately fairly narrow and therefore biased practices which prevailed for half a century – of total risk (total volatility) and total factors and consequently – as an attempt to saturate it. This field is intertwined with a universe of inefficiencies which are all the more pronounced since, rightly, they were not subject to a clear *consciousness* and an investment strategy. The arbitrage cycle produced by these new approaches will probably lead to a new market (regime) status which will in turn call forth others. These approaches thus form a market dynamic. Finally, although all these approaches seem to be based on a positive point of view (i.e. they seem to contribute something, risk-adjusted return or total risk/volatility, in particular), they seem to raise a normative and theoretical difficulty (i) when compared to certain, fundamental, theoretical propositions which seemed to be established: low-risk investment strategies should produce relatively low returns; a market cap weighted approach to equity investment should be consistent with the Capital Asset Pricing Model (CAPM) and the portfolio should be mean variance efficient, *assuming that the market itself is efficient*; in order to be consistent with the modern theory of the portfolio, approaches like Mean Variance should postulate that expected returns on all individual stocks are equal; however, these “alternative” approaches seem to support the theoretical assertion that passive exposure to a source of risk (factor) provides a higher return than that from cash (risk premium); (ii) between the premise advanced by a particular alternative strategy and that which observation seems to indicate: in the case of the so-called Maximum Diversification or Risk Efficiency approach, the premise that the more volatile a stock’s return, the higher the future average return, or the higher the risk (whatever the measure), the higher the expected return (with the idea that the investment is rewarded for taking a stock specific risk) is confronted with occasionally conflicting observations.

All the observations seem to indicate that (i) all the alternative strategies to the classic market cap weighted index approach produce *on average* a better risk-adjusted performance; (ii) this is not true for a certain number of sub-periods. It can be inferred that (i) this is a robust result which can be considered as a sort of norm or law; (ii) on the contrary, this is a matter of chance (a certain number of analyses show, however, that the result imposes itself on a mere random walk) or that the longest period under observation remains nonetheless an "exception", i.e. a particular, macro-financial *regime* which is unfavourable to the classic approach and favourable to others (in this case, sensitivity analyses to a certain number of macro-factors and/or macro-scenarii are required, in order to try and identify the polarisation trends of such classic or alternative strategies as compared with given macro-economic situations or variables; for example, the period of disinflation, "great moderation", associated with falling nominal and real interest rates is arguably a distinctive feature of the regime which started in the 1980's); (iii) the result is normal, in the sense that it highlights a market inefficiency (classic approach) which should be reduced over time by the alternative strategies (one should then observe a reduction over time in the risk-adjusted outperformance of the so-called alternative strategies).

Institutional dilemmas and choices

Points (i), (ii) or (iii) make the institution responsible for deciding and implementing the strategies, whether classic or alternative, when faced with a certain number of difficulties and what could be called *institutional dilemmas* (it can never be stressed enough that the production of the investment, and therefore of the associated performance, is an institutional act which cannot be understood or analysed without taking into account the socio-institutional conditions of the entity which is responsible for producing them, within the context of the various structures (organisation, governance, regulatory environment ...) and of the men and women who are responsible for them). Accordingly, points (i) and (ii), which should ideally produce a favourable incentive for alternative strategies can only be reconciled in the context of an institutional structure which has defined a risk-adjusted performance policy for a certain number of investment universes within a sufficiently long-term time framework, after bringing all the institution's internal governance (front office, CIO, CEO, Board ...) into alignment, in order to accept the non-zero probability that such alternative strategies may be temporarily disappointing (and temporarily may mean a number of years). If this is not the case and the front office manager is, for example, aware that the *real* temporal framework for the valuation is the calendar year, then the institutional structure of incentives will produce a sub-optimal result (from the point of view of the absolute results obtained): while being aware that, in all probability, the market cap weighted strategy will weaken the institution's long-term risk-adjusted performance, with occasionally even the certainty or the intuition that the outperformance of the classic strategy during a sub-period which is more or less long will ultimately prove to be illusory (fake alpha: capturing risk premia on future hidden fat tails), the classic strategy will, however, be chosen in a sort of preference for the present which refers less to investment matters than to the institutional structure which makes decisions. The same will be true of the choice between a passive or active strategy for a given investment territory. In the absence of an objective determination over time of an active or passive policy, which has been brought into line with the institution's governance, the unclear incentive will produce a preference for the passive strategy, which is easy to relate to governance (there is nothing simpler than reading the result of an index) and politically neutral (the market bears the responsibility and erases that of the person). Overall, by combining these two dimensions alone (the choice between an active or passive strategy, the choice within the passive approach between a classic market cap weighted strategy and alternative strategies of mean variance, risk efficiency or maximum diversification), the incentives structure will potentially produce a sub-optimal decision in respect of the investment universe itself (by remaining passive, we deprive ourselves of the active production of performance in a universe where there is potential) and in the choice of passive management (market cap weighted is preferred). Point (iii) may then at least serve as a pretext (unless it is a conviction in the institution's established policy) for the more or less rapid erosion of the inefficiency permitted by the alternative strategy, as compared to the classic market cap weighted approach, but does not justify making it a central pivot for long-term investment. Ultimately, active and passive are fragile concepts since, whether active or passive, they both incorporate an "active" exposure to some factors, whether conscious or not. All investment strategies are, in this respect, active strategies.

Long-term arbitrages of inefficiencies

However, investment only seems to be justified in the context of a conviction that possible arbitrages of inefficiencies exist and are anchored to a long-term temporal policy. A so-called long-term investment strategy is only justified by the use and correction of a form of mispricing. Whether the mispricing issue is explicit (e.g. the price of carbon) or not (adopting a mean variance strategy means first using the inefficiency produced by the market cap weighted index, before becoming a so-called change of style or allocation), whether the institution wishes to adopt a Socially Responsible Investment (SRI) or Environment, Social, Governance (ESG) strategy (there are multiple possibilities for deploying long-term investment strategies in an investment universe which has not yet integrated correct expectations regarding the occurrence of environmental, societal or governance risks) or wishes to pursue, in general, a policy for the extraction of alpha, there is an alignment between the investment strategy, the status of the long-term investor and the search for a return from the strategy. Accordingly, it is not appropriate to contrast the SRI/ESG strategy and the profitability of the strategy since, if the strategy is relevant and correctly calibrated, it will result in the reduction of an inefficiency and will therefore deliver alpha (from this point of view, the ESG/SRI approach must be thought of as a participant in a general alpha policy – the incentives strategies and the strategies for changing an investor's attitude, such as L-shares and loyalty shares, also form part of this). SRI/ESG is taken here as a positive investment strategy, differing from the usual normative approach. One can consequently understand, conversely, the extent to which the accumulation of assets parked in classic passive management (market cap weighted index), if it represents a line of reasoning which can be described as rational, in view of a given institutional environment in which the individual decision-maker seeks to optimise the given constraints of a real or perceived investment horizon and an aligned governance status, barely contributes to an improved optimality of not only the functioning of the market but above all the pursuit of long-term investment objectives which are both profitable *and* societal.

A strategy to make use of inefficiency represents a market failure. This failure may concern a set of issues which are related to a price (carbon) or a particular market segment (sector, stock). It often refers to a structure of flows and channels of savings or reserves, which is itself sub-optimal. The theoretical vision of the market as a unitary and liquid pool providing access to all possibilities is a figment of the imagination. In real life, accumulations of assets can co-exist, within segments which provide a low return and which do not serve any express long-term objective for the purposes of alpha and the use of mispricings (like the enormous allocations to government Treasuries which are deemed to be the safest, although the utility function linked to their liquidity may provide a justification for this), with established financing requirements and investment opportunities in segments in which savings are not placed, unless there is a framework which enhances the risk and an appropriate incentive structure (such as the infrastructure projects in a certain number of emerging markets).

The bias of the flows structure (financing gaps, misfinancing) and the sub-optimality of the price structures (mispricing) constitute two identical faces of one and the same question. The concepts of liquidity and value can be found here. Liquidity always refers back to the trade or to the difficulty of determining the trade (that which evidences the implementation of a relationship is liquid) and the concept of liquidity is based on a definition of the economic Subject whose fundamental structure is that of a disposition for others (exchange). Conversely, every so-called liquidity crisis is a disruption of this structure of otherness. The concept of value, in turn, refers back to a substance which constitutes an entirety, a being-in-itself of that which contains value and, at the same time, indicates the distance from this substance at any given time (that which is en route towards this substance has value), a gap which can never be reduced or crossed unless it can be maintained, because the value is enshrined within the framework of a temporality. Value is both substance and the path towards substance and, in the real life of the economic Subject, the path is predominant and creates the economic and financial dynamic. Although the substance contains the promise and the requirement for the long-term (which is merged *ad infinitum* with the disappearance of temporality), the path towards that substance constantly exerts a force back towards that which can in a word be reduced to "short-termism" but which, as can be seen, is less an anomaly in the structure of economics and finance than one of its fundamental constituent elements and its spirit. One can also understand the extent to which the concept of the long-term, for the same reasons, is marked by impossibility, which is a source of efforts, debates and discouragements.

Because value is, in the real life of the economic Subject, as much a path towards the substance as the substance itself, the concept of value and that of liquidity tend to converge and merge. The path towards substance can only be thought of in and through the determination of the relationship between the economic Subjects and therefore the trade of which liquidity is the marker, the witness and the name. A liquidity crisis contains within it a disruption of value. These brief reflections are developed in greater detail in our earlier works (see on this, *Philosophy in Economics* and *La Valeur – Substance, échange et prix*).

These few theoretical reflections enable one to understand the general operating framework in which a long-term investor may find himself. There is, at any given moment, a reference to a substance, whether it concerns an institution (long-term objectives, criteria or references which help define a rationale) or individual investment strategies (such as the determination of an alpha policy for the whole of the assets managed or, more particularly, of investment in a given stock or value). There is also, simultaneously, a path towards the substance which takes the form of the determination of a relationship, of the exchange with the other players, which are often summarised, by way of description and analysis, by the terms flow and liquidity. These two dimensions produce dynamics by rubbing against each other. The whole is, finally, encased, first, in an individual institutional framework (the relevant entity) and a general institutional framework (the other institutions) which is defined by and which produces norms, rules, incentives, disincentives and constraints of a diverse nature (regulatory, governance, internal or external management of the investment universes or political ....) and, second, in the decision-making structure of the individual or collective (the team, the entity ...) economic Subject which belongs to the long-term investor institution. The two frameworks produce, in turn, a dynamic, frictions and conflicts by superimposing themselves on the first two dimensions discussed above, of substance and the path towards substance (value and liquidity).

PART II

THE DYNAMICS OF THE FINANCIAL MARKETS[7]

[7] Part of this work was published in 2008 in *Carnets monétaires,* Economica. It contained columns and notes from the years 2000-2005. Certain passages are from an earlier date.

Essay 5

VALUE, LIQUIDITY AND STOCK MARKETS

The macro-regime, from disinflation to excess liquidity

Disinflation and a structural decrease in nominal interest rates were central to the appreciation of financial assets during the 1990's. They also caused the US credit bubble. The inflation in the price of financial assets and the expansion of the Price Earnings Ratio (PER) progressed as classic inflation and interest rates withdrew. Fear of deflation then continued the trend, the "Japanese" path which goes from disinflation to deflation along with the bursting of a bubble which was sufficient to locate the US risk. From 1960 to 1995, there was indeed a strong, stable link between this monetisation rate and average inflation in the G7 countries: increased monetisation of the US public debt preceded an acceleration of inflation by about three and a half years. In 1995, this link was broken. The financial markets, and not the markets for goods and services, can be repositories for unwanted cash. In fact, as from 1995, valuations of numerous financial markets departed from classical valuation metrics.

Disinflation cannot be invented twice. Without necessarily fearing a strong, sudden return of inflation and, in its wake, a noisy disruption of the bond markets, one needs to be convinced that the fundamental driving forces of the downward trend of nominal, and then real, interest rates in the 1990's, are exhausted; and that the low level of risk premia at the end of a period of disinflation, together with the abundance of liquidities, now determines the medium-term risk of inflation and interest rates to be increasing.

For the last thirty years, and even longer, the preference between shares and bonds – a function of the current relative return – is the principal adjustment variable between the two asset classes, and the determinant of the cyclical fluctuations of the stock markets. Shares are the most attractive bonds – especially when interest rates are falling – and the two asset classes are interchangeable. Interest rates dominate the behaviour of shares and the value of shares is essentially relative. The mere expectations of profits, especially when they do not exceed a horizon of one or two years, have a limited explanatory force. Given a lack of expectations of profits in their non-cyclical component part, which are the only truly relevant ones for the long-term valuation of shares, the preference between shares and bonds prevails.

This preference is in fact the principal reason for discounting a good later performance of the stock markets, after a (pronounced) drop in long-term interest rates and in the price of shares. It should, however, be borne in mind that the relations which are considered to be normal between interest rates and shares become weaker when the inflationary risk disappears (e.g. in the 1950's-1960's) and/or when the risk of recession/deflation increases (e.g. in Japan in the 1990's). The two asset classes then become complementary rather than interchangeable. If one accepts the modest probability of a bleak deflationary scenario, there remains the possibility of a more structural revision of the equity/bond risk premium. After all, the period 1970-2000, which is often taken as a reference, was exceptional, driven by the inflationary years. The longer-term reality is a hierarchy of returns which reflect more clearly the fact that shares are riskier than bonds (government bonds here; the sovereign debt crisis calls into question the hierarchy of risk, in favour of corporate bonds). The increase in credit risk (default) in the developed world will, in turn, review the absolute value of bonds.

If one lines up all the cuts in interest rates decided on by the four corners of the global village since, about, the mid 1990's – for different but converging reasons, from the stimulation of growth to the central banks' practice of lender of last resort – there is no doubt that there was an intense international monetary easing. This considerable increase in the means of payment, in a lack-lustre economic climate, generated substantial excess liquidity. Available for the financial sphere (i.e. for the price of assets), such excess liquidity had every reason to pour into it, in a rotation orchestrated by the relative price of some compared to others, the only real limit being the violent bursting of a bubble which appeared in respect of one or other of such asset classes, and/or a sudden withdrawal of liquidities by the central banker.

Liquidity as a stock, a preference, an exchange, a path

The paths of liquidity are like the *Holzwege* in the great German school of philosophy. More often than not they are cluttered by undergrowth and suddenly come to a stop on a path which has not been cleared. Heidegger discusses this topic well; to be on a *Holzweg*, on a path which leads nowhere. At the bottom of the economic cycle, the easing of monetary policies increases liquidity (fall in interest rates), which then grows faster than the requirements of the real economy. This excess liquidity pours into the financial markets, where it stimulates an appetite for risk (one of the markers being the outperformance of shares by comparison with bonds, of emerging markets, of so-called cyclical values, i.e. all asset classes or market segments with a more pronounced risk profile) and expectations of growth and inflation. Secondly, the effect of acceleration on economic activity, and then on prices, leads to a tightening of monetary conditions and then to a slowdown. Aversion to risk increases. The circle is undone, in a more or less ordered manner, according to the excesses committed during the expansion phase. The stock markets are purged at the top of the cycle by interest rates (i.e. the contraction of liquidity), the slowdown commences, announced by a clear under-performance of shares (and, more generally, of the riskiest asset classes or segments), bonds enjoying a safe haven status when the slowdown is confirmed and the central banks stop increasing their rates (cut in long-term interest rates), or when the markets expect that they will fall.

Fundamentally, it is therefore a monetary shock (an increase or restriction of liquidity) which produces a shift in the appetite for risk, distorts the relative prices of financial assets (i.e. since these liquidities are injected into the financial markets, the first impact is on such markets) and then reaches the real sphere and distorts the relative prices of goods and services, from the very outset (the price of semi-processed goods) up to the final consumer prices. Therefore, and because they are the first to be affected by the monetary shocks, the prices of financial assets incorporate the expectations of later real evolutions. Moreover, the rise in power of the so-called "patrimonial growth" regimes, which are characterised by real wealth effects and/or psychological effects, assigns to developments in the financial sphere an increasingly relevant function as leading indicator for the real cycle.

Liquidity, value and *momentum* are without doubt the conceptual pillars of this process. The appeal of an investment is optimal when abundant liquidity focuses on an overvalued asset and the price of the latter starts to rise (*momentum*). One must, however, first agree upon the concepts of this triptych. Essentially, the value approach for a financial asset (here shares, bonds) must involve seeking to reconcile the asset price and the memory of the critical economic variable for that variable (e.g. inflation for bonds, profits for shares), such memorisation (over a period and with weightings which may be variable) constituting the synthesis of an adaptive-type expectation, in which the future fundamentally remains a component of the past, modified by a factor of forgetfulness.

The liquidity approach is a more delicate matter. Liquidity is one of the most often discussed concepts but also, without doubt, one of the least well-defined. The sources of liquidity and the attitude of the economic player may offer several angles. Money (monetary creation) and savings constitute the two fundamental sources of liquidity, savings being, theoretically, a counterpart to monetary creation; but, in fact, we live in economies where monetary creation, *ex nihilo*, is commonplace. The financing game played between the US economy and the central banks of emerging markets is a flagrant example thereof. The US economy exports capital which it has not saved, in proportion to the capital lent by the emerging central banks (the product of interventions on the forex markets under a fixed exchange rate or so-called floating exchange rate against the dollar), such capital itself being the product of the exports of capital from the US economy. This closed-loop system maintains capital at an artificially low price at both ends of the chain.

Money and savings open up the field for a certain number of possible liquidity measures: monetary base, money aggregates, foreign reserves ... insofar as money is concerned; elements of the balance of payments for savings (or, at least, the macro-economic relationship between savings and investment for the current account balance, or the sum of the said current balance and the long-term capital balance for a basic balance approach). For savings, as for money, it is difficult to define in pure terms the concepts which allow liquidity and the price of financial assets to be linked. The equilibrium between savings and investment (current account) is an example thereof. For money (or monetary creation), the link between the monetary unit (of monetary creation) and the economic cycle (e.g. growth) or financial cycle (transactions on a market) will give an idea of the velocity of money (its circulation) in the real sphere or in the financial sphere. The velocity of money and the savings/investment equilibrium may enhance the approach to money and savings alone. Since this is somewhat ambiguous, it is essential to provide an explanation in any approach.

The link between sources of liquidity and the price of the financial asset may be established by comparing/measuring their respective evolutions or the difference in behaviour of the two variables. In all instances, one can relate a status of liquidity at a given point in the cycle to the behaviour of the financial variables. This approach may be refined by analysing the behaviour of the market players through the preference for liquidity, a Keynesian concept which has the merit of linking the individual (and his expectations) and economic life, and placing this duo at the centre of what is and becomes liquidity. Liquidity, irrespective of its source (and, in particular, if monetary), results as it were from the choice made by the individual in an uncertain context and in connection with interrelations with others (exchange). This approach differs from the classical analysis of the pure sources of liquidity (money, savings), sources which precede, as it were, choices and preferences, the latter only being expressed during liquidity's journey through the economy and the financial markets.

In some way, the preference for liquidity may be compared with appetite for risk (or aversion to risk). This shortcut may permit the intensity of choices to be measured. That said, one sees more often an estimate of risk appetite/aversion indicators which merely add together all the risk premia recorded on the financial markets. This information is precious but only includes the price of the financial asset (which, admittedly, as some people think, may encompass all the available information). Since it is not practicably possible to understand the preference for liquidity as such and to allocate it an indicator or measurement, this approach remains of interest. Another way, which can be described as more classical, leads to money aggregates, their segmentation and the analysis of the relative evolutions of the various aggregates. The link can be made to the financial variable.

As can be seen, many liquidity roads lead nowhere. Adopting the path of an analysis of the sources of liquidity (money, savings), of the circulation of such liquidity (velocity) and of the preferences for liquidity (or aversion), related to risk: these are the paths which one may travel along, where one may progress. On each of these paths, the link to the price of the financial asset has to be established, which remains a delicate matter. It is possible to try to estimate the point up to which a financial asset incorporates/reflects (through its price) a status of liquidity or of preference for liquidity. A status of liquidity (or of preference for liquidity) can then be compared to a status of the asset price.

Whether one is dealing with value or liquidity, the necessary characterisation of a status of variables or their relations leads to a normalisation of the statuses.

Added to the two pillars of value and liquidity, which have led to a standardised characterisation of their relations with financial asset prices, is that of *momentum*. The estimation of market dynamics only requires the asset price, which is the explained variable and the explanatory variable. The deviation of the price by comparison with its own history (which may be the shortest or the longest), within a self-referential approach in which today's price fundamentally refers back to yesterday's (the asset contains, as it were, the memory of itself), remains the most widespread. The approach remains fundamentally the same, whether it leads to following the investment trend or, on the contrary, to adopting a "contrarian" approach.

Liquidity, value and *momentum* constitute three fundamental dimensions for the understanding of the financial markets and of the action which takes place there. A more in-depth analysis of these pillars and, especially, of their roles in the formation of financial prices, remains a priority for contemporary research. They are the essential pillars, since they lead, in particular, to questioning the links between real and financial spheres, the temporal referentials (the time of the real economy, financial time, psychological time), through, in particular, expectations and effects of memory.

From monetary stimulation to bubbles

The strong dose of monetary stimulation administered to the worldwide economy during the emerging markets crisis in 1998 provides an interesting example of the liquidity process. It first hit the financial markets in 1999: adjustment of inflation expectations for the bond markets, of growth in profits for the stock markets; explosion in the volume of transactions, increase in the price of financial assets and then of real estate assets. At the end of 1999, these liquidities started to rekindle the real sphere. The prices of semi-processed goods increased in the wake of those of industrial raw materials, while underlying inflation remained prudent. This period therefore underwent a distortion of relative prices.

The tightening of monetary policies at the end of the year triggered a symmetrical reversal of these sequences (restriction of liquidity, aversion to risk, underperformance of the stock markets, slowdown of activity).

The global cycle of liquidity – a formula which is practically redundant, since it is the fundamentally global nature of liquidity which results today in the existence of a global cycle – may be characterised, for want of anything better, by a rudimentary ratio between real activity (e.g. international exports) and available means of payment (central banks' foreign reserves, in the absence of a satisfactory money aggregate). Variations in this ratio are appropriately correlated to those of the long-term (US) interest rates. When means of payment increase faster than real activity (i.e. the demand for means of payment, traditional cash as well), during a period at the low end of the economic cycle and/or a period of easing of monetary policies, there appears an excess of available liquidity for the financial markets, which drives the interest rate down. Going back to our example, it can be seen that the sequence was present during the emerging markets crisis and that it returned in the summer of 2000. Conversely, in a phase of accelerated activity and then of monetary tightening (1999), the price of liquidity (interest rate) rises.

The financial markets fundamentally enhanced the disinflation process during the 1990's. The stock markets, especially in the USA, surfed the decline in nominal interest rates and then real interest rates (even if the stock markets are, in many respects, victims of a nominal illusion). However, disinflation cannot be invented twice. This is probably a reason for questioning why one cannot extrapolate returns on stock market investments which may have seemed exceptional.

It is essential to bear in mind that the period which commenced at the start of the 1980's, with the mandate to central banks to fight inflation given by a social system which, in fact, therefore indicated that it no longer intended to put up with the inflationary consequences of a macro-economic regime of monetised government debt and a distribution of added value which was very favourable to wages, came to an end at the close of the century. This period, during which a structurally long position in bonds *and* shares was successful (downward trend of bond risk premia *and* expansion of the PER on the stock markets), saw inflation and its volatility slide from the real sphere towards the financial sphere, that of financial assets, also saw central banks gradually adopting a new possible choice, to fight inflation in the price of financial assets – which fundamentally means questioning a distribution of added value which had become very favourable to profits, the disinflation in the real sphere "costing" pressures on asset prices, the transmission belt being held by the interest rates.

The disinflation years were share years. A story of interest rates. The expansion of the PER during the 1990's obtained a twofold benefit from the disinflation movement. From the point of view of valuing shares, the fall of inflation, of expectations of inflation and their volatility made the future evolution of profits less uncertain. We know that the equity risk premium is fairly well-correlated to inflation and its volatility. The perception of risk resulting from the traditional forces of the economic cycle (more growth, more inflation, more monetary tightening by the central banks) gradually diminished. However, it did not disappear, since the effects of the memory of an inflationary past (the 1970's) continued to drive inflationary fears, when from time to time petrol prices increased, even though the impact of such prices on inflation was no longer what it had been twenty year earlier. With the inertia which characterises the adaptive expectations and the progressive erosion of the past from memories, long-term interest rates have, at each phase of pressure, expressed this memory by means of a hiccup, each additional hiccup reducing in intensity in the same way that a noise fades in the distance. In a way, it is such bond market movements, which are excessive in the light of the actual risk and borne mainly by expectations and memory, which make the activation of the cumulative inflation process less probable in absolute terms. At the same time, however, the gradual weakening of the impact of the past, i.e. fundamentally the act of forgetting, beyond what becomes the effective link between petrol and inflation, will gradually create a surprise for expectations whose memory of inflation have been progressively eliminated. For the time being, however, generally and through the 1990's, the decrease in the perceived risk of inflation sustained a rise in stock valuations, the fall of nominal interest rates playing the role of transmission belt from disinflation to share value through the intermediary of the preference between shares and bonds.

From the point of view of liquidity which is available for the financial markets, there is no doubt that the disinflation movement acted as a liquidity pump, the central banks maintaining an accommodating bias in the absence of an established risk of inflation of the price of goods and services. The increase in the price of assets accelerated as classic inflation and nominal interest rates decreased. This mechanism reached its peak in the USA, sustaining the formation of a credit bubble, at least part of which was used to fund the purchases of stocks. In many respects, the 1990's in the USA were more the years of *debt culture* rather than those of *equity culture*, which are often commented upon. The use of debt leverage by companies which sought to inflate their ROE and reduce their equity capital (in particular by buying back their own shares) was a salient factor. For one dollar invested in the buyback of their own shares, US companies contracted three additional dollars of debt between 1996 and 1999. This is singularly demonstrated by the escalation of debt in non-financial corporations compared to *cash-flow* (ratio), together with a constant rise of bond risk premia in respect of profitability and then solvency, up until the known final crisis.

Two major perversions accompanied the dynamics of the credit bubble. A confusion between the escalation of debt and the increase of liquidity and a confusion between savings and money. Are we so certain that the Asian miracle was based on high levels of savings, when such countries had current account deficits? Was it really savings that US households invested on the stock market, if their level of savings was nil?

Disinflation therefore played a key role, both in itself and also because of its consequences (central banks' monetary policies and nominal long-term rates). Although part of its positive effects on stock market valuations seems legitimate (profits environment less uncertain), it is probable that the central banks unwillingly created conditions for excess through monetary policies which remained too flexible for too long. In both the USA and Europe one could only feel a sense of unease, when witnessing the rise in share prices, as growth projections were revised downwards after the shock of the Asian crisis (1997-1998), and therefore as inflation and interest rates fell at the same time. The interest rate effect then reached its limits, from the point of view of stock valuation.

The 1990's were the years of compression of risk premia on the financial markets, in particular the stock markets. Investors expected returns from developed markets, which matched the risk taken on the emerging markets. This increased pressure on companies to increase their profitability and may also have led them to adopt unreasonable management practices. The revival of the price of risk, first on the private bond markets and then on the stock markets, put an end to any illusions which may have suggested for a time that shares could provide annual long-term double-digit returns and at the same time represent less risky investments.

An economy can only give the financial markets what it has. In economies which are growing at around 2/3%, with the same amount of inflation, it is mechanically impossible for all companies, in all sectors, to record a sustainable annual increase in profits of more than 20% and a similar average increase in the price of their shares. Certain companies can, as can certain sectors, but not all. It is even probable, in such a scenario, that certain companies will, temporarily, look for flattering illusory effects through the taking of risk and the consequences of debt leverage. Others will even go so far as fraud, for want of a better way, once they have reached the end of the road, in order to satisfy unreasonable commitments to the market. The simple truth is that the average increase in shares cannot extricate itself on a long-term basis from the increase in profits, which in turn cannot distance itself from the increase in the economy.

It was improbable, in the second half of the 1990's that, in a global economy where real growth and inflation did not exceed 3%, the earnings of all companies would increase by 15%. There was also a risk, against a backdrop of a return to growth, that interest rates would rise, blocking the liquidity pump. This finally happened in 2000.

In many respects, and although history does not repeat itself, it is tempting to make a comparison between the Japan of the 1980's and the USA of the 1990's. At the origin of the two stock market miracles, ten years apart, was a deep-seated movement of disinflation, a spectacular fall in long-term nominal interest rates and very accommodating monetary policies, because the inflation of the price of goods and services then seemed to have disappeared. Two credit and over-investment bubbles, which ended up bursting. If Japanese history is used as a guideline, it will be noted that a long period of positive correlation between interest rates and share prices had then commenced, against the backdrop of a liquidity trap. Disinflation and its real and financial consequences then finally led to deflation. It can also be noted that successive injections of liquidity had maintained false hope that the economy and financial markets would recover, with Japan plunging from weak rallies into relapses, until it drew the conclusion of an inevitable restructuring.

All stories of credit bubbles started with good years but ended badly, since the authorities lost sight of the delayed effects of their policies. Moreover, when the bubble bursts, additional injections of liquidity cannot hide for long the need to remove the imbalances and create conditions for a true recovery.

Are shares always bonds?

Are shares always bonds? In the crash of 2000, which was extended by the events of 11 September 2001, a positive correlation was noted between bond yields and share prices, which were falling. This evolution is inconsistent with what had been noted, on average, for about thirty years. In a context of growth and recurring inflationary pressures, shares resemble bonds, especially when interest rates are falling (and therefore the price of bonds increases). Since 1960, the correlation is high and negative, together with on average a slight six-month lead, which dissolved in the 1990's. An exception to this rule appeared in Japan, after the bubble burst, when the long-term interest rate and the share price followed a downward trend, hand-in-hand, over a period of ten years. This is a deflationary correlation, sometimes improperly referred to as "Gibson's paradox" (the economist Gibson had essentially noted a positive correlation between interest rates and the general level of prices). The negative correlation between long-term interest rates and share prices is fairly largely based on the positive link between equity risk premium and inflation (together with the volatility of inflation). During the inflationary period of the 1970's (the turning point occurred in 1982-1983), there was a strong perception of risk fostered by the sequences of the cycle (from inflation to the withdrawal of liquidity by the central banks). This perception then diminished, in particular because the sequences of the cycle seemed, without altogether disappearing, less marked, more transparent, less painful. The fall of inflation, of the expectations of inflation and their volatility made the future evolution of profits less uncertain.

Long-term interest rates have a statistically significant influence on the performance of stock markets, especially, as we have seen, when bond yields are falling (average performance is good and shares outperform bonds). This does not mean that the stock markets cannot experience an increase when bond yields rise; on the contrary, although the situation is admittedly less clear. This may suggest that, over fairly short horizons (one to two years), i.e. the so-called cyclical fluctuations of the stock market, the financial elements (monetary creation, savings and liquidity factors, of which the nominal interest rate is one expression) are essential, indeed certainly more significant than the real elements whose dividends or earnings may validly be used as a proxy. Consequently, much will therefore depend, with regard to the overall performance of shares, on whether shares are attractive as compared to bonds and therefore on the relative value of shares (i.e. as compared to bonds).

The preference between shares and bonds

The preference between shares and bonds is an explanatory factor of the cyclical fluctuations of the stock markets, this relative performance incorporating the expectations of growth of real activity, which is verified by observation. The relative performance of shares precedes the business cycle by around ten months, with a suitable degree of strength. This observation invites one to meditate upon the function played by the financial markets in integrating the available information and acting as a crossroads for expectations. The robustness of the relationship between the financial sphere (which contains the expectations) and the real sphere (which produces the activity), even if subject to certain limits (bubbles fall outside the relationship, due to their fundamentally atypical nature), provides support to those who wish to believe that (almost) all the information can be found in the financial markets (over and above the information, it should be noted that market evolutions produce real effects, e.g. through wealth effects).

It is not therefore unreasonable to try, in order to value shares, to estimate the preference function between shares and bonds, i.e. the relative value between the two asset classes. This preference, which is also a function of risk appetite (or risk aversion), is one of the principal variables for cyclical adjustment between the two asset classes. This preference may thus be approached and defined in the context of a stable "regime", in particular whilst the expectations of long-term growth and inflation are themselves stable. This regime, which marked the period 1975-2000, defines a period where the two asset classes are interchangeable and where the difference in yield between shares and bonds is a relevant indicator of the relative value between the two asset classes and of relative performance as well. The switch to a deflationary regime or even to a regime where inflation remains low over the long-term, with low volatility, may modify the 1975-2000 regime, marked by the strong memory of an inflationary period and therefore the close link between the price of liquidity and share prices.

Value is only relative. Over "short" horizons (cyclical fluctuations), the absolute value of the stock markets (indicator of the future performance of shares as compared to a risk-free asset) may be seen as the combination of two value components: the relative valuation of shares (as compared to bonds) (indicator of the future performance between the two asset classes) and that of bonds (indicator of the future performance of bonds as compared to a risk-free asset). The first may be based on the difference in current yield between the two asset classes; the second may use the difference between the nominal interest rate and long-term inflation and/or nominal *long-term* growth (long-term expectations are proxied as an adaptive function of the memory of the variable's past behaviour, with a factor of forgetfulness). It must be possible to normalise these differences, i.e. compare them to a relevant average over a period which defines a regime, through the homogeneity of its characteristics. The stock market will then offer an optimal value, if shares are attractive as compared to bonds and if bonds are themselves attractive (i.e. as compared to a risk-free asset).

The preference between shares and bonds is a function of liquidity. The key role of interest rates in cyclical stock market fluctuations reflects the importance of liquidity, of which the interest rate is the price, as it were, in the determination of the preference between the two asset classes. It is, in particular, at the bottom of the business cycle that injections of liquidity by the central banks (fall in interest rate) generate surplus liquidity which is available for the financial markets, when the requirements of the real sphere are depressed. The stimulation of appetite for risk by the actions of the central banks (i.e. low return on risk-free investments) will normally end up causing a switch from the bond asset class to shares (preference), with transmission delays of approximately two quarters. It is in such a context, when the increase in means of payment is much higher than that of the real activity, that the equity asset class may generate an outperformance – other than in a deflationary-type scenario. It is also a financial crossing point (expectations of growth) and real crossing point (wealth effects) for an acceleration scenario of the real activity, the financial cycle of the shares/bond preference function pre-empting the real cycle by two to three quarters on average, in a normal regime. The interest rate plays the role of a transmission belt between the distortions of liquidity (e.g. those of the relationship between means of payment in circulation and growth of activity) and those of the preference between shares and bonds, of which it is in fact the principal determinant. The sequence of expansion of available liquidity for the financial markets makes way for a normalisation of the appetite for risk and, subsequently, for shifts out of government bonds. Preference is a function of the relative yield, which leads to a comparison between a real notion (return on shares) and a nominal notion (bond yields), since the stock markets are victims of a nominal illusion.

Valuing the Stock Market. A practical attempt

It seems vain to try and value the stock markets based solely on dividends or earnings over fairly short cyclical horizons, of one to two years; even more so when it involves expectations over at best one or two years, a form of external disruption to the fundamental determination of the value of shares. Moreover, analysts underestimate short-term earnings growth on a fairly systematic basis, thus accentuating the cyclical bias.

The holder of a share undoubtedly pays more attention to the whole sequence of earnings, which are spread over several cycles – or at least one full cycle (about four to five years, on average) – than to the earnings of this year or next year alone. The same is true of inflation in the valuation process of bond markets. Unless the cyclical fluctuation helps update a more fundamental element, purely cyclical information is non-information for valuation purposes, good and bad news cancelling each other out over a full cycle. The almost total lack of predictive capability of the so-called "classic" indicators for valuing shares (PER, Price to Book Ratio, Dividend Yield ...) highlights the extent of the difficulties and the limitations of the traditional approaches.

It is necessary for any reflection to be placed within the perspective of a full cycle and that cycle within a homogenous set of several cycles. The cancellation of cyclical noise over a full cycle does not, in fact, permit the equilibrium regime to be characterised over several cycles, such regime being, in turn, determined by the very characteristics of the macro-financial regime which make a set of cycles homogenous.

There are numerous difficulties. The gap which appeared in the USA in the 1990's between the average annual increase in share prices, which was very high (14%) and the average annual increase in corporate profits, which was scarcely above its long-term trend (7.5%), bears witness, in its own way, to such difficulties. The market ignores the underlying trend of profits (long-term earning power), the extrapolation of one or two exceptional years acting as a regime of long-term expectations, which does not allow the powerful effects of memory (and forgetfulness), which are at work in the determination of long-term expectations, to be captured. In addition to this confusion, there is an expansion of the PER resulting from an "interest rate effect" (fall in nominal interest rates). The expansion of liquidity and its move towards shares, due to the higher relative returns, are dominant factors.

One may consider that, during this period, the valuation of the stock markets is not really concerned with the regime of profitability and related long-term expectations, despite rhetorical appearances. It is the structural drop in nominal (and then real) interest rates, which is fundamentally driven by the powerful worldwide disinflation movement and its impact on the share/bond preference, which inflate capitalisations. From this point of view, the share bubble is above all a bond bubble. Liquidity dominates value. Consequently, it is not surprising that the interest rate reversal in 1999 was the starting point for the downturn and the bursting of the bubble.

One should be interested in the non-cyclical component of the expectations of earnings and inflation when considering value. The difficulties in obtaining a satisfactory indicator for shares may justify the combination referred to above of a bond valuation and of the preference function between shares and bonds. This is an operational compromise which results, however, by construction, in granting significant weight to liquidity (and therefore to the interest rate), which is subject to limits, when the economic context is flirting with recession or indeed deflation. This was, for example, the situation in 2001, after the terrorist attacks. It was reasonable to assume that the relative yield on shares might return to a more normal, multi-cyclical equilibrium level, due to the collapse of interest rates, but this assumption was linked to a scenario of economic slowdown which would not degenerate into a recession and would result in a modest recovery in 2002. In this case, the return to normal of the gap between equity/bond yields preceded the recovery of the real activity. It is clear that the share/bond preference function, even if it seems to be determined solely by the yield, is ultimately based on an assumption of growth, even if cyclical (one to two years).

The influence of interest rates on the valuation of shares is not unlimited. Although the cyclical fluctuations of the stock market have followed those of the equity/bond preference for almost thirty years, this has not always been the case. This regime, which is now perceived as "normal", is fairly generally based on the observation of a high (negative) level of correlation between interest rates and share prices. If one looks at the relations between the two variables since the start of the century, things are less clear-cut. This correlation diminishes when inflation, the expectations of inflation and their volatility are themselves weaker and/or the risks of recession/deflation increase. The 1930's, but also the period 1950-1960, offer a few examples thereof. It has already been pointed out that the two asset classes of bonds and shares are then no longer interchangeable but complementary.

In an economic context where inflation is low over the long-term and not very volatile, it is probably normal, not only that the bond risk premium is low but also that the required return on shares is clearly higher than that of bonds. This fairly healthy hierarchy of risks, and therefore of yields, was shaken up by the inflationary period of the 1970's. Viewed against the background of the 20th century, these years are an exception and not the rule. The bond risk premium was partly adjusted to the disinflation movement which commenced in the 1980's. Only partly, since the fall in nominal rates was less pronounced than that of inflation, real rates remaining fairly high; at the same time, the stock markets surfed on the wave of disinflation (with the nominal illusion referred to above). Overall, at the end of the decade, the hierarchy of yields and risks between the two asset classes might suggest that the perception of bond risk was still too high and that of the share risk too low. The twofold movement of the fall in long-term interest rates and in the share price, which commenced in 2000 with the stock market crash, triggered, to a certain fashion, a more long-term normalisation of risk premium as between shares and bonds.

The historical parenthesis, commenced in the 1970's, came to an end. This period which is often used as a reference and which includes the inflationary years (1970-1985), was in many ways exceptional. The longer term reality is less inflation, business cycles which are more pronounced and a yield structure which reflects more clearly that shares are riskier than bonds. In such circumstances, what may have been interpreted during the crash of 2000-2001 as a very attractive relative yield of shares as compared to bonds may not be quite what it appeared. It is arguably the start of a structural review of the premium between the two asset classes, the negative correlation between long-term interest rates and shares will weaken over the long-term, as will the mechanisms of the equity/bond preference which have applied since the mid-1980's.

This would mean a change of regime. The equilibrium level of the nominal and real interest rates falls and that of the share risk premium increases, all of this defining a new risk/return equilibrium within a macro-financial regime determined by new characteristics. The reasons for justifying a new equilibrium for real interest rates can be found in the evolutions of inflation (also of volatility and expectations), of global liquidity (excess liquidity), of the return on capital, of the debt/GDP ratio, of demographics and of the efficiency of capital markets themselves. The question of the equilibrium of the share risk premium cannot ignore the determinants of the equilibrium of interest rates, in particular the regime of inflation. Disinflation has been a powerful force driving down the share risk premium. Even without fearing a return of inflation, the fact alone that disinflation cannot be invented twice marks a limit, not only on the continued drop of the share risk premium but also on maintaining the equilibrium of a very low level of share risk premium. The growth regime (return on capital), its weaknesses (indebtedness) and its context (geo-political) are also taken into consideration.

In this type of rebalancing, a slowdown of the global economy without inflation is very likely to be accompanied by an *aggiornamento*. The erosion of the share price, with unaltered long-term interest rates, continues until a hierarchy of yields is restored which is more consistent with long-term macro-economic trends and realities. In this scenario, the argument for a revision of expectations of earnings dictates, for the purposes of valuing of the stock markets, an argument for a cut in interest rates. This option could be reasonably selected at the end of the crash in 2001. One cannot, however, exclude the possibility, in this kind of fragile configuration, that the return to normal may take an extreme turn. If the global economy does indeed enter a recession and if the deflationary expectations gain the upper hand, the preference function between shares and bonds then acquires what can be described as a Japanese appearance; a positive correlation between share prices and interest rates is required, where the principle of disappointing earnings alone prevails. At the end of such an extreme movement, the equity/bond risk premium returns, after the excesses, to a long-term view which provides a slightly improved reflection of the hierarchy of risks and returns.

Everything takes place as if, within a particular macro-economic regime, the long-term growth expectations were stable. The less such expectations are questioned, i.e. the longer the significant effects of memory continue, the more the shares/bond preference will act as a driving force for the cyclical fluctuations of the share and bond market and as an essential element of the valuation of shares. This means that a stock market crash or increasingly frequent or numerous cracks indicate a change of regime and expectations. These changes in equilibrium lead one to reconsider the foundations of the valuation of shares, since the referential of memory, and therefore of expectations, together with its points of reference, are modified. In this context, the only approach for the value of shares is that of this referential and the rest is nothing but distraction. It is no doubt necessary to be able to distinguish, in a special stock market situation, between that which forms part of the regime (referential, equilibrium, memory) and that which, within a regime, is only its cyclical respiration (share/bond preference function), once one is interested in such strange things as stock markets. A regime remains valid so long as the expectations of long-term growth and inflation are themselves stable. A switch to a deflationary regime, or even to a regime where inflation remains low over the long-term, with low volatility, may modify the regime without, moreover, excluding the possibility of a return, in the medium-term, to an inflationary regime. The recent rise in the volatility of real variables, after a long period of anaemia, may perhaps indicate a change.

The preference between shares and bonds encapsulates both a liquidity effect (interest rate) and a growth effect (profits), the latter effect containing both a purely cyclical dimension (fluctuations of profitability within the cycle) and a heavier and more inert dimension, determined by the memorised (and therefore expected) reference to a norm of profitability (and therefore of growth) within a regime which has an equilibrium. The pressures which may appear within a regime, i.e. within a referential which links growth, profits and share prices, may prove to be untenable. When the preference function between shares and bonds ends up leading the share price into territories where it enters into conflict with the norm of the equilibrium regime, a market disruption may occur at any time. As already noted, the divergence, since 1982, between the annual average increase in the price of US shares (14%) and that of earnings, close to its long-term average (8%), was untenable. Such a divergence is not of itself a novelty. Over the long-term (1922-1996), the annual increase in the price of shares and that of corporate earnings were, unsurprisingly, close, i.e. almost 8% for the period in question. This long-term regularity includes divergences in opposite directions, which form the same number of sub-periods, a divergence in one direction always being corrected by a divergence in the other direction. When, between 1982 and 1996, the share price increased more quickly than the earnings on shares, there was an extreme expansion of the average stock market PER, taking the latter 50% above its long-term average (its average value has been estimated at 14 since 1871). There was then a tension within the equilibrium regime, the determinants of the share/bond preference function leading the absolute performance of shares into areas of contradiction with the elements of equilibrium of the regime and its underlying assumptions. This then results in phases of divergence in the opposite direction, the share price then increasing at a slower rate than earnings, and the long-term mean reversion equalising the two variables is thus guaranteed. A sub-period of lower annual profitability is then unavoidable. One can see a return to long-term equilibrium, provided that, and this is essential, the macro-financial characteristics of the long-term regime remain relevant.

The long-term mean reversion was guaranteed during the crash by a sub-period of annual profitability which was temporarily very low, although the choice does not, however, alter the main characteristics of the long-term regime (growth, profits). Once this risk (global deflation) has been avoided, the share/bond preference function may direct the interaction within the regime.

Extrapolating year-on-year, average, annual profits on shares of 15% (i.e. an increase of 13% per annum in the share price, after deducting a Dividend Yield of 2%) means more or less discounting the fact that the return on physical capital may experience an annual increase of the same amount. It therefore means betting on a significant increase in productivity when, furthermore, the upward trend of the workforce, the capital stock and the share of capital in the national income do not enable the equation to be completed. This was one of the major questions of the 1990's. The regimes of corporate profitability and of the average return on shares must adjust to a global context delivering 2% to 2.5% of growth in real GDP and the same amount of inflation. In this world such as it is, investment must accept that it will be difficult for all companies in all sectors to generate an average annual increase in earnings which is well above 8% or 9% and must be satisfied with returns on equity investments in the same proportions. There is often a great temptation to avoid the regime's equilibria and norms by means of risk, debt leverage and, ultimately, fraud.

Essay 6

THE CYCLE, LIQUIDITY AND INTEREST RATES

The yield curve and the real cycle

The relations between the yield curve and the real cycle are those of the cycle and liquidity. Whether they are "normal" or more exceptional, they state the fact that the yield curve expresses a status of expectations of growth and inflation. Since the long-term interest rate is a composition of expected short-term rates, monetary conditions constitute its principal theoretical determinant. The more restrictive they are, the more the slope flattens, since the response of long-term rates to rises in the key rates is not one for one (credibility effect of the central bank, expectation of a slowdown in future activity). Since the higher cost of capital reduces the demand for credit and investment projects, this form of flattening (or inversion) usually comes before a redirection of activity and prices. Conversely, a positive slope comes before an expansion phase. The curve also reflects the central bank's credibility, since the response of the long-term rate to a movement in the key rate will be weaker, the more credible the monetary authority. Finally, the curve expresses the conditions of demand and supply for credit on markets which are now global and integrated, where non-resident capital flows may play a key role (the phenomenon of flight to quality, in respect of the government debt of developed countries during the Asian crisis). Although the short part of the curve remains largely determined by the movements of national (or regional) central banks, the long part is influenced by the movements of international savings and investment. In this regard, the long-term rate becomes a composition of a global interest rate (especially US) and a domestic factor.

These few comments of a slightly theoretical nature must be put into perspective, that afforded by observation, but also by the accelerated transformations of global finance. The gap between a system of national/regional central banks and the global, open nature of the capital markets raises serious questions regarding, in particular, the transmission of monetary policies, the general efficiency of such a system and the increasing limitations of a monetary power, which is admittedly prestigious but inadequately coordinated (the authority of the Federal Reserve itself is challenged by the significant *ex nihilo* monetary creation by the Asian central banks). When, moreover, the financial flows hold sway in terms of weight and speed over the exchanges of goods and services, the strictly real link between the liquidity cycle (i.e. the interest rate) and the business cycle, has to ease. The curve, the structure of the interest rates, their formation and distortion, then come within an increasingly autonomous and self-referencing sphere, the financial sphere of liquidity. Simultaneously, the link between the curve and the real cycle, which is maintained by the function of expectations, expands in turn. The over-use, as it were, of the yield curve provides one explanation for this, if all the players use the same variable as a tool or point of reference for the expectation. However, the increasing over-determination of the curve by the financial sphere of liquidity is an even stronger explanatory element. What seems to be a disappearance of the curve's ability to anticipate (the real cycle) is instead a manifestation (consequence) of the loss of control by the monetary authorities of the financial sphere of liquidity and therefore of a certain form of emancipation of the liquidity function.

The predictive power of the curve has only partially been revealed, whether it concerns, for example, the impact of a variation of 1% in the yield curve on the increase in the real GDP or the proportion of the latter explained by the yield curve. With regard to this latter indicator, it is in the USA, France and Germany that this predictive power has been the most marked (at least in the last thirty years of the 20th century). It was almost nil in Japan. The essential part of this predictive capability, which is much weaker with regard to inflation, is expressed for a one-year horizon and may continue for up to three years.

The anomalies are particularly interesting. The anomaly lies in the breakdown of the link (of expectation) with the business cycle and not in the link between this same curve and liquidity. The phases of anomaly are periods during which the curve is only stimulated by a liquidity which is, as it were, disconnected from the real sphere, whether it concerns manipulations by a central bank (as in Japan during the 1990's, when the central bank played the role of last resort purchaser of debt), or global market factors and financial flows, carried along by waves of appetite for or aversion to risk (inversion of the US curve in 1997-1998, resulting not from an increase in short-term rates but from a sharp drop in long-term rates; this atypical profile led not to a deceleration but rather to an acceleration of activity).

The empowerment (and the self-referencing) of the financial sphere and the global liquidity cycle are increasingly less anomalies and rather characteristics of the contemporary economy. The debate regarding the predictive function of the yield curve, because the latter constitutes, as it were, a status of the conditions of (monetary) liquidity faced with reality (the transmission to the economy and the financial markets of the liquidity effect, by the financial markets) and faced with uncertainty (the construction of the players' expectations), is in many ways emblematic. The relations of the real and financial spheres, but also the autonomous mechanisms only at work within the financial sphere, have increasing economic significance. While retaining the idea of a journey taken by money towards and within the real economy, one cannot ignore the mechanisms which make money reflect on itself by transforming it before, in turn, transforming the activity and, more generally, the real economy.

The price of liquidity and the global economic cycle

The relations between the real cycle (e.g. international growth) and the price of liquidity (e.g. the long-term interest rates) certainly refer to the fundamental question of the journey of money (liquidity is money/savings which are making a journey) within and towards the real economy. They also refer to the question of the globalisation of the two variables, growth and interest rates, i.e. to the forces which, in the period of international interrelations which has developed since the end of the 20th century, take precedence over the domestic, national or even regional determinants. An observation of these relations during this unique period would suggest that the global forces which affect the long-term interest rates are determined by the intensity of international growth and by the degree of synchronisation of the regional cycles. The contradiction between the limited operating framework of the majority of central banks (national or regional at best, since only the Fed has a broader function granted by the dollar status) and the more global realities of the determination process of the majority of the big market variables, is increasingly evident. This is undoubtedly one of the fundamental contradictions of the structure of globalisation; this internal contradiction will give rise to more radical upheaval and changes than the majority of pressures which are usually commented upon because they are more visible. At the very moment that independence was granted to the central banks, the latter's sovereignty function was disintegrating.

Although the level of short-term interest rates continues to be determined by the independent central banks, on the basis of considerations which are fairly generally domestic ones (this is a major issue and a source of considerable ambiguities regarding the transparency of monetary policies), that of the long-term rates reacts increasingly, during globalisation, to global factors, especially US ones. A consideration of the correlations between the USA and the rest of the world (Germany, Japan) since 1975 is enlightening. The correlation between short-term rates has weakened. The coefficients which were very high during the years 1975-1980 then faded away to a negligible quantity during the 1990's. Simultaneously, the long-term rates are increasingly connected. The different economic shifts between zones, marked by a significant desynchronisation (German and Japanese problems), explain the sharp divergence in short-term rates, i.e. the additional divergence as compared to a situation which can be described as normal, which is already marked by discrepancies (synchronisation is the exception). This is not the case for long-term rates, which makes the consolidation of this link all the more striking. The links between long-term rates are strong in a situation of synchronised global recovery (e.g. at the end of the 1980's), but remain tight in phases of desynchronisation (the 1990's). They only show a marginal shift in direction.

The determining weight of the US variable on such relations is partly due to the fact that it aggregates, as it were, the new area of emerging growth within globalisation (including, primarily, Asia). The approach to worldwide growth by the USA, Germany and Japan alone found its limitations at the end of the 20th century. The USA and Asian emerging markets are not only synchronised in terms of activity (as compared to Japan and Germany) but, above all, there emerges a financial axis comprising the USA and Asian emerging markets, governed by the dollar status, as a fundamental centre for the creation of global liquidity. The interaction between the need for external US funding and the central banks of emerging markets which agree to monetise it, is undoubtedly central to the globalisation of the long-term US interest rate. This centre for the *ex nihilo* creation of monetary liquidity at the two ends of the spectrum (USA, Asian emerging markets) results, at the same time, in an almost-synchronised monetary stimulation of a USA/Asia axis of activity which is fairly largely integrated and in the creation of a fairly advanced financial integration grouping of market variables. This dollar block attains a certain degree of coherence through activity and through finance. This evolution places European and Japanese monetary policies in a difficult position by dispossessing them, as it were, of the full effects of monetary sovereignty (one aspect of which being the link between the key rate and the long-term rate). This is the most visible aspect of the globalisation of the long-term rate, which is set to disrupt the function of monetary determination and reaction for economic blocks which have remained outside the axis. The mandate for a monetary policy to be transparent and to restore confidence enters into conflict with these new realities and contradicts them.

There is another less visible aspect, in the USA itself. The area of financial globalisation represented by the USA-Asian emerging markets admittedly incorporates the US long-term rate within a broader interaction but it also deprives the Fed of part of its direct monetary sovereignty in the creation of liquidity, which is as much if not more the result of foreign exchange interventions and the accumulation of reserves by the central banks of emerging markets than the autonomous expansion of the US monetary base alone, directed by the Fed. As from 2008, the implementation of quantitative easing (QE) increased the intensity of monetary creation by the Fed alone.

The direction and the volatility of long-term rates depend on international growth but within a real and financial global interaction to which the emerging markets are being admitted, such markets playing the dual role of driving economic activity and being a source of creation of monetary liquidity. This means that the real determinants (growth) of the long-term rate, while remaining present, must increasingly accommodate the autonomous forces behind a global interaction of liquidity, and such interaction may distance the interest rates on a more or less long-term basis from their equilibrium references.

Since 1970, there is a high correlation between the weighted average of the G5 bond yields and international exports, which is an approximation of growth; the rate movements advancing those of real activity by about three months. The long-term rates recorded on average a fairly significant upward trend, when exports exceeded their trend rate. Similarly, the volatility of long-term rates rose with the growth of real activity, as compared to the average level recorded when the growth of exports was zero year-on-year. This is one of the keys for understanding the 1990's: the average global growth was too low to exert pressure on the production capacities and the available means of payment. Global growth governs the triptych of interest rates, inflation and their volatility and rate movements come before shifts in the real cycle.

The role of (de)synchronisation of global growth

That said, the absolute level of global growth is less important than the level of (de)synchronisation of the regional business cycles. The reduction or increase in the growth differentials between the USA and the rest of the world constitutes the key determinant for the direction and volatility of long-term rates and inflation. An acceleration of activity in Europe and Japan as compared to the USA has, for example, had a bullish impact on such variables, the volatility of the long-term rates rising on average, as well as the volatility of the spreads of long-term rates between regional blocks. Conversely, a widening of the growth differentials between principal regions resulted in a fall in level and in volatility of the long-term rates and in the spreads of long-term rates. In particular, although strict domestic considerations could have justified higher long-term US rates, these rates fell during the second half of the 1990's. The desynchronisation of global growth was deep-set, which enabled the US expansion to be financed at low levels of interest rates, with a high dollar and without inflation.

There is therefore a global long-term interest rate, a combination of the global growth equation for regional blocks (large developed zones, to which the Asian block is added, whose function is as much financial as real). The relative interaction of growth between blocks is a determining factor, like the interaction of pistons and communicating vessels which exert pressures and dilations on global liquidity. This interaction of pistons takes place within a global system which is distinguished by a fairly high average level of liquidity due to the creation of liquidity occurring on the USA/Asian emerging markets axis and is principally linked to the monetisation of US external debt by the central banks of the emerging markets. The means of determining interest rates therefore remains fairly classic, an international interaction of the available means of payment and of economic activity, even if the price of liquidity is now determined globally. What seems much newer is both the *ex nihilo* nature of monetary creation adopted in the production of global liquidity, the appearance of an abundant global monetary creation on the USA/emerging markets axis, which does not come under the authority of any particular, identified institution, a sort of invisible, central bank which, like a monetary hand, multiplies the means of payment, and, finally, the excess liquidity of the global system which results from this monetary interaction, a long-term feature of the contemporary regime of the global economy and finance. The separation of savings and money, of the classic inflation of goods and services and the inflation of the price of financial assets, of the real sphere and the financial sphere forms one whole, i.e. one regime. The excess liquidity of the regime dominates the whole. Admittedly, it is still necessary to synchronise global activity, in order to obtain a global rise in the price of liquidity (long-term rates), but the upward pressures are increasingly cushioned by excess liquidity, a phenomenon which is accentuated by any dose of desynchronisation of global activity, which is enough for a global downward pressure. The somewhat artificial lowering of the cost of liquidity enables growth to be maintained but with increasing financial imbalances.

Speed and duration rather than direction. Non-linear movements in asset prices

The question of interest rates is too often approached through that of direction. Time, i.e. the speed and duration of movements, is just as relevant or indeed more relevant. Essentially, the long-term interest rates (market price for global liquidity) do not rise faster than they fall. This is, however, the case during major trend reversals, and/or when extreme movements occur. The non-linear nature of movements within time and the contraction or dilation of time and duration within finance are fundamental phenomena which have to be linked to the function of memory and that of expectation, closely connected by duration, forgetfulness and acceleration, as if inertia co-existed with the sudden jolts in the regime.

The question of the speed of movement of the price of financial assets is a determining factor, in particular for the investor. We already know that, borne by expectations, the movements of long-term interest rates come on average before the shifts in the real cycle and that, moreover, the direction and volatility of long-term rates depend upon global growth and its greater or lesser degree of (de)synchronisation. The confrontation between the means of payment and the real activity at international level drives the price of liquidity. It can, moreover, be observed that such rate movements may occur very quickly.

An observation of long-term interest rate movements, as a monthly average, in the principal developed countries since the end of the 1960's allows one to analyse their speeds, i.e. the estimated movements in basis points, as compared to their duration expressed in months. The distribution obtained for such speeds suggests at first that, on average and for a very large majority of movements, rises and falls are equally split and both occur with a moderate degree of intensity, in the order of 10% to 20% per month, the average duration of such phases lasting between two and three quarters. With regard to Europe, and principally in order to eliminate the convergence effects of the Southern countries, the historical behaviour of German rates may reasonably be used as a reference for that of the euro rates. There would accordingly be no reason, still on an average basis, to fear a faster rise in interest rates than a fall. An investor would have time to organise himself in order to capture a large share of the movement.

The observation of distribution tails (i.e. extreme movements) reveals an interesting asymmetry. Extreme upward movements are twice as numerous as downward shifts. Furthermore, these extreme rises are very fast, completed on average within the space of three months, i.e. twice as fast as extreme falls. One can probably assume that this acceleration of time (the non-linearity of the time of finance is a fundamental factor) has all the more chance of occurring, if the interest rate is distanced from its territory of equilibrium or neutrality. Overvaluation is corrected very quickly, abruptly and by means of acceleration; by means of a sudden movement. It is probably this very speed itself which produces the cyclical corrective effect. This acceleration is that of expectations, whose temporal structure is non-linear; its fundamental framework is constituted by memory/past time with, accordingly, a significant degree of inertia and a tendency to make adaptive adjustments. However, a sudden movement can occur when the regime of expectation is faced with a new element (i.e. one which disrupts the regime and its assumptions), within a special context where it is distanced from equilibrium. The energy of memory, accumulated at a fixed point (which is that of the maximum distance from equilibrium) is released, unwinding like a spring.

It is not possible to define what constitutes an event in finance without examining the distributions of extreme phenomena which are non-linear in temporal terms. This reality remains fundamentally linked to the existence of a cycle, the existence of an equilibrium (and, therefore, to its permanent absence, i.e. to its constant transformation into imbalances), to the existence of powerful effects of memory linking the past, present and future, but also and above all time (that which is captured by memory) and matter. The only point of reference is that or those which come to memory like a capture of temporal mass. The economic or financial event is, fundamentally, a breach, a questioning or a change of regime, the regime being understood as a piece (territory) of temporal mass, where the inertia of the coagulated past represents a certain status of matter. The breach of the regime produces acceleration. Time maintains a very close link with value to the very extent that the acceleration (contraction and then dilation) of time indicates that either there is a return to equilibrium within a regime, after having been distanced from it, or there is a breakdown of the regime and a possible transfer to a new regime. As such, the movement of the cycle is distinguished from the crisis.

Shares, unlike long-term interest rates, rise on average faster than they fall. Since 1970, as many rises have been observed as falls, with a positive average speed which is above the median value. These conclusions are not fundamentally altered by the consideration of the positive long-term trend of shares and dividends. Compared to this upward trend, shares rise even more quickly than they fall. The observation is even clearer between 1982 and the end of the 1990's, the period when shares rose sharply. Finally, an extreme rise or fall is, on average, followed by a less intense movement in the opposite direction, with a drop in speed, once again on average.

With regard to interest rates, phenomena of acceleration (contraction/dilation) are noted at the extreme points, with a predominance of increases, i.e. releases of energy-time from over-valuation zones. Everything seems to take place as if the dilations and contractions of liquidity were asymmetrical at the extreme points, with a strong reversal in the price of liquidity back to equilibrium and value. Shares do not seem to experience such asymmetry. However, they do play the same role as the interest rate in the general economic and financial framework, the latter being, in numerous respects, one of the central regulators of the temperature of the cycle and of value. The interest rate creates a link between time and value within a referential which is not linear and where the forces which pull back towards equilibrium are asymmetrical. The future is anticipated there in the same way that the past is remembered or forgotten. The present does not seem to have any reality or substance. There is an analogy between the matter which is or seems to be liquidity and the economic memory (e.g. status of the demand).

This asymmetry of speeds as between shares and interest rates can be explained by the determining role of the preference between shares and bonds in the cyclical fluctuations of the stock markets. This is particularly true in phases of economic recovery. The rebound of shares is then based on an attractive risk premium (e.g. the comparison of current yields on shares and bonds), upward revisions of the expectations of earnings, all against a background of a more pronounced appetite for risk. The interest rates rise and the central banks and real economy absorb the excess liquidity. Shares end up suffering the negative effects thereof but the fall is on average less pronounced and less rapid, since the expectations of earnings play a cushioning role, marked by a certain degree of inertia, and are therefore only gradually revised downwards. All of the above applies to so-called normal periods.

There is a fundamental link between time (memory, duration, expectations) and value (equilibrium). The link is not linear. It is one of the reasons why economic and financial events exist.

Equilibrium in the macro-economic and financial regime

The question of equilibrium regimes is fundamental. This is probably the main objective of research. The regime, which overflows or exceeds the notion of a cycle within time, contains a certain number of macro-economic characteristics – which should be understood in the widest sense, including institutional transformations. These characteristics form a set of determinants and this determination function is essential in the formation of equilibrium values for the financial variables within the regime (e.g. interest rate or share risk premium but, in fact, more generally any financial variable for which the question of value is posed). The concept of a regime is a moving target, as are the characteristics which define the equilibrium values for financial variables.

Value is only relative and there is a need to clarify what one means by this in all sectors of the economy and finance. The concept of value is relative within a temporal referential, which may be the history of the variable itself or the history of neighbouring or even distant variables. The concept of value may also prove to be relative within a spatial referential, which may be illustrated by a comparison between two regions. There is only value by comparison to a given point of view of the relevant variable. This point of view requires a fixed reference point and therefore a regime.

An observation of the first decade of the 21st century allows one to identify some characteristics which, when put together, may form a regime. Certain of these characteristics come from far away and from other regimes, if only because they are created from a reaction to (a rejection of) a past regime. This is true of disinflation. For example, the macro-economic regime, for an observer of, let us say, the mid-decade, includes, in the context of growth, elements of a return to normality post-bubble (growth which is close to its potential, certain weaknesses and imbalances), of a return to better fortune for Japan and Germany, which were struck off the economic map for almost fifteen years, of a return to calm in the emerging markets sphere after a decade of upheaval. The macro-economic regime, against a backdrop of a global theme of return to normality, includes the experience of disinflation. Classic inflation of goods and services seems to be dead, although perhaps it is only sleeping. The monetary sources of inflation are very present in a system which has a structural excess of liquidity but the monetary stimulation of prices is lost en route, on the financial markets, leaving bubbles there like the scars of rising inflation. However, a distribution of added value which is favourable to earnings (as compared to wages) and a mix of globalisation and technology, whose "globalogical" remainder exerts a diffuse pressure over the end consumer prices, adds to the overcapacities and the disinflation exported from the emerging markets sphere, which are two fundamental characteristics of the regime.

The distribution of added value between earnings and wages is a central element at the heart of the regime, its management and its regulation. This distribution (its distortion in favour of earnings) is one of the pillars of what can be called a form of patrimonial capitalism, which appeared in the USA in the 1990's and has since spread to the rest of the world. The equity asset class probably constitutes its foundation, supported by the elevated share of earnings within value and the fall in interest rates permitted by disinflation, which is itself sustained by wage moderation. This distribution goes hand-in-hand, moreover, with a high level of private debt, attracted by the relatively low equilibrium level of interest rates within the regime and, also, by the prospects of a happy triptych mixing wealth effects, credit and consumption. Governments probably benefit from low interest rates, which make the structural reduction of public debt painless or less painful and also make them less urgent. This relative benefit stops here: the inflationary monetisation attempts have little chance of succeeding in the current regime, which is no longer that of the 1970's. The wheel may perhaps turn. To a certain extent, there is a monetisation of the US government debt and only the US debt, by the central banks of emerging markets, but this produces financial inflation and not the classic inflation of goods and services and its inflationary effects are mixed with those of the monetisation of private debt on the financial markets, which are, in turn, a fundamental characteristic of the regime. The various QE (quantitative easing) transactions conducted by Western central banks have added a new dimension of monetisation, which is more autonomous and more direct, although one can still not speak of emancipation with regard to the monetisation by central banks of emerging markets.

Debt is central to the macro-economic regime. The excess liquidity (structural excesses of liquidity) of the regime is, to some extent, merely its reflection in the mirror. The regime is characterised by a sharp increase in debt, both private and public. Excess liquidity accommodates this increase. The heart of the regime lies in the credit granted to households (especially) and (to a lesser degree and in any event of less concern since the purge of the years 2001-2003) to corporates, the counterpart for which is monetisation on the financial markets in the form of wealth effects, a consumption regime which is gradually freed from the realities of savings and the necessary accommodating conditions of liquidity (moreover, the disinflation which is unique to the regime enables this). This excess liquidity postpones (moreover) the efforts of governments to reduce their debt. Public and private debt cannot increase forever, with an increasing number of imbalances (financial bubbles) and subject to permanent, increasing injections of liquidity. Someone in the system will indeed have to save money once again. The crisis of 2008 and its aftermath have added further to this conundrum.

Excess liquidity is, in many respects, the principal vault of the regime's structure. It renders debt tolerable, is sustained by disinflation (since it frees the central banks from their anti-inflationary vigilance) and forms a link between consumption and wealth effects. The classic origin of this excess liquidity lies in the monetary policies of the G7 countries and its less traditional sources form part of the monetary consequences of the interventions by the central banks of the emerging markets on the forex markets. This excess liquidity is a fundamental element of the regime, since the monetary policies of the G7 countries have a structurally accommodating bias (in a context of a low risk of inflation), and an asymmetrical approach as between a rise and fall in rates (in a context of financial imbalances, including bubbles); it is also a fundamental element, since the financing axis of the USA/emerging markets (in fact, Asia), which is based on the monetisation of the US external debt by the central banks of the emerging markets and the absorption of dollars by the rest of the world, therefore based on the dollar status, is itself an essential element for understanding the contemporary financial economy. Things may and indeed will change, but, for the moment, provided the so-called dollar convention remains intact, this is how things are.

These few elements which define the contours of the macro-economic regime determine a certain (equilibrium) status of the financial variables. The case of interest rates (or bond risk premia) is probably one of the most interesting. The majority of the elements discussed during the characterisation of the regime are in line with lower real (natural) equilibrium interest rates. A drop in inflation and its volatility, an excess liquidity which is non-inflationary (apart from financial inflation) imposed by the stimulation of the growth regime, by the risk of financial breakdowns and the explosion of bubbles, by the global mode of financing guaranteed by the dollar status: if one wishes to add demographic elements (ageing) and the efficiency of capital markets, one arrives without difficulty at an idea of lowering the reference points of real (natural) rates within the regime, in particular in the European case which, in addition to all these points, shows a weakening of the growth potential. The determining elements of the regime are the disappearance of classic inflation of goods and services and the monetary transformation of inflation into various financial bubbles, which make deflation rather than inflation the ultimate risk prevailing over the regime. To a certain extent, the lowering of the equilibrium level of real (and nominal) interest rates states in its own way that the ultimate risk of the present regime is a deflationary one, since the journey, which necessarily passes through an unwinding of the debt/financial asset price/economic activity triptych, has reached the limits of sustainability and may, moreover, include a (transitional) phase of inflationary pressures – it then represents a trap for central banks, since any indiscriminate monetary tightening will only accentuate the final deflationary risk. There are, however, many other elements which should, all things being equal, be in line with higher real rates, higher returns on private capital or an increase in the public debt ratios of the G7 countries as a whole. The fact that this is not the case means that there are even stronger factors at work. The excess liquidity of the regime which is (for the moment) not inflationary is no doubt this factor, holding the others in the palm of its hand.

Equilibrium. A positive approach to real interest rates

The question of the equilibrium regime of (real) interest rates remains deeply linked to that of excess liquidity. The undisputed lowering of the equilibrium level of real rates (the easing of the monetary constraint which affects liquidity, because of disinflation, played an essential role in this) does nothing to solve the question raised by interest rates, which are projected well below any new equilibrium level which one might estimate (and lower than one might estimate). Excess liquidity probably has something to do with this and, in such circumstances, the equilibrium differential permitted by excess liquidity helps explain a few cyclical dynamics and, in particular, the expansion phases of the PER (the 1990's demonstrated this in spectacular fashion and then the post 2008 crisis). The legitimate, structural reduction phase of bond risk premia (essentially in the 1990's) does not raise any insurmountable issues. A possible excess reduction is of more concern, since such an imbalance will, sooner or later, require a correction and result in a cycle.

One must bear long cycles in mind when considering real rate regimes. The reduction of equilibrium levels, which were seen from the mid-1990's onwards, occurred within a regime of real rates which were even higher. Taking only the usual inflation of consumer prices, the IMF identified three real rate periods for the G7 countries. The figures are of far less importance than the illustration of the principle of regimes: 1960-1972 (average real long-term rates: 2.8%; 1973-1980: 0.4%; 1981-1993: 4.7%). The remainder of the decade and then the start of the 21st century saw the completion of the transmission of disinflation experiences to nominal and real interest rates, the equilibrium regime of real interest rates being lowered, moreover, by (additional) adjustment of the nominal interest rates, once a context of low long-term inflation with little volatility was reached.

The globalisation of real interest rates is now a reality at the turning point of the 21st century. The confrontation between the global supply and demand of capital on the integrated markets and the existence of a global business cycle are some of the elements which supported the movement. After consolidation of the global economy's interconnections, the long-term European interest rate is, in turn, a function of the global real rate (especially the US rate, in fact) and of a domestic constant (or risk premium). The real long-term European (German) rates were historically, and on average, higher than the real US rates, this risk premium reflecting the dollar status but also the situation of the European state finances. It will require some time for the euro to obtain a status comparable to that of the dollar, and the European budgetary efforts, if confirmed, will also need to be taken into account.

No one has ever been able nor will ever be able to observe a real interest rate. Unlike a nominal interest rate, a real rate is a concept which cannot easily be approached. Its somewhat obscure nature helps explain the fundamental role which may be allocated to it, in particular within the cycle. Whether its origin is "real" or financial, the concept of the real rate remains essential. The approach to the real rate through normal inflation (annual or sub-annual variation) is unsatisfactory, since it includes volatility, the purely cyclical distraction of inflation and ignores the long-term expectation of inflation, which alone is relevant for value (bond value, in this instance). It is because the real interest rate establishes a deep link with time (memory, duration, expectation are three connected functions within the determination of value), that one must define precisely what one means by a long-term expectation of inflation. The real interest rate is a fundamental concept and therefore a pillar of the structure of any economic and financial regime, because it expresses, in concise terms, the merger of linear segments of the past, present and future within a duration, a matter of memory, which is elastic (dilation, contraction) and malleable. The bridge between time and value is traversed by the concept of a real interest rate, since that which has value (for tomorrow, in expectation) is that which expresses what has been, continuously (or discontinuously), within a form of duration and inertia which does not exclude either a breakdown or an acceleration. The non-linearity of the special forms of dilation and contraction of time is, in many respects, central to the value process.

To return, strictly speaking, to the strict question of the real rate, medium- or long-term inflation (what indeed are the medium- and long-terms? Let us take here a period of ten years, i.e. the average maturity of a long-term bond, since we are examining the real interest rate) is the principal risk for the holder of a ten or thirty year bond, which is expressed by the so-called Fisher equation by, essentially, reducing the nominal long-term interest rate to the sum of the real rate and of *expected* inflation, two unobservable variables, as if they are obscurely hidden away within the fundamental foundations of that which "appears", i.e. the nominal interest rate. There is, within this presentation, an in-itself/for-itself, being/the being structure which marks a breach between that which is (real rate, expectation of inflation) and that which will appear within the being. That which forms part of being (of that which is) is not observable here, but maintains a close link with time (that of expectation, i.e. that of memory, which cancels over the duration the artificial differences between present, past and future). This close link with time is a close link with value. Value, time and being are fundamentally linked within everything which is essential for the economic discipline but cannot be directly observed. The observable is the being, and the economic discipline, rather than losing itself within the infinite technical observation of the beings, must look for the foundations which, within the being, speak about that which is from an origin. The concept of the real rate, and together with this, the question of long-term expectation, say nothing more.

Rather than using current, normal inflation, one can approach long-term expected inflation using a long-term average of inflation. Expectations are, therefore, a function of the past here, affected by a coefficient of forgetfulness (the future is discounted in the same way that the past is forgotten) and characterised by a certain degree of inertia. Unsurprisingly, on markets where the effects of memory are powerful (in fact, memory is in many respects the very matter or raw material of the financial markets), nominal interest rates are better correlated with this type of average than with normal inflation, particularly since normal inflation, expected inflation, long-term inflation and the central bank objective all converge. When one states here that normal inflation is not relevant in the approach to long-term expectation and that of the real interest rate, one is in fact stating that the present as a temporal segment does not exist within economic and financial time; that the past dominates; that the whole, of duration and of memory, dominates the overall package. When one states that time is central to the economy and of finance, one means that the links between value, time and being determine the essential questions of these disciplines. One also means that there is a financial time, dominated by the effects of memory and forgetfulness (there is a symmetry) within the determination of that which is coming (the expectation) and that which has value (that which has been to a certain extent, i.e. within a certain lapse of duration for memory). The expectation of that which is coming and the apprehension of value (memory and forgetfulness, of that which has been) constitute two, probably symmetrical, sides of the same phenomenon.

Long-term inflation is not the only risk for the holder of a ten-year government bond. Since a given level of inflation has a different meaning, depending on whether nominal growth is strong or weak, such growth constitutes a second risk. In an uncertain economic climate, the long-term, nominal, equilibrium interest rate is, in principle, equal to the rate of growth of the average (i.e. past) national income as a nominal value, increased by a risk premium which represents a certain factor of uncertainty. Accordingly, there exists an equilibrium risk premium which, within a given regime with special macro-economic and financial characteristics, may validly be used as a reference. This reference means that the values taken over time by the risk premium may fluctuate around the equilibrium value of the regime, such cyclical fluctuations not affecting the status of the equilibrium value, provided that the regime itself is not questioned. This approach, using the national income as a nominal value fundamentally means, over and above what is specifically represented by this business variable, that any expectation is a memory (whether complete or forgetful) of a certain past and that the raw material of the economy and finance (in particular of the financial markets), i.e. time, is essentially a memory of that which has been projected into that which is coming, without being able to distinguish any of the sequences. This approach also means, essentially, that economic and financial behaviours are dictated or influenced by what has been and that there is probably no economic or financial variable or magnitude which cannot be understood through the history, i.e. memory (i.e. duration) of that same variable, or by the memory of another variable, which is close or distant. This memory, which determines that which is coming and the action which develops within that which is coming, is steeped in a sort of temporal matter, one may say duration, which grants such matter the toughness and inertia of that which is, compact. It is from this in-itself foundation, the principal characteristic of which is "being" that the Subject will deploy the act of projection and detachment, the act and memory forming one whole.

The concept of bond bubbles and the deflationary risk

It is difficult to talk about a bond bubble in the same way that one might for shares. In the latter case, the speculative demand is more easily identified. However, the bond markets also experience phenomena of *hubris* and imbalances. Such imbalances, which are less apparent, less commented on and which attract less media coverage than those involving the equity asset class (although they are both often linked), in particular because the psychological or real wealth effects are not the same, are nonetheless fundamental, since they bring into play the interest rate and its essential nature of issuing signs (the economic and financial truth, that of prices, of economic activity, of capital ...), of steering the expectations of the Subject and the economic and financial action and of regulating the cycle which witnesses the chain of expansion and contraction phases.

Whether or not the term bubble is the appropriate one, it is unclear whether we can, in all circumstances, consider a bond-type investment as absolutely certain. One bubble may conceal another. The economies of our financial markets are made up of connecting vessels. One imbalance is rarely closed without opening another. This is true of the forex markets. There will, accordingly, be a US current account deficit for as long as there is an external demand for dollars. This demand may, ultimately, shift towards the euro, with the appearance of a European deficit. In the absence of an international currency, there can only be shifts of deficits from one zone to another. This is also true of the two main competing asset classes, shares and bonds. During the clear-out of mirages at the end of the 1990's and the associated aversion to risk and panic, the connecting vessel of shares was emptied and that of government bonds was filled.

It is not unusual for nominal and real interest rates to be positioned below their equilibrium levels when, all things being equal, the real economy is not itself at equilibrium. This was all the more true when the global economy came closer to deflationary territories, after the bubble burst at the end of the 1990's. The most intriguing thing is that, after having averted the risk of deflation and having returned to growth, the global economy maintained an interest rate structure, in particular for long-term interest rates, which has more in common with deflation than with an economic context of synchronised global growth. Everything seems to take place as if the bond market, over and above the tangible realities of the supply and demand of liquidity (a robust explanation of the situation), had retained a memory of the fear of deflation, had as it were "imprinted" it. The objective risk of the current economic and financial regime is indeed deflationary and, from this point of view, the financial market means something. This interpretation is fundamentally different from that which sees, in the anomalies of low bond yields at the start of the 21st century, essentially an irrational imbalance combining excess liquidities and a captive demand – pension funds seeking to match their liabilities, the central banks of emerging markets forced, by the dollar status and the latter's position in their foreign reserves, to agree to buy government bonds, independently of any consideration of price and therefore of rational investment.

This memory of deflation, which is as it were "imprinted" in the market and in the interest rate structure, does not mean that there is deflation nor even that the risk of deflation may transform into actual deflation. This memory states, as it were, that the current regime contains an end risk of deflation, since the breakdowns or explosions caused by the association of debt and over-valued financial assets (characteristic features of the regime) destroy liquidity and wealth; when debt ceases to be inflated by the inflation of the price of assets, the excesses slow down and over-leverage strikes. At the end of the 1990's, that which was called liquidity on the markets was principally debt. When the crisis erupted, the indebted players suddenly sought to liquidate their liabilities and the demand for precautionary cash balances skyrocketed. Deflation is an evil which takes root gradually. The movement which anchors deflation occurs through a fall in the general level of prices, which precipitates a rise in real interest rates, since inflation falls faster than nominal interest rates, and a contraction of credit and the money supply, with a reduction in the speed of circulation of the stock of money within the economy. This whole process ends up stifling the real economy (bankruptcies, unemployment) and blocking the financial system. It is not easy to make a diagnosis of deflation, since there is often a degree of confusion between the general level of prices and relative prices. Certain prices may fall sharply, both in the real and financial spheres (shares, manufactured goods), but others may simultaneously rise (e.g. real estate or services). Equally, the largest money aggregates may continue to increase at comfortable rates, even though the economy is exposed to a risk of deflation. This is particularly true of growth in the central banks' monetary bases. The difficulty in making a diagnosis was evident in the quasi-deflationary territories in which the global economy found itself after the internet bubble burst.

The risk of deflation is the final risk of the macro-economic regime at the start of the 21st century, final because it summarises the very nature of the growth regime and its interrelations with debt and the price of financial assets. This risk of deflation is the basis for serious bond anomalies and disruptions to the essential role of the interest rate. The start of the 21st century has seen two major central banks (the Fed and the Bank of Japan, the ECB ultimately joining the party) struggle in a difficult post-bubble situation. Monetary activism then failed in Japan (liquidity trap, deflation and credit crunch) and was suspended in the USA (credit-rationing in the USA and almost-zero key rates). The US recession was only cushioned in the early 2000's at the cost of an additional deterioration of the financial situation of households, which would have to be paid off sooner or later; at a time when the Bank of Japan, finding itself out of ammunition, inflated its balance sheet by purchasing shares directly and when the Fed discovered fresh room for manoeuvre, at least in theory or rhetoric (direct purchases of government bonds). At the time of the Japanese difficulties in the 1990's, there emerged a perverse idea that the bond market could be withdrawn (by a beleaguered central bank which was short of ammunition and arguments) from market forces. The positions expressed by Mr Bernanke in the USA after the internet bubble burst open up, in turn, this range of possibilities to the Fed, i.e. the direct purchase of segments of the yield curve (and possibly more, e.g. private bonds, shares or real estate assets), the ultimate means for creating "central bank liquidity" and inflating the monetary base. This desperate monetary counterpart for budgetary policies, which were accordingly granted a certain laxity (there will be a captive demand in such a regime for government bonds), will justify an accumulation of government debt and will probably have crowding-out effects on private spending. The only alternatives to such choices are sub-optimal options which, at the end of the day, offer the same outcome, a dangerous rise in interest rates which will have to be managed or suffered, by accommodating it as best as possible. If such attempts are ineffective, the deterioration in the quality of government debt will lead to a risk premium (interest rates, currency). If they prove to be effective, in an economic context of global growth which is at least more promising, the bond market will be handed back to market forces and the central bank will not only cease to play a role of last resort bond purchaser but will commit to a difficult monetary normalisation process. It is then hard to avoid the monetary asphyxiation of an economy which has been heavily subsidized for a long time.

A macro-economic regime which contains within it a risk of deflation undergoes a permanent distortion of the fundamental interest rate functions. As such, it is a "blind" regime, since the perversion of the interest rate is a perversion of the essential link between time and value, which determines the expectation and therefore the very possibility of action. The perversion of the interest rate, a concise way of stating the distortion of the fundamental link between money (liquidity), price and activity, is one of the characteristics of the contemporary era. The fact that this distortion occurs at a time when the independence of the central banks is asserted reveals the urgent nature of the issues and is also worrying. This distortion contains a more serious forgetfulness of the origins and foundations of that which is expressed within the concept of the (real) interest rate and states that which "is" within the link between time, value and being. The forgetting of such foundations has made room for a manipulatory function of the interest rate, a technical variable/utensil working for the benefit of the action. It is essential that our era pays attention once more to that which, within the concept of the (real) interest rate, speaks from an origin of economics which is located well beyond the technical transformation of the economic discipline of the modern era into a quantitative means of appropriating the world within (economic) action.

What is the fate of a macro-financial regime which is at risk of deflation? Is a significant bond correction conceivable in a global economy which experiences deflationary pressures? Can the central banks take control of the bond market?

The last thirty years of the 21st century created a reference regime which connects business cycle, central banks and bond market around three pillars which are sufficiently recurring to be legible. They are first the consistent relations between the yield curve (the differential between long and short maturities) and the cycle of growth and inflation. The stylised description shows an increase in the slope of the curve before the recovery of activity, from the bottom of the cycle and through the short part of the curve (fall of key rates), up until the confirmation of the acceleration and through the long part (pressures on the long-term interest rates, in expectation of a rise in inflation and of the first monetary squeezes). The slope levels off before the actual economic slow-down, from the top of the cycle and through the short part (rise of key rates) and right into the downturn through the long part (fall in long-term rates), a reversal forming part of the possible outcomes. Aware of this information content, the market players used the curve to read the intentions of the central bank and the central bankers used it to identify the expectations of the markets. As a result of this interaction, played out within a closed-loop, the information contained in the curve has perhaps been weakened.

There is then an effective steering of the curve by the central banks, rhetoric (communication) and/or more effective (movement of the key rates). The delicate operation represented by the preparation of the financial markets prior to monetary movements is the best-known example thereof. The credibility of the central bank is at stake, which enables the impact on long-term interest rates of a movement in short-term interest rates to be controlled or indeed limited (when interest rates are rising).

There are also communicating vessels between shares and government bonds, close links where valuation and the cyclical fluctuations of the stock markets are strongly dependent on long-term interest rates (and therefore on the central bank to a fairly large extent), within a period which is marked by inflation and then by disinflation. The preference between shares and bonds, a function of the appetite for risk (or the aversion to risk) and of the differential in current or expected yield as between the two classes, of assets and of earnings expectations, plays a major role in the relative direction of the two asset classes and, consequently, in that of the expectations of growth and of the business cycle and, ultimately, in that of the real and financial cycles. The movements in stock market risk premium express the permanent arbitrage between the two asset classes.

It is, finally, the self-regulation of the economic cycle by the bond markets, within a regime where inflation remains (remained) a concern. The reactions of such bond markets, borne by expectations, make it more difficult for inflation to appear, since they prevent the cumulative process of inflation to unfold, possibly by killing the business cycle. It is not therefore the lack of inflation which makes a bond correction unlikely but the bond corrections which make a pronounced, sustainable reappearance of inflation more unlikely. Here is one example, among others, of the fact that time (and, more specifically, memory) is the raw material of the financial markets and that the referential is temporal. Memory is financial matter and, at the same time, maintains a deep link with "real" matter, which it distorts and modifies through the very dilations of time and expectations, and which also distorts such "real" matter when an event occurs which calls into question a regime of given memory. The interactions are such that the difference between memory (financial matter) and (real) matter gradually diminishes. The strong development of the financial markets has highlighted this diffuse reality.

Although this regime is still current in certain respects – the cycles and regimes are long – some changes directly question its foundations. It is first of all a macro-financial regime, whose ultimate risk is now deflation, which threatens a global economy in disequilibrium with regard to debt and an inflation in the price of financial assets which conceals it and which, in general, has to deal with the heritage of financial crises which have unfurled over almost two decades. The meaning of price risk has changed. The risk of inflation is no longer the key determinant of the bond yield curve. What does a yield curve look like as deflation approaches? Our generation has no references. The term "risk" in respect of inflation is probably inappropriate, since inflation is then (in the 1970's, in short) the principal means of regulating the macro-financial regime, characterised in particular by a government debt monetised by the public authority and a distribution of added value which is very favourable to employment and the employee. Things have changed, the regime was, as it were, questioned before being overturned. The regime has changed but the effects of memory are, once again, powerful. The current regime at this start of the 21st century, which is deflationary, continues to be haunted, at a distance, by the memory of inflation. The behaviour of the players, whether a mere investor or the central bank, continues to be marked by a certain degree of inertia, when faced with something which has, however, changed and is no longer. Inflation was, during the 1970's, the risk and the means of regulating a given economic and financial regime. The start of this century has made deflation the risk for the new regime, while inflation of the price of financial assets is its means of regulation.

It was then the central banks, representing another change to the regime, which, at least in Japan and the USA, came close to a zero key rate. In such areas, the effectiveness of monetary policy and, consequently, the credibility of the monetary institution, are coming increasingly under pressure. Added to this is the feeling, admittedly open to discussion, that the Fed (at least the Fed) has often, since the 1990's decade, found itself lagging behind the financial markets rather than at the helm, agreeing to what was demanded. It is, moreover, possible that, as a result of demanding too much and ever more from the central banks, their credibility is finally challenged. Far too much is expected from monetary policy, since it was a prominent feature of the regime implemented in the 1990's. One tends, at the same time, to underestimate what monetary policy can do (the stimulation of the component parts of internal demand, which are indeed sensitive to the interest rate) and to overestimate what it cannot do (e.g. increase the growth potential or clear situations of over-leverage and overcapacity); what it should not do (the symmetry in the price of financial assets can only be abandoned at the cost of a difficult moral uncertainty); what it can no longer do or do alone after a certain point: e.g. the transmission channels leading to confidence remain hypothetical, in absolute terms, particularly below a very low level of interest rates, when there is a global deterioration of the economy.

There is little doubt that the macro-financial regime which was introduced at the end of the 20th century contains a monetary policy crisis or is at least a serious challenge to monetary policy. It is one of the most remarkable characteristics of the regime, an institutional element and therefore an element of crisis, since it is the memory held by the institution (in this instance, vigilance against inflation) which is hit with full force by an acceleration (dilation/contraction) of economic and financial time. In a certain manner, given that they have been "too" credible, since the successful fight against the inflation of goods and services, central banks (which probably bear part of the responsibility for the period's imbalances) perhaps came closer to a certain paradox of tranquillity, where a gap was formed between the expectations of the reality of their resources, their assignments and their efficiency. The unbalanced attitude of the central banks towards the financial markets (benign neglect during the bubble, interventionism during the crash) clearly has something to do with this, since it sustains bubbles but also postpones or delays – although does not eliminate – the unavoidable adjustment which, when it finally comes, leaves the monetary authorities only a few resources with which to respond. These are the zones where the long-term interest rates may free themselves from their traditional determinants.

There is, within the current macro-financial regime, a monetary crisis, i.e. strictly speaking, the start of a renewed thinking of money which, beyond the technical instrumentation of monetary policy for the benefit of action (of economic policy), returns to that which, from the outset, has not ceased to traverse monetary action.

Consequently, one can understand why the central banks, the Fed itself, may have considered unconventional action relating to the yield curve, in order to maintain long-term rates at artificially low levels. The objective, which is to take direct control of long-term interest rates, is probably more difficult than would appear. When, faced with the potentially deflationary consequences of the bubble bursting, the Fed makes an intellectual commitment to adopt this path, since the words, concepts and discourse of central banks are never innocent, the Fed is in a way validating the expectations of global deflation by reinforcing them, to some extent. This is a cocktail for the creation of a bubble. Investors purchased bonds in the expectation that the central bank was likely to do so. The long-term interest rates dropped like stones. What risk is there in bearing bonds, when the central bank plays the role of bond purchaser of last resort? The risk is that it will cease to do so and that interest rates will soar. Long-term interest rates cannot be taken outside market forces with impunity. This new context makes the central bank's communications exercise more complex and difficult, market expectations possibly more volatile and the efficiency of monetary policy more uncertain. Finally, the encounter between an increasing need for financing (twin US deficits, more general state finance problems within the G7 countries) and an active search for returns by investors creates a new dynamic. With a key rate close to zero and long-term interest rates historically low, the appetite for other asset classes may increase, in the same way that there may be an increase in the price required for holding public debt. Withdrawals from bonds may accelerate independently of a fundamental assessment of the economic situation or future monetary policy.

It is difficult to reverse monetary policy in a regime where the ultimate risk is deflation. It is not an easy matter to disconnect the monetary infusion of an economy flooded with liquidities, without running the risk of causing a relapse, especially if the central bank is committed, whether in fact or even in spirit, to a path of unconventional action. If this path is abandoned, together with a more promising climate of growth, which therefore warrants a form of monetary normalisation, it may cause pressures on bonds, especially if the central bank's communication is not sufficiently prepared or is inadequate. The probability of a brief recovery would be more likely, an area of growth closed by the interest rates on imbalances and numerous weaknesses. The self-correcting nature of the bond movements is expressed in this type of configuration. It is also possible that one may see long-term interest rates continue to increase, even though the central bank, aware of the limitations of such a fragile recovery, does not intend to reverse the monetary situation and raise its key rates. Expectations of market growth, even if unfounded, may suffice. However, another scenario may be considered, which is far less comfortable, where the external financing requirement of a heavily-indebted economy – namely the USA – sustains pressure on bond yields, against a backdrop of a strike by creditors, or a backdrop of doubt, and when, especially, everything else is equal, i.e. independently of a context of growth and inflation which justify such pressures. Such an economy may find itself on a path of weakened growth (e.g. imbalances being purged or bubbles burst), while being affected by an atypically steep yield curve, a privilege of periods of sustained growth and inflationary risks in former times. This is a way of saying that a central bank which ventures into the key rate zero zone may lose not only its conventional means of action but also its control over the whole of the market and part of its credibility. The central banks will then only be left with the weapon of rhetoric, which remains formidable: to give credibility to the spirit of recovery without sparking a crisis in the bond market, to note the weakness of the structure without acknowledging in detail their profound doubts.

The question of the monetary regime is fundamental within the broader concept of the macro-financial regime.

Essay 7

EXCHANGE RATES, PRICES WITHOUT EQUILIBRIUM

Beyond the illusory adjustment towards equilibrium value

In exchange rate regimes such as ours, it is somewhat illusory to expect an adjustment of currencies towards their equilibrium value. Monetary flows do not match transactions of goods and services and there is a considerable number of short-term capital flows. An exchange rate may remain below or above the so-called fundamental values over a long period. The very concept of what is fundamental is in fact weakened, since the real reference for a reflection on the exchange rate is dominated and probably overwhelmed by a strong monetary reality. This victory of the monetary dimension is only partly apparent, since it is not money which triumphs but, fairly generally, its distortion in the global and correlated phenomena of *ex nihilo* creation of liquidity (monetary creation). The fact that there is no (unique) global currency or, at least, a undeniable value standard, accentuates the phenomenon. The dollar currency has ended up as a standard, in the same way that the law enters forcefully always and everywhere, even though there is no value reference to the intangible dollar and though the dollar "value" is fairly generally self-referenced within a series of mechanisms of monetary duplications and multiplications of which the USA-Asia axis is one of the major pillars. As such, the forex market has seen a deindexation of money, value and the exchange rate. There is no instability on the forex market but rather a monetary instability (cause) reflected by the erratic movements of currencies (symptom). As such, if the international coordination of the exchange rate does not seriously tackle the causes of such bad habits, it will not achieve conclusive results.

The question of exchange rates is fundamental, since it is central to the mechanism of relative prices and therefore of value, which is always and ever a relative concept. The globalisation period which commenced at the end of the 20th century makes exchange rates into an economic and financial reality, where the interaction of currencies is a channel for the transmission, redistribution and adjustment of value. The offset or shifts from one region to another of savings deficits or surpluses by comparison with investment (current account balances) and the interaction of exchange rates are intertwined, although the causal link between them is not clearly identified. At the same time, the interaction of currencies tends to become independent within a monetary and financial process which distances itself from other real and more traditional determinants.

A positive approach to value on the currency markets

The approach to value on the currency markets remains improbable. The best predictions struggle to apply to mere random movements. The word random is important, the forex markets are inhabited by chance, which is neither risk nor uncertainty.

Approaches other than the most traditional ones remain to be explored with humility and without any illusions. One approach may involve considering the question of the exchange rate as a problem of holding *cash.* Holding a currency is, for the most part, like holding liquidity, whose preference function is complex (reasons for the transaction, for holding, for speculation ...) and is probably closely linked to the apprehension of risk (appetite, aversion). These aspects of the issue of currency are insufficiently explored. Within the function of preference for liquidity, which is involved in the holding of a currency, currencies may constitute an asset class in their own right. The question then arises whether an investor is well or badly remunerated for holding a currency which is over- or under-valued, by comparison with another currency, since it is only a relative value. A rational investor may benefit from holding a currency whose fundamental situation is unbalanced or risky. This approach treats currencies like an asset class for which the risk/return pairing needs to be characterised or, rather, the remuneration of the risk in relation to a certain idea or value reference, which remains very difficult to estimate.

Another approach may be interested in more monetary phenomena, in the abundance (rarity) of one currency by comparison with another, placing the emphasis on liquidity aspects. It may involve estimating the new net supply or the new net demand of a given currency. A currency has more chance of coming under downward pressure, the higher its net supply (which the markets must absorb). This net offer can be approached through the balance of payments and in particular the basic balance, the sum of the current account and the long-term capital balance. The first reflection seems, *a priori*, more aimed at the question of value and the second more exclusively at the liquidity equilibria. However, the first approach, by accommodating the return of the currency asset (and, in particular, the "currency" liquidity), opens itself up to monetary phenomena. At the same time, the second reflection, because it is open to the question of the abundance (rarity) of a currency, may be compared with the question of value. One can see, in this example, the extent to which the bridge between money and value is lacking, so-called phenomena of liquidity and determinants of valuation. The empowerment of the action and of the monetary phenomena under the label of liquidity seems to have distanced the question of value to such an extent as to cause it to expire. The second approach discussed above, almost paradoxically, returns to the question of value, which has fallen into oblivion, through liquidity itself and through the very basis of the reflection on value, abundance and rarity, of monetary unity here. This approach, which seems at first sight to yield to the "all-liquidity" fashions, returns to the origin of the questioning of value in its relationship with money, the magnitudes and perversions of which have always been linked to relative rarities.

Why hold currency **X** *as opposed to currency* **Y***?*

An investor may be well remunerated for holding an over-valued currency, which can also be called (more) risky, even though the term refers to other realities as well. The risk/return pairing consequently constitutes a more complete area of investigation of value (of a currency, of an exchange rate).

One can reduce the holding of one currency as compared to another to a search for a response to the following two questions: am I well or poorly remunerated, as an investor, for holding currency *X* as compared to currency *Y*, in terms of the risk taken? Is currency *X* under- or over-valued as compared to currency *Y*? We are attempting to weigh a risk premium (return) against an element of risk (inflation in an approach which reduces the question of holding the currency to a question of holding liquidity) and an element of value (valuation), which may, moreover, itself incorporate the dimension of inflation (e. g. real effective exchange rate), this latter element of value being also an element of risk (which is high when the currency is over-valued), which is weighed against a global return. The value of the currency (in the strict sense of the word), in its traditional meaning, is incorporated within the larger question of return and risk, the value (and its most classic indicators) being compared to the concept of risk. This approach at least has the merit of raising the question of value (question 2) and in relative terms (the valuation of one and only one currency in absolute terms makes little sense, although the economic discourse contains an abundance of absolute judgements; value, fundamentally, is difference and otherness), while admitting that the under- or over-valuation is probably necessary, in particular for the detection of a future trend, but is not enough. The fundamental unbalanced situation of a currency does not constitute an obstacle to holding the relevant currency. This is, moreover, one of the reasons why such situations of imbalances may persist.

One must first be able to obtain a measure of each of these two dimensions. The question of holding *cash* (a risk-free asset) or liquidity, adopted as a means of access to the question of holding one currency as compared to another, thus leads to the relative remuneration as between two positions invested in a risk-free asset, which is considered here as an asset class as such. When an investor wonders whether he is well or poorly remunerated for holding a currency *X* as compared to a currency *Y*, he is comparing the difference in nominal remuneration between two investments in *cash* (a risk-free asset) and his expectation of the inflation differential between the two reference economies (currencies). In fact, despite an unfavourable inflation differential (in respect of currency *X* as compared to currency *Y*), an investor may be better advised to maintain his confidence in the first, if the short-term interest rate differential was higher than the inflation differential. This reasoning is verified *ex post* in theory, the expectation *ex ante* – and its measure – are in practice harder to grasp.

The example of the dollar/yen exchange rate between 1980 and 2000 may illustrate this point. Consumer prices increased faster over this period in the USA than in Japan. Unsurprisingly, the dollar depreciated as compared to the yen. However, an investor would still have been advised to hold cash in dollars, if the differential of the nominal short-term rates was higher than the current inflation differential. This was effectively the case during the relatively brief sub-periods (1980-1984, 1988-1990, 1995-1999), when the relative performance of *cash* in dollars was better. Equally, and despite a trend over a long period which was favourable to the yen as compared to the deutschmark, it was rational to hold *cash* in marks rather than yen during the sub-periods 1988-1989 and 1992-1998. For the same treasons, it was wise to hold dollars as compared to marks in 1981-1983, 1990-1992, 1994-1999.

Accordingly, everything takes place as if the market evolutions represented a rational formation of the aggregated expectations of the players. Although, *ex ante*, the individual expectations of the market players are not necessarily rational, this seems to be the case *ex post*. This coherence is largely based on the relative inertia of the regime of expectations of inflation. The disruptions to the regime of expectations (non-linear jumps due to shocks) can be considered to have a non-negligible link to the crises or disruptions noted on the forex market.

By following the approach discussed above, it should be noted that the difference in nominal remuneration between two investments in *cash* may simply be provided by the nominal spread of the three-month interest rate. The expectation of the inflation differential between the two reference economies is, for its part, harder to measure. An average history of the inflation differential will be preferred to the current inflation differential alone, the former being more inert, since it incorporates the effects of memory and smoothes out the purely cyclical variations of inflation. A real spread of short-term interest rates is thus obtained. This approach, which is used for other asset classes, postulates an adaptive expectation. Nor is it far-fetched to state that this is a rational expectation, in the sense used when one states that "it is rational for an investor to ...". As such, a fundamental form of equivalence is established between reason and memory (reason and time) within the economic process itself. This goes well beyond the formation of expectations alone. It is suggested, more fundamentally, that it is impossible to understand the economic phenomena outside a temporal regime of long, or instead dense, time in order to state its inertia. This dense time is both the matter of memory which "rationally" grasps the economic object/phenomenon and the memory-matter of the economic object. The expectations are rational to the full extent that reason is memory and memory is matter.

It is not enough to obtain a real spread which incorporates the memory effect of inflation, since the investor is not yet in a position to qualify this variable by comparison with an equilibrium regime within which the variable fluctuates around equilibrium. If one wishes to be able to state whether this real spread is high or low, it should be compared to an equilibrium level which one may be able to estimate using a multi-cyclical average. This deviation from the equilibrium level, which is standardised and expressed as standard deviations, provides an element of response to the original question: when the real *X/Y* remuneration differential is greater than its equilibrium level, the investment is correctly remunerated by holding currency *X*, for the risk of inflation which is taken. In fact, it can be noted that this type of situation tends to result (after a delay of about one year) in a nominal increase in currency *X* as compared to currency *Y*. There is therefore a (cyclical) process of a return to equilibrium (a mean reversion) which fundamentally constitutes the consistent operation of the market, without excluding the possibility of disruptions in equilibrium and linearity. It is suggested, consequently, that contrary to what is often thought, paths of rationality do exist on the forex markets. The premise that the investor is rational on the forex markets, which is somewhat fragile *ex ante* for each of the investors, retains a practical sense *ex post*.

Such a tendency for mean reversion (return to equilibrium) of the real spread (an interesting example is the case of the dollar/yen exchange rate between 1980 and 2000) gives the investor the possibility of a rational expectation of an evolution in the nominal exchange rate. Such a movement has all the more chance of occurring, if currency *X* is under-valued by comparison with currency *Y*. The degree of over- or under-valuation can be estimated using the effective real exchange rate for *X/Y*, which is positioned in this way, when compared to an average long-term equilibrium value. This approach to value, which is fairly rudimentary, is linked to that of the remuneration of risk discussed above. More specifically, an estimation of value which is disconnected from the Subject's expectation (e.g. effective real exchange rate, which can be compared to the method of purchasing power parities) can be linked to an estimation of value in which the risk and its remuneration, from the "rational" viewpoint of the Subject (or the investor), are essential. By linking the two approaches, there are accordingly four situations which may potentially arise, ranging from that which characterises a currency which is well-remunerated and under-valued (as compared to another currency), up to the opposite situation. These four stations represent the same number of stages which follow on from each other within a full cycle, driven by the process of the return to equilibrium, excluding crises which are, indeed, often sudden, evolutionary leaps in the fundamental parameters of the equilibrium regime.

The abundance of a currency and its price

The question of currencies and exchange rates is relative – as is the concept of value – and not absolute; this question may be expressed as an approach to an asset class by an investor and therefore based on the risk and return pairing; the question of value is both that of the future expected erosion of a purchasing power – and the remuneration of the associated risk – and that of the (relative) rarity of the monetary unit represented by a currency, which is a liquidity variable (abundance, rarity) as much as it is value in the strict sense of the term.

The abundance of a currency determines, to a certain extent, the evolutions on the forex markets. The supply of a currency, which the markets have to digest, cannot, like other goods, be unrelated to its price, which in fact measures its rarity. The estimation of such a supply is a delicate matter. Often the current account balances alone are called on for assistance (the greater the deficit, the larger the supply) but such an approach remains partial. It does not take account of the long-term capital inflows and outflows (direct and portfolio investments). It is the basic balance (sum of the current balance and the long-term capital balance) which seems closest to the notion of the supply of currencies. A basic balance deficit means that the new net supply of a currency which the market will have to absorb is increasing. This net supply is the result of current account transactions in goods and services and transactions relating to long-term, direct and portfolio investments. Its counterpart is the movements of short-term capital, i.e. capital account inflows. In order to attract such capital, the currency has to fall, particularly when it is poorly remunerated by comparison with other currencies. The opposite is true in the event of a basic balance surplus –

i.e. the net demand of currency which is covered by short-term capital outflows caused by a rise in the currency. Since one currency only evolves by comparison with another currency, it is the relative movements of the basic balances which should be monitored.

The price of the currency (exchange rate) adjusts the basic balance by the same amount that the latter determines the fluctuations in the price of the currency. From the investor's point of view, it is a matter of estimating whether the remuneration of the risk of future depreciation of the currency is sufficiently attractive. This means, in particular, that a significant imbalance in the balance of payments may persist for so long as the risk of future depreciation (expectation) and the remuneration of that risk continue to form a pairing which represents an acceptable compromise for the investor. The forex market remains fundamentally a market of expectations since it is, at each moment, the risk of future depreciation/appreciation which is weighed and which receives as it were a probability and a price. What is meant here is that behind the mass of flows or stock (flows make stock) which, almost mechanically, seem through the interaction of equilibria and imbalances between supply and demand, to determine the evolutions on the forex markets, there is fundamentally a confrontation of expectations – of regimes of long-term expectations more precisely – and of risk premia. This is why foreign exchange is an asset class.

The exchange rates constitute an interaction of relative prices which contribute towards a "general" equilibrium on the forex markets. The variables constituted by the currencies do not refer to underlying assets which are strictly comparable to those of other asset classes. This is true of earnings for shares, even if, from a macro-economic point of view, growth – or growth differentials – may often be discussed or commented upon with regard to foreign exchange, although it is not really sure what the valid reason for this is. Foreign exchange seems, from the point of view of value, to be closest to the bond asset class, since the expectation of (long-term) inflation – which is absolute and, especially, relative, since the analysis concerns a pair of currencies and therefore an exchange rate – is central to the estimation of the risk of a (future) reduction in the purchasing power of such a currency (by comparison with another currency). The traditional approach puts the emphasis on inflation and purchasing power, as the underlying asset for value. This approach is not unconnected, quite the contrary, with the question of the risk of a future depreciation/(appreciation), which seems to us to be fundamental to the operation of the forex markets and of the relative prices of currencies. What we mean is that the risk of future depreciation is greater than might be indicated by the interplay of expectations of inflation alone. Behind the long-term expectation of the depreciation of a currency there exist numerous determinants which constitute a regime and which borrow from numerous categories, whether economic or financial, where the effects of memory and more purely psychological effects play a non-negligible role. The interplay of currencies is an interaction of relative prices which encompasses, absorbs and surpasses the mere interaction of relative prices defined by the relative evolution of classic inflation indexes. The fundamental question of foreign exchange is the apprehension of the risk of future depreciation. This risk forms part of a long-term, multi-criteria expectation, such criteria forming a regime which is characterised by a certain degree of stability/inertia, but also by shocks and discontinuities.

It is, therefore, through an "overload" of one currency (by comparison with another currency) that one can approach the world of foreign exchange (bearing in mind that the factors of supply and demand are themselves fairly broadly adjusted by the risk/return pairings on a form of efficient foreign exchange frontier). The multiplicity of equilibria obtained at any time on an infinite number of efficient frontiers, and the same number of possible investors, forms part of the elements of determination of the forex market. The adjustment of quantities through prices (the risk, the return) is probably an acceptable premise.

The example of the launch of the euro

The estimation of the "overload" (i.e. the abundance of the supply of one currency) thus led, between 1998 and 2000, to the launch of the euro and to considering that the European basic balance was in deficit, its two entries being both in deficit: appearance of a current account deficit (recovery of internal demand; increase in the price of oil) and net long-term capital outflows, with more numerous determinants which were harder to grasp. The appearance of a current account deficit was a surprise to some extent, since, at the launch of the euro, most scenarii for a stronger euro were based on the existence of a structural surplus in savings by comparison with investment in the eurozone (i.e. current account surplus). Faced with a US economy with a net structural deficit (having moreover played the role of consumer of last resort during the emerging market crisis), the bullish fate of the euro/dollar parity seemed to be sealed. A comparison was willingly made between the eurozone and Japan in this context.

The net supply of euros was very abundant at the time of the launch of the European currency, which was unfavourable to the price of the European currency, if indeed one considers a fall in price to be unfavourable. The eurozone was thus destined to be a net capital exporter within the global village. This role was respected to precisely the same extent that the recycling of European savings was effective (the eurozone debt crisis led to an accumulation of national "non-cooperative" current account surpluses and a challenge to recycle them both across the eurozone *and* outside it).

Net long-term capital outflows rely first on a mechanical effect of a search for diversification resulting from the very appearance itself of the euro. The crushing of the ghost of intra-zone returns (equalising effect) precipitated portfolio adjustments by resident investments. This movement was fairly generally completed between 1999 and 2001. Added to this was a restructuring of the landscape of European firms, which led a certain number of players, from a domestic base which was henceforth expanded to Europe, to target the acquisition or constitution of market shares outside the zone, sustaining capital outflows for direct investments.

In order to allocate a long-term characteristic to such phenomena, one must probably assume that the investors will be convinced (i.e. will expect, since foreign exchange interaction remains fundamentally an interaction within time and expectations) of the possibility of generally obtaining, outside the eurozone, higher long-term returns on investment. The demand for the euro depends in part on the expectations of real and financial relative returns offered by the zone (and, therefore, to a certain extent, on reorganisations and investments which ultimately refer back to the conduct of the policy mix but, more generally, to the conduct of the national and European economic policies). What is at stake is fundamentally a regime of long-term expectations on the future trends of the European, US and Asian economies – the three pillars of the global foreign exchange market. The determinants for such regimes of long-term expectations reflect those of the regimes of (long-term) growth and productivity of these principal economic regions. The over-interpretation of simple, cyclical, short-term oscillations, like the medium-term extrapolation of laudable intentions to restructure and make progress, represent an equivalent number of interpretation traps, but also, since that is the way the regimes of expectations are made, very real sources of volatility and disruption on the currency markets.

The euro still has before it both its future and the paths which may trace its destiny there. The first few years will not exhaust this subject but will instead indicate a direction. The effect of liquidity (downward trend for currency) has dominated what one might call the value effect, which will in turn prevail over the long-term, over and beyond the various cyclical oscillations. The euro has disturbed the structures (portfolios, markets, businesses) in the manner which we might have expected. In particular, even if the euro has not challenged the dollar as reference currency for international trade nor as the currency in which the central banks' foreign reserves are denominated, it has captured the lion's share of the market as currency of issue. The euro has played a (its) role in expanding and deepening the European market base. Accordingly, the supply of euros was abundant, consolidating its role as capital exporter from the zone. There was, accordingly, a contradiction between calling for the rapid construction of a European financial market (first, principally, a bond market) which was to be a deep and liquid market, and expecting a sharp increase in the euro; without, moreover, undermining, quite the contrary, the fundamental arguments of such a diagnosis, over the medium-term.

The cumulative effects of the adjustment of portfolios within the eurozone (diversification effect), of direct investments (restructuring effect) and the deepening of the European bond markets (issue effect), have prevailed over the diversification of private and public non-resident portfolios and capital inflows through direct investments (demand effect). These three factors may be grouped under the heading liquidity effect. The total impact of this liquidity effect was a fall in value of the currency and was under-estimated.

This liquidity effect may or not have stabilising virtues for the US economy and the dollar. Much depends on the form taken by the recycling of surplus European and Japanese savings, which are the principal creditors of the US economy. A current account surplus may have two sorts of counterparts. They may be financial investments, purchases of T-bills (and/or private bonds) or direct investments in the USA. The first are possibly (potentially) stabilising, the second allow the external debt of US companies to be eased and constitute a counterpart which is *a priori* less reliable. For example, the recycling of Japanese surpluses in the 1990's took the form of financial investments instead. The recycling in Europe took the form, above all, of direct investments. One way of mitigating the impact on the dollar of the accumulation of US external debt might require US corporate borrowers to obtain their funding in yen or euros.

More recently, the relative strength of the euro, despite established deflationary pressures, is largely due to the accumulation of current account surpluses (to which can be added the net capital inflows, portfolio flows into European stocks as part of a rebalancing of global portfolios). The lack of any recycling of such surpluses (i) within the eurozone (from the core countries to the periphery and ideally through direct foreign investment rather than capital flows as during the first decade of the euro's existence) and (ii) outside the eurozone (the natural role of a net exporter of capital is not fulfilled).

Is the prevailing price such that there will be a modification of stocks held?

What we have called the "liquidity effect" and "value effect" overlap their influences in the determination of the fundamental forces which are at work on the forex market. The value effect is, most often, a mix of the estimated remuneration of the risk for holding a currency and the valuation of a measure of purchasing power (and, therefore, of its erosion), e.g. through inflation of the price of goods and services. The liquidity effect is, in turn, interested in stocks (of savings, of monetary creation), in flows (the same) and, even more, in the preferences which determine the distortions of the portfolio structures. Liquidity, irrespective of the analysis, is always a function of preference. Liquidity includes, incorporates and assimilates, at the heart of its operating mode, the viewpoint of the (economic) Subject, that of its preferences in the context of exchange interactions. Value is different in this regard, for the majority of its definitions.

The said liquidity effect and value effect can be organised, regrouped and arranged in many ways (by regional, macro-economic themes such as those of the "raw material" currencies, "dollars", etc.)

and it is possible to identify the cyclical rotations of currencies (or, rather, of the currency pairings), driven by the two dimensions of liquidity and value (and, also, probably, *momentum*). It is also possible to identify the currency pairings which, two by two, are less correlated than others: the investor then incorporates information which is precious for the structure of the portfolio and its preferences. It remains, in any event, the expression of a preference for the structure of the portfolio (liquidity) within the context of remuneration of risk (i.e. of risks, including inflation) (value).

The existence of a worrying US current account deficit, which is often cited in order to anticipate a fall in the dollar, must not hide the fact that, as a counterpart for this deficit, USA Inc. assigns, to some extent, real and financial assets to the rest of the world (long-term capital balance). Ultimately, everything takes place as if there had not been any increase in the dollar supply which had to be absorbed by the non-resident investors.

The arguments concerning flows cannot ignore the accumulated stock levels. A currency is in danger, if the capacity for absorption at a given price (i.e. the exchange rate) is *saturated*. The currency market is a flexible price market. As on other markets, the prevailing prices, which seem to be determined by the prevailing demand for "currency-merchandise" and the new supply which flows into it, are more often determined by stocks. The question is whether the prevailing price for a currency is such that investors wish to modify the stock which they hold.

Long years of current account deficit have considerably damaged the net, external US situation. Stocks of assets denominated in dollars are an edifying example. Investors are mainly non-resident, both public and private. The central banks, at least up until now, have been captive "bearers", this attitude being largely based on the quasi-monopoly of the dollar in their foreign reserves, which enables the US economy to obtain its own credit finance almost automatically. These institutional attitudes (the strategic positioning of institutions and the preference functions of the latter are fundamental elements of the forex economy) are linked, more essentially, to the "dollar convention", the acceptance of a certain number of operating modes within the exchange, which is central to a medium-term macro-financial regime. The "dollar convention" also includes a form of dissuasion equilibrium through the commercial interweaving of exchanges and the financial integration of the Chinese holding, in particular of treasuries. China thus has power as creditor but has absolutely no interest at all in causing a dollar crisis of which it would be the main victim.

Private investors hold a stock which is at first essentially made up of treasury bonds and then by private bonds and, to a lesser degree, shares. These private investors hold a large part of the US government debt and the majority of them are Asian. The role of these investors forms part of a debate which is not only a theoretical one. The question is whether the current account deficit steers the capital account or vice versa. In the first case, the funding of the current account results in adjustments to the interest rate and exchange rate. In the second, it is the capital flows which direct the current account. Optimists will not see any particular problems in funding the US current account deficit at "acceptable" or reasonable levels of interest rates and dollar price – if they do not question the reality or relevance of the current account itself – or will put the concept of the deficit into perspective, through the identification of surplus global savings, which is, however, an aberration in accounting terms in a zero-sum world, which owes more to *ex nihilo* monetary creation than to the merits of hoarding. Those who worry will put forward a risk scenario which is specific to emerging market economies: a marginal modification (the "delta", i.e. the rate of accumulation, is more important than the stock) of the capital inflows (which would have a strong impact given the level of the current account deficit) or, in the extreme, of the capital outflows, would end up forcing an improvement of the current account at the cost of a collapse of internal demand. And of the dollar.

The strong dollar, and its rhetoric, are a close counterpart to the net capital inflows which finance the internal US demand. For an economy which has a net structural deficit with regard to the rest of the word, the desire for the currency to fall amounts to endorsing a reversal of such capital. The dollar remains an indicator of the confidence of global savings in the long-term growth potential of the US economy. This relates to what can be called the dollar "convention", the fundamental structure (or form) of which is that of belief. Economics is a language precisely to the extent that there is a (causal) arrangement of factual sequences. However, the economic fact only comes completely into (economic) reality inside a structure of beliefs which gives it meaning (i.e. interpretability, transparency). Belief is the vision of the other, of others, a vision of the Subject's consciousness (whether the Subject is an individual or an institution). This vision (belief) gives meaning and value. Value comes, in the modern era, from this vision. In the modern era, there is only an economic fact (meaning) for the consciousness (of a Subject) which thinks it (intentionality). This economic fact, constituted in this way, only attains value in the act of vision of the consciousness (which is itself in conflict with the consciousness of others). The economic fact is the consciousness (of) of the Subject's world. Economic value is the vision of others regarding the Subject's consciousness at work in the world.

It is fundamental to understand why, on the forex markets, the "price" is not formed on the basis of current supply and demand. Such an approach, which has the benefit of a certain simplicity, does not state how the adjustment is made. The said adjustment results, essentially, from a decision (i.e. f(expectation)) of the economic Subject, an arbitrage between various structures of preference(s). This decision relates to the stocks of currencies held (whilst the approach through current supply and demand eliminates the decision, as it were, which is fundamentally an expectation, and the stock, which is a function of the past). In fact, what is often wrongly considered to be the essential element in the operation of the forex markets is the residue or a sort of consequence of the essential phenomenon: the decision whether or not, for a "price", to modify the stock held. This price expresses a decision whether or not to modify that which is (has been) – a stock –, on the basis of an expectation. The price evolves (i.e. the exchange rate evolves) when the former price has led to the economic Subject's desire to modify its currency stocks. There exists a link between one price and another, which passes through the stock. The former price is rejected on the basis of a risk of sharing/remuneration of a given stock, for the future. The current price is only rejected in the name of an expectation (of a new price). The former price (the current price) is only rejected for a certain stock carried by the Subject (and a structure of preference for risk/return/stock). At any given time, the price of a currency expresses a global structure of preferences for the modification of stocks. At any given time, this price incorporates a global expectation regarding the determinants of the stock and regarding the (future) equilibrium price (balancing the preferences for the modification of stocks). It is the price which triggers the decision to modify the stocks (and therefore leads to a new price), this price being triggered on the basis of an expectation of a new price which balances the preferences for the holding of stocks.

Fundamentally, this means that the price emerges from a tension between an expectation (of price, of the risk/return pairing) and memory (past function) of stock, with numerous, precise characteristics. At any given time, on the market, the projection (towards a new equilibrium) is as it were "retained" by the force of inertia of the stock and its characteristics. The effects of memory of the stocks which the Subject (investor) carries in its decision are not visible enough. The extent to which the price (the exchange rate) collides, at any given time, with the memory of stock held by an investor, until it possibly leads to a modification of the stock, is not visible enough. Repeated on an infinite basis, this collision contributes to the determination of a market equilibrium. This memory regime is relatively inert and adapts slowly. This helps us understand in part the sudden disruptions, the non-linearities that can be seen on the forex markets, where the dams yield like claps of thunder in a clear sky. A disruption is a major modification of the regime of stocks (i.e. of the regime of preference for/acceptance of a certain structure of stocks). The price is both the witness which records this respiration/disruption of the regime and also what produces them at the end of an adaptive process. Contrary to what is often said or believed, the forex market is not a spot market (image of the trader), but instead a market of expectations and fairly onerous effects of memory. The structure of stocks and the memorisation of this structure play an important role. Once again, there exists a profound similarity or symmetry of forms as between the memory/forgetfulness of the structure of stocks and the expectation of future prices. The future price (i.e. the exchange rate) is always a memorised function, affected by a factor of forgetfulness, which is more or less powerful, of the stocks of currency which are held.

Within the function of memorisation (and of forgetfulness) of stocks of currency can be found various characteristics, including the past elements of risk and return. These risk-adjusted returns form the fundamental layers of the memory regime of stocks. More generally, the memory regime of stocks (and all its characteristics) can be incorporated into the global macro-financial regime of an economy. The current prices arrive at any moment, like drops of rain on a pane of glass, to question the regime.

The history of a currency, which is *a fortiori* new, cannot be summarised solely by the changes in its exchange rate. The extreme attention paid to the phenomenon in the case of the euro was atypical. In many respects, the (initial) depreciation of the euro seems to have resulted from the very effects of introducing the currency and, a paradox which is only apparent, from its very success. The mechanical effects of searching for returns, which resulted from the appearance itself of the euro (portfolio adjustments, more general effects of diversification, overall effect which can be described as "liquidity") merged with the new status as a bond issuing currency, which the European currency acquired on an international level from the outset. This global liquidity effect prevailed (because of its consequences, i.e. net long-term capital outflows) over the diversification of the non-resident private and public euro portfolios and the capital inflows through direct investments in the zone. There was, in particular, a contradiction between calling for the rapid constitution of a European bond market which is deep and liquid and expecting an immediate appreciation of the European currency. The euro supply factors dominated, when a strong demand was expected. The euro played the role which was expected of it, namely that of shaking up the structures (portfolios, markets, businesses) and the euro zone played the role of net capital exporter within the global village.

The "dollar convention" will probably last as long as the (favourable) regime of long-term expectations of greater returns on real and financial assets denominated in dollars (also as long as Asian growth regimes continue to be not sufficiently independent). However, although the net dollar supply remains of particular concern and although the elements for a stronger demand for euros are being promptly organised, there is room for doubt. The advent of a "European" period cannot come as a complete surprise – viewed within the alternation between the USA and Europe of the major productivity cycles. Its impact on the dollar continues to cause more concern and is more uncertain. The euro-dollar exchange rate, despite the (relative) closed nature of the two economies has a good chance of becoming one of the most important prices in international economics. As a structuring force of the international monetary construction site, the appearance of the euro is also an explosive force within a global monetary landscape which has endured.

Essay 8

SEARCHING FOR REFERENCE POINTS INVESTING IN UNDERSTANDING

The loss of (search for) reference points is probably one of the important phenomena of the turn of the century, on the financial markets and within central banks; an estimation of equilibrium values for some, the definition of relevant objectives for others. The difference in rhythm and regulation as between real economies and financial markets complicates the exercise.

Is normalisation impossible?

The same is true of the co-existence of real, desynchronised economies (within a global, and therefore globalised, village) and of financial variables which are (increasingly) integrated. Three elements, namely the desynchronisation of global growth, disinflation and the advent of a new (US) era of technology and productivity, were in many respects only three ways of discussing the same thing. The weakness and desynchronisation of global growth provide the key to the fall of inflation, of nominal interest rates and, especially, to their volatility. They also provide the key to the seamless financing, without inflation and with a relatively firm dollar, of what was perhaps not an American "miracle" but at the least an exceptional economic and financial performance. They also provide a fairly broad explanation for the spectacular expansion of the PER, in a world where, suddenly, the future profits environment is perceived as less risky. Finally, they are sufficient to reduce the volatility of growth by reinforcing the idea of a permanent smoothing of the economic cycle, or indeed that of its abolition.

The apparent withdrawal of the global cycle and its sequences (traditional sequence of expansion, inflation of the price of goods and services and of monetary tightening) helped create an environment which is apparently less dangerous. The anaesthesia of risk and the stimulation of risk-taking form part of this special moment. For those minds which are (rightly) marked by the ravages of the inflationary years, the calm waters of the 1990's (calm waters in terms of the "real" inflation of the price of goods and services, not that of the financial variables which, from the successive crises of the emerging markets to the stock market bubble, were characterised by sharp volatility) had all that was necessary for a relaxing of vigilance. History, which is always repeated, suggests that price stability rarely goes hand in glove (over the long-term) with financial stability, since it encourages artificial paradises. The major financial bubbles all occurred in times of (classic) almost-zero inflation. There is a distortion of the global/general structure of prices in the sense that the reduction or lack of pressures (both directional and of volatility) on "real" prices is accompanied by financial pressures. There is a distortion of relative prices, since certain elements rise and others fall (the link being fairly generally provided by the fall in nominal interest rates). This presents a challenge when the objective is to stabilise (or preserve the stability of) relative prices, since institutions are not equipped to consider the distortion of relative prices (which remains central to their mandate), over and beyond the chain of formation (and deformation) of the prices of goods and services. Once again, history repeated itself, with the bursting of the bubble in 2008 and the start of a period of deflationary pressures.

Fundamentally, the financialisation of the global economy – i.e. the role of allocation, distribution and regulation performed by the financial market as a central institutional form – forces one to consider the interpenetrations of the real and financial spheres and to reconsider the concept of price (and therefore that of inflation). The concept of price – and therefore of the deformation of relative prices, as the cycle progresses – is modified as is that of value. This transformation lies at the heart of the turn of the century. The twofold transformation of the concepts of price and value leads to an expansion of the basis of their definition so as to include that which is literally "said about it" by the financial market (in the pure form of information or material form for the creation of wealth); helps one see that a necessary link exists between the real and the financial, the alternation of which (the volatility of one results in a lack of volatility of the other) constitutes a "fatal" determination of the economic cycle (i.e. the deformation of relative prices, which are expanded to include "financial" prices, is essentially cyclical); helps one grasp, within this transformation, the confrontation of two onerous institutional forms, the financial market (the producer of financial variables, by regulating it in part) and the central bank (which regulates the real variables and is partly responsible for producing the financial variables). The transformation of value – which is fundamentally that of the concept of price – complicates a reconfiguration of the field of institutions which organise and regulate the interaction thereof.

The risk is highest when it is close to certainty. The elimination of inflation as an immediate threat – even if it can be interpreted, from a long-term perspective, as a return to normality after an exceptional phase – leads to new challenges because it leads to a series of paradoxes of tranquillity. A globalised economy, but one with national/regional growth cycles which are poorly synchronised, from which inflation has disappeared and in which the central banks continue (for a time) to pursue price objectives for goods and services which are close to zero inflation, such a global economy changes growth regime and risk regime. Low interest rates, private debt, market finance and financial volatility form its asset structure. In such a regime, the periods of resynchronisation of global growth are difficult and short, often swept along by the cocktail of their consequences (rise in interest rates, in particular) on the inherent financial weaknesses of such a regime. The risk of the regime is deflation or, on the other hand, the bubbles which form an integral and necessary part thereof.

The transformation of the concepts of value and price is, fundamentally, central to the evolution dynamic (or, possibly, the disruption dynamic) of the macro-financial regime, of growth and regulation. This transformation causes part of the traditional institutional forms, which accompany and control the concepts of value and price, including the central banks, which are probably the best known aspect thereof, to become outdated. In particular, the practice of QE after the 2008 crisis – before any inclusion in the central banks' official mandate, even before the formulation of the theory of the reaction function incorporating asset prices – introduces a change to the DNA of many central banks (objectives, guidance, reaction function, tool box ...) which brings the Volcker period to a close. This pressure, which comes from the market, contains within it necessary evolutions and connections between the traditional institutional forms and the financial market. These connections form the institutional structure of the new macro-financial regime. The frictions and cracks at the seams of these connections are, fundamentally, the reasons for the economic and financial crises and malfunctions. The crisis stems, within this new macro-financial regime, from the weaknesses of these connections between the institutions and the market (the market being the rising institutional form). The linear breaks within such a macro-financial regime (i.e. the cycle, the crisis, inflation/deflation ...) stem from the conflict between the market and the (traditional) institutions. Accordingly, it is not easy, far from it, to stabilise a global economy whose regional growth cycles are fairly generally independent and poorly synchronised, the models of the central banks being focused on domestic indicators and objectives, even when the bottom part of the balances of payment and the principal financial variables are liberalised, global and integrated. Furthermore, and we shall come back to this later, the use of QE after 2008 precipitated a (possibly structural) change in the DNA of Western central banks or at least certain of them.

The transformation of the macro-financial regime, which takes the form of a loss of reference points, is also the opportunity for essential questions which return to the very origin of certain concepts (value, equilibrium...).

Accordingly, in a floating exchange rate regime, it is still difficult to adjust the dollar to its equilibrium value, since the monetary flows do not represent transactions in real goods. The possibly massive movements of short-term capital noted in the balances of payment make this fairly illusory. Matters are complicated by the juxtaposition of the liberalisation of short-term capital flows, of real economies which are still generally closed (share of net exports in the GDP) and of central bank models which are focused on domestic variables. It is, accordingly, in many respects, the Asian central banks, through their (*ex nihilo*) creation of liquidities, as much as the Fed, which sustain the global financing circuits, including at the very heart of the US economy, and also their financial excesses.

In the same way, it can be seen that many of the reasons behind the financial bubble at the end of the 1990's (credit, investment, financial assets) – more specifically businesses/(over-)indebtedness/(over-)investment/stock market (over-)valuations – were related to the fact that the cost of capital was too cheap, which disrupts the allocation of capital and to the fact that the monetary interest rate was, in the USA, lower over the long-term than the equilibrium level which enables savings and investment to be equalised. This is hardly revolutionary in terms of the diagnosis itself – a completely classic credit bubble -,and this classic form noted, at the end of the 1990's, for businesses underwent a shift (through the fall in interest rates) to households – (over-)indebtedness/(over-)consumption/real estate (over-)valuations. The fate of the years 2000-2010, including subprime, was written. The form and the diagnosis (artificially low level of the interest rate) are hardly revolutionary, but can this equilibrium level be achieved, at least defined in outline, in a (US) economy which is financially open, which has a net structural deficit with regard to the rest of the world and which is financed by its own currency on the basis of a "dollar convention"? The determination of the optimal/neutral level of the US interest rate is as much in the hands of the non-resident investors as in those, strictly speaking, of the Fed. The equilibrium level of the interest rates is lost in the sands of globalisation.

The forms of imbalance and of the crisis remain classic (credit bubble in the case of the example taken) – there is, fundamentally, a permanence and continuity of the essential forms – but the characteristics of the macro-financial regime – and its transformations – require a transformation of the concept of equilibrium. Furthermore, the imbalances and cracks occur, as we have seen, when the financial market and institutions (central banks, the Fed or Asian institutions, the "dollar convention") interact. The "dollar convention" constitutes one of the major anchors of the macro-financial regime, since it enables interactions and connections of expectations (time), of prices in the more general sense (value) and of the institutional forms (central banks, stakeholders in economic life and the financial markets). Interactions and connections form the structure of the regime's equilibrium (of the equilibria). Although the "dollar convention" is one of the essential dimensions of the current macro-financial regime – to a certain extent, it reflects it, summarises it and expresses it -, the fact remains that the cracks in the regime are also those of the "dollar convention". A macro-financial regime is, fundamentally, a belief (a set of beliefs). The "dollar convention" is the most striking aspect thereof but not the most long-lasting.

Finally, and so as only to take one more example, in the domain of the valuation of financial assets, much still remains to be done in order to start to understand, and only to start, the path taken by the value of a stock market. It is not a question, certainly not, of understanding the most traditional measures which seem to direct the markets through the distraction which they cause. It is, instead, understanding that which within value cannot, fundamentally, be brought within the confines of the share asset class; that which constitutes the mechanism of expectations within the stock market, i.e. the manner in which time is perceived and apprehended (memory of the past, expectation of the future). It is doubtful that we have fully considered the consequences on the valuation processes of the structural drop in interest rates. This drop in interest rates has largely concealed the requirements of a fundamental approach to the valuation of shares. Once exhausted, this drop could only leave the investor, over the long-term, facing the need for an intellectual reorganisation. Interest rates cannot eternally (there is here a cyclical medium-/long-term dimension) dominate the expectations of profits within a regime of the valuation of shares. This valuation constitutes, together with other elements, one of the fundamental pillars of a macro-financial regime.

Disinflation (and the risk of deflation, in the context of inflation which is stabilised at low levels and with no marked volatility) forms part of the macro-financial regime which unfolded with effect from the 1990's. The powerful effect on the preference between shares and bonds of the downward trend in interest rates has dominated any earnings component. This is in any event what is shown by a performance attribution taking elements of profitability which are at least recorded (published earnings) or, often, expected (from one to two years). These profitability elements show only an uncertain relationship with the increase in stock market prices. It is easy to conclude from this that interest rates suppress profits in the (*ex post*) understanding of stock market movements and this probably contains an element of truth. However, it is also quite possible that we only reached this conclusion because we continue to refuse to look at the right thing, for example the expected component part of profits within its non-cyclical dimension.

We remain fairly blind, when faced with stock market evolutions, because we are not willing enough to consider time within the stock market universe as we should. Stock market time is a time of memory and of forgetfulness, of duration and also of discontinuity. One expects in the same way that one remembers (more or less well, and accordingly in the same way one forgets, as well). The present does not exist. There is only a lapse of time, a *continuum* of duration filled with the past, which is the true raw material of the stock market universe and of the value of shares. There is, fundamentally, an analogy between value and memory, memory and duration, expectation and memory/forgetfulness within the stock markets. The instant result (the present is not or, rather, it is in a state of non-being) and the expected result for the year to come (the future is memory and duration) have no real meaning. One can at best accept, in a situation where memory is reduced (and therefore the function of expectation is shortened), that one may end up with a regime of expectation based on a very short memory (one year) and therefore on a strong degree of forgetfulness.

This constitutes a fundamental point. Value is an increasing function of memory in the stock markets. The future is anticipated there in the same way that one remembers the past and/or forgets the past. It is this very premise which allows one to envisage an approach to value and the development of measures of value, which show a certain efficiency of interpretation and reading of the stock markets. However, memory and forgetfulness are not symmetrical with regard to value. There is in fact an asymmetry between memory and forgetfulness from the point of view of value. Value will be all the more important, the more developed the capacity of memory (e.g. of earnings) and the denser, literally, the stock market "matter". This can be estimated. Conversely, and this is true of many other things in many other sectors, forgetfulness is a leak, a leakage of value, like a hole which is pierced in the bottom of a barrel. What this means, from a practical point of view, has two dimensions. First, the construction of value indicators for the stock markets involves, fundamentally, the estimation of a function of memory (expressed, for example, in years) of the market, a function which must show a certain stability. This function of memory includes, by definition, a factor of forgetfulness, which is more or less strong (and which is itself a function of the more or less distant nature of the past). It will be noted, in this exercise, that some or other market contains a longer or shorter memory than some other market; this is also true of some or other segment of the market, as compared to another. This constitutes the first dimension of the approach to value, from a practical point of view, since it enables one to understand, to explain and, possibly, to predict stock market evolutions.

There also exists, and this is the more essential dimension, a form of benchmarking of the "density" of the value of a market by comparison with a pure value criterion, where such criterion is an increasing (non-linear) function of memory. The practical approach to the value of a stock market consists fairly simply of estimating the function of memory/forgetfulness, with the objective of explaining/predicting/acting in the universe of stock market evolutions. The pure approach to the value (of shares) involves "classifying" as it were this function of memory/forgetfulness, by positioning markets, stock market segments, stocks by comparison with the density of matter-time (non-cyclical memory of profitabilities as an approximation of the expectation function). This pure approach may have practical implications. It is, in particular, probable that a stock market with a decreased memory (strong forgetfulness) function is more fragile than another. The dilation of the function of memory/forgetfulness must therefore be analysed.

The causality of the fundamental relations, which is also central to the question of the valuation of shares, may be disrupted, or even reversed, within a particular macro-financial regime. The essential relation of causality thus unfolds from profits, or from profitability, towards the stock markets, i.e. their price. There is in fact something powerful and certain in the idea that the price is an (expected) function of profit [$P = f(Pr)$]. The price is distorted, modified – within the financial sphere – by the event, the fact, the cause which occurs within the real sphere. There is, in fact, a fundamental idea that what is real comes before what is financial. There is something even more essential, in this idea, which concerns the relationship of the Subject with the world, i.e. the relationship of the economic Subject, economic being the name rightly given, as from modern times, to this relationship of capture/appropriation which is maintained by the Subject with the world, within/through the action.

We have explained this elsewhere. With the arrival of the modern turning point, economics becomes the technical "science" of the action of projection/appropriation of the market by the (economic) Subject. This projection (intentionality of the consciousness which obliterates) places the action of the Subject (of the consciousness) before (in the ontological sense) the world. This projection, in the modern era, is increasingly financial, in the sense that the financial market becomes the dominant form of the intermediation of the projection (in fact, origination, intermediation, execution). In the modern era, what is financial comes before what is real.

This fundamental turning point involves much more than the question of the valuation of shares alone. However, it can be seen, in this instance, that the "usual" causality which unfolds from profits to the stock markets is reversed, if there is a strong exposure of the earnings of numerous companies to the stock markets. The profits then depend on the direction of the financial markets. The markets scrutinize the profits of companies which scrutinize the markets. With this reversal, which is only one aspect of a more fundamental reversal, that which unfurls at the heart of the modern era is accomplished: financial comes before real, in the sense that the (intentional) design of the transforming consciousness comes before the world which it transforms through technique; in the sense that the Subject and its design (will, expectation) impose themselves upon a "targeted" object (in fact, the object no longer has meaning other than in the fact that it is, rightly, "targeted"). The price ends up coming before the profit, because the profit is predetermined by the price; because the price is, *ex ante*, already a design of expectation and therefore of transformation of what is real (the profit is the form taken by this design of transformation). It is also the price which ends up, to a slight extent, leading to the price, in the same way as a will which wills itself.

Finance comes before reality (the world) and this ontological precedence is fundamentally the essence of economics in the modern era, if one is willing to see in that which is called finance the technical and appropriating projection of the Subject aimed at the world.

The concept of liquidity, which is difficult to define, dominates the macro-financial, modern regimes and shows a tendency to impose itself, always with a certain amount of confusion, on that of value. At the modern turning point discussed above, value is as it were the product of the (economic) design of the Subject within the world. The design itself, i.e. the transforming projection (the movement, the temporality), fundamentally encounters itself in liquidity, which expresses various elements, including, in particular, money as a transforming design of the Subject. This can be seen in the various ways in which the concept is evoked or called upon, liquidity is, fundamentally, the (monetary) movement which transforms over time, either defined or approached by money itself (liquidity is then as close as possible to the monetary flow which accompanies the action), or defined by the action of the Subject itself and more directly (the preference for liquidity is probably the best example thereof, a mode of action of the Subject aimed at/in the world throughout the exchange and with the other. Liquidity is a function of the exchange. The relationship and the exchange dominate the strict underlying matter of liquidity. Liquidity is that which brings about the exchange of money).

These are, in our opinion, the fundamental elements which should be considered when reflecting on the multiple forms taken by liquidity. Its manifestations are numerous, as are the questions which it raises. Accordingly, and without being exhaustive – we will, moreover, come back to this – the preference for "Keynesian" liquidity does not state what the counterpart for such liquidity is (credit, savings, credit matched by savings, *ex nihilo* monetary creation). It is often an abundance of liquidities which leads to a liquidity crisis, in the sense stated by the preference for liquidity. The confusion between credit and savings, savings and money and that between liquidity and debt are probably perversions which play a role in a certain number of imbalances and crises. International over-liquidities add to the confusion. Since the dollar status allows for monetary creation in countries which generate positive overall dollar balances, without a symmetrical reduction in the means of payment in circulation in the USA, there is *ex nihilo* monetary creation at both ends of the chain. When the majority of the counterparts of monetary creation consist of stocks, the explosion of stock market transactions results in a strong demand for means of payment. The circulation of money accelerates within the financial sphere, maintaining an inflationary dynamic. With money, one can also buy stocks. The symmetrical nature of the circulations of money in the real and financial spheres can be found in the fundamental analogy which may exist between "real" inflation (of the price of goods and services) and "financial" inflation.

The fundamental reversal of the modern era (financial comes before real) is applied in the very transformation of the forms of inflation. Moreover, it can be seen that the multiple confusions discussed above (liquidity, debt, credit, savings...) fundamentally express the appropriation of the conceptual field of economics by that which forms part of the expanded concept of liquidity. The domination of liquidity can essentially be linked to the fundamental structure of economics in the modern era. Liquidity contributes to the action. As a projection of the Subject towards the world, value is what comes after the action, at the end.

Central banking policies. The end of the beginning

We are faced with an unprecedented lack of visibility regarding (i) macro variables, such as growth and inflation, (ii) central bank policies, (iii) the equilibrium levels of asset prices faced with various sources of distortions ranging from QE (quantitative easing) to the euro zone debt crisis.

Considering the end of QE became the focus of consensus in 2013/2014. We would argue that it is the end of the beginning and that QE is here to stay for longer than many people may expect.

Tapering has certainly never meant a contraction of the balance sheet, at a time when Japan and Europe are likely to do more rather than less. Even in the case of the USA, the cyclical objectives of QE have not (yet), in early 2014, been met and some key elements are missing from the chain (on the employment participation rate – and wages front) in a pattern of recovery, in which the consumer has been supported by wealth effects derived from the influence of QE on the housing market. QE has three objectives (i) to break the link between asset prices and deleveraging, (ii) to keep long-term interest rates low; and (iii) to consolidate growth and profits into a positive self-reinforcing loop including investment and employment, thus ultimately justifying increases in asset prices. Item number (iii) is still missing to some extent in early 2014 and the jury is still out on the full cyclical equation.

Our point extends well beyond cyclicalities. There is a structural shift at work in the DNA of most major Western central banks. We are witnessing the end of the Volcker period – one tool, i.e. leading interest rate; one or two objectives, i.e. inflation/growth, and a transition to a multi-tool (including QE) and multi-objective regime. QE may temporarily cease but it will return as a structural piece of the equation when growth/asset prices falter or when the next crisis hits.

Most Western central banks are faced with a credibility paradox, because we are in such a transitory phase. All investors have become, so to say, "long" central banks during the crisis period and its aftermath and have expected them to fix the problems. This at a time when, to take some examples, the Fed's reaction function or its objectives have never been so unclear or difficult to define. Investors have indeed received "Forward guidance" from the Fed – involving risks of miscommunication. However, notwithstanding the lack of clarity or details regarding Forward guidance (multiple moving indicators), FG seems to contradict the rational expectations hypothesis which has been built into the Fed models – in a market driven by experts, FG should be less effective. The bottom line is that we may realise *ex post* that we were going through a transition in the period starting in 2013 – a learning process during which it was very hard to tell who, out of the Fed or the markets, was driving whom.

There is also an *implicit*, structural change at work in the mandate of most Western central banks: asset prices are considered to be part of the monetary equation and of the reaction function, within a framework where the general level of prices will matter more than the prices of goods and services only when multiple monetary tools – including asset prices taken as a monetary element – replace the unique, official, leading interest rate.

This change has not yet been made express. Theory often comes after practice. It will do so here. Exceptional measures which last become policy. Non-conventional actions which last become new conventions. The central banks will in turn have to declare their objectives openly.

Ultimately, the *real and effective* mandate of such central banks has always been to stabilise relative prices; they cannot ignore the fact that liquidity in a modern economy is injected into financial markets, through various transmission channels, such as wealth effects, which may sometimes be effective or even powerful, where they can play a role or stay trapped fuelling bubbles; or the fact that it was sub-optimal to have a restrictive definition of prices and a unique tool for everything. In particular, if one adopts an appropriate definition for a real, long-term interest rate (a nominal rate of interest minus the *expected level of general prices*), one will agree that, when prices of goods and services are in a downward, deflationary spiral, as they were after the crisis in

2008 (a rising *component* of the real interest rate), one may consider targeting a *lower component of the real rate for asset prices*.

The problems are various and include (i) the fact that asset prices are over-determined: target, tool, outcome, instrument ..., (ii) the asymmetrical approach to asset prices by the central banks, (iii) liquidity-driven bubbles with a compelling "Austrian" argument: fiat money, monkey paper, capital misallocation, distortion of value and time preferences: time is bought, it all ends in tears. Central banks, as it goes, are trapped in a framework of no return/from bubble to bubble. The longer the process, the higher the price to be paid, particularly when any termination of steroids runs an apparent, asymmetrical risk (too soon, too late). In monetary matters, we are still experiencing the consequences. This would seem to indicate a *decade where normalisation will prove to be impossible.*

This is certainly relevant for investors, at least as one of the scenarii. There are dilemmas and challenges to investment beliefs, which are linked to the so-called end of QE: (i) Should one buy or avoid QE-infected assets? Should investors participate in what could, optimistically, be described as "rational bubbles"? We should not forget the years 1996-2000, ranging from the diagnosis ("irrational exuberance") to the bursting of the bubble. Is it rational to buy, because there is a buyer of last resort? This is at cross-purposes with beliefs in the long-term, i.e. value/mean reversion. There is no long-term investment without a presumption of some normality (normal = equilibrium level = value reference point) and, at the same time, new policies have introduced a change, in the sense that normalisation may prove to be a trap or a false friend. Investment policies have to adapt.

QE and the so-called end of QE introduce the issue of a change in anchor (i.e. volatility of the anchor) – see the example of the impact of tapering on emerging assets in 2013-2014 and the general rebalancing of global portfolios in the new anchoring regime. Normality is a relative concept, relative to an anchor.

Diversification, liquidity, risk. In periods of QE, volatility is abnormally low and is increasingly expected to remain low (i.e. investors are *not* protected against a spike in volatility). QE helps sustain fake alpha: capturing risk premia on hidden fat-tails, the problem stemming ultimately from (i) a change in anchor for the risk premium, e.g. central banks' reference rates, (ii) the symmetrical and procyclical aspects of volatility as a measure of risk – add to the position when volatility is high and reduce it in times of crisis. As stated above, downside volatility and drawdown management are more effective. Idiosyncratic risks will prove key (country, sector, stock). In times of QE, there is a false impression that everything is liquid, which is clearly incorrect. Moving into smart beta strategies may help counterbalance the procyclicalities of such periods (remember 1996-2000) and the concentration biases.

Asset managers, corporate investment banks, central banks. The regime of the long-term financing of the economy

The crisis reveals the limits of a long-term financing regime for the economy and, more generally, of a macro financial regime, which led to the disruption in 2008. The inevitable changes which it entails set forth a schedule for transition.

We should put into perspective the financing difficulties of the banking sector during the crisis and the role of asset managers and the CIB (corporate and investment banks). It can be shown that the problem is the long-term, global financing of the economy and that the solutions require a mobilisation of all participants for the purposes of achieving market solutions.

The general feeling of a stalemate, experienced during the crisis, is largely due to the change in method of financing the economy during the past decade. For example, consider the majority of the economies of continental Europe. The economy was, up until then, financed principally by the banking system, with a gradual contribution from the financial markets and asset managers during the 1990's, the latter through the intermediary of monetary assets held in bank CDs (certificates of deposit) and in stocks. For the last ten years or so, financing witnessed a withdrawal by the banking system and a sharp increase in the role of asset managers, through, first, the corporate credit asset class and, second, a new generation of products and instruments, linked in particular to securitisation (CDS, ABS, CLO, CDO …).

Against a background of favourable liquidity, asset managers have in fact replaced the banks in their traditional transforming role. In so doing, they have introduced the characteristics and challenges thereof, committing to daily liquidity for long-term assets and taking credit risk. There was, accordingly, a mismatch, or dissymmetry, between, on the liabilities side, total liquidity and, on the assets side, instruments or classes which might prove to be non-liquid or barely liquid, *a fortiori* when such instruments are not listed on organised markets.

The crisis manifested itself by a generalised aversion to risk and an unlimited preference for liquidity and cash. Products with low liquidity or uncertain valuations (mispricing) were completely and suddenly terminated. Asset managers therefore saw a sharp increase in money market funds whilst long-term asset classes (including corporate bonds, shares), particularly those which ensure the long-term financing of the economy, were withdrawn in a significant manner.

Regular monetary funds represented around 450 billion Euros on the Paris market, in 2008. Two-thirds of this amount was made up of bank CDs. The whole of these monetary funds increased significantly during the crisis, by almost 100 billion Euros, and the share of bank CDs remained at least stable against the backdrop of an increase in issue programmes. The crisis did not therefore create a short-term financing problem, as one may have been led to believe, and asset managers continued to play their role in full.

The crisis destroyed the financing method described above, hastening a return to a factual situation which is similar to that which prevailed up until the middle of the 1990's: financing must once again be provided only by banks through their balance sheets. The financing market component was brought to a sharp and sudden halt.

The situation created by the crisis therefore means that the issue of financing the economy is transferred to banks' balance sheets alone, at the very time when such banks are subject to an increasing number of prudential regulations, in particular regarding their internal capital.

The crisis has in fact raised a problem for the long-term, global financing of the economy, which extends beyond the difficulties of the banking sector alone. The aversion to risk which encouraged monetary investments has accentuated the difficulties for the long-term financing of the economy, shifts which have been imposed upon asset managers by the economic context and over which they have no direct control.

If one adopts the diagnosis set forth above, the priority must be to redirect savings toward the long-term financing of the productive, economic sector. Three possible routes must be explored at the same time.

Since aversion to risk lies at the heart of the difficulties affecting financing through long-term financial assets, a significant drop in interest rates is likely to make the remuneration of short-term monetary investments less attractive. It is the responsibility of central banks, or the European Central Bank in the case of Europe, to remunerate aversion to risk less well.

It is up to the asset managers to reinvent long-term investment products which offer an adequate guarantee of liquidity. The participants are aware of the issues and of the need for disruption; there are a number of possible solutions, e.g. by distinguishing a completely liquid part and pockets which, although less liquid, have lock-up clauses for a given period. These products may clearly be inserted into the various possible forms of incentive for long-term, precautionary savings, in particular for retirement purposes.

This is because a high level of savings does not possess, far from it, a sufficiently long structure, i.e. invested in corporate underlyings, in order to ensure a drain of capital towards the financing requirements of the real economy. This requires a set of incentives to generate appropriate investment solutions, in particular tax incentives, which are more favourable in terms of time scale, risk and liquidity. Already existing products may be used as a convenient repository (group pension plans, personal equity plans...). More generally, the unequal distribution of savings and international surpluses assigns to Western asset managers the role of recycling savings generated in the emerging country sector and steering them towards long-term investment projects in both debt-fuelled so-called developed economies and so-called emerging markets.

Finally, it is the business of the CIB, within the context of organised markets, to consolidate the liquidity of financial assets and, therefore, of fund assets managed by asset managers. Whether they are CDs or a more general standardisation of securitisation products, there are a number of possible courses of action.

Since the issues are global, all participants who are involved are affected. It is up to asset managers to ensure the construction of simple, liquid, long-term products – which may justify a charge for such liquidity –, it is up to the world of the markets to provide liquid instruments on the assets side, it is up to the central banker to stimulate appetite for risk by discouraging aversion, it is up to the government authorities to encourage the development of attractive, regulatory and fiscal provisions in order to channel long-term financial savings towards the economy.

Such necessary action will be all the more likely to succeed, if any misguided ideas are put aside. Accordingly, one must be convinced that there is no way of avoiding reintermediation. Such a step backwards would only result in fresh problems for banks' balance sheets, in particular with regard to the management of their own capital.

All this at a time when the crisis process (deleveraging of the CIB) is likely to push businesses towards market finance and, moreover, leads asset managers and investors to manufacture debt funds (e.g. medium-sized companies, loans) from the balance sheets of the CIB, in respect of which the CIB retain a share of risk, thus transferring part of the financing function to the sector of investors.

A structural reform of the markets is, moreover, desirable. Securitisation has perished due to the banking system's lack of transparency and accountability, the banking system having created the debts and sold them to asset managers. Renewed confidence will require the implementation of true, organised markets, which consolidate the liquidity of financial assets within the context of a more general standardisation of securitisation products. It will also require an obligation on the part of the banks to retain a share of the risks, which is an effective way of encouraging them to select such risks more carefully. More generally, the capacity of asset managers to steer the final holders of savings (which they know well) towards solutions of various originations and *ad hoc* financing rounds which represent real needs, suggests that a "from investment to originate" model may gradually be implemented.

The only possible solution is to prime the pump for the long-term financing of the economy through the market. This task will require a contribution from all participants. This was true back in 2008 and is, in general, still true six years later, despite a mobilisation which still leaves much to be desired.

Inflation as a total phenomenon

One needs to go back to the 1930's in order to find an international cycle threatened by an excess of supply and overcapacities and not by the *hubris* of demand observed after the Second World War. The Asian crisis was an overinvestment crisis, the "internet" crisis revealed overcapacities, the subprime crisis and, later, that of sovereign debt disclosed weak balance sheet positions on the part of both households and States.

These deflationary forces (debt deflation), combined with a competitive, international environment and technological breakthroughs weighed upon the international inflation indexes. If inflation in its classic form seems to have died, it survives in financial forms (asset market).

Disinflation cannot be invented twice. The sources for a downward trend of interest rates are exhausted. The low level of risk premia, the abundance of liquidities and a deterioration in the solvency of certain Western States place the medium-term risk slightly higher for inflation and interest rates, a classic cyclical risk (growth and inflation) or credit risk (debt/GDP). In addition, the hierarchy of risks, as between businesses and States, is disrupted by the sovereign debt crisis.

At the start of the 1980's, the central banks were given a mandate by society to fight inflation which thus meant that society no longer intended to put up with the inflationary consequences of a macroeconomic regime of monetised state debt and a distribution of added value which was favourable to wages. A position which, in structural terms, was long in bonds *and* equity was profitable (downward trend in bond risk premia *and* dilation of the PER on the equity markets). This period saw inflation and its volatility shift from the real sphere to the financial sphere and central banks gradually adopted a possible new choice, to fight against inflation of the price of financial assets within a monetisation regime of private debt and a distribution of added value which had become favourable to profits. The sudden emergence of the crisis generally accommodated the risk of financial inflation as a result of the monetary largesse granted.

Extrapolating an average year-on-year annual yield from shares of 15%, namely, after deducting a dividend yield of 2%, an increase in the price of shares of 13% per annum, amounts more or less to expecting that the return on physical capital may experience equivalent annual growth. It therefore means gambling on a significant increase in productivity, when, moreover, the increase of the workforce, that of capital stock and that of the share of capital in the national income mean the equation cannot be completed. This was one of the major issues of the 1990's for the West. The regimes of corporate profitability and of average equity yield must then adjust to an overall context which delivers 2 to 2.5% of growth of the real GDP and the same amount of inflation. It is, consequently, difficult to expect an average annual increase in profits which is much higher than 8 or 9% and one must be satisfied with yields on equity investments of the same order, year-on-year.

Therefore, and because they are the first to be affected by monetary shocks, the prices of financial assets incorporate expectations of later, real evolutions. Moreover, the rise in power of the regimes driven by wealth effects, which are characterised by real wealth effects and/or psychological effects, assigns to developments in the financial sphere an increasingly relevant function as a leading indicator for the real cycle.

Our analytical framework includes a stock of money, two economic spheres (one, which is real, including goods and services; the other, which is financial, including all financial assets) and a circulation of the stock of money (i.e. the velocity of the stock of money, understood as the number of transactions, whether real or financial, per unit of monetary stock). The circulation takes place within each of these spheres, producing classic or financial inflation, and from one sphere to the other, in the form of what is known as a "transfer". There is a balancing mechanism, in the sense that an expansion in the demand of means of payments within the sphere of goods or within that of financial assets presupposes/requires a reduction in expenditure in the other sphere. An imbalance in one of the two spheres will ultimately be corrected by a return to neutral equilibrium in the other sphere, unless it is accommodated, for a certain amount of time, by monetary expansion and credit[8].

Since the cycle is a movement of relative prices, inflation, i.e. the dynamic for the distortion of prices between and within goods,

[8] Since the stock of money is not constant and velocity has a multiplying effect, the equation proves to be even more complex.

services and financial assets, maintains a close link with the distortions of value given to time (memory and forgetfulness, which make expectations), and therefore the arbitrages and substitutions which occur within the real sphere and within the financial sphere, as preferences are transformed. This means that, unless one adopts a broader definition of inflation, i.e. one which includes the real sphere and financial sphere, the inflationary phenomenon cannot be fully understood.

The inflationary phenomenon is understood as a total phenomenon ("general" within the meaning of the general level of prices). Inflation is indeed a product of the velocity of the stock of money (liquidity), but the velocity unfurls, and must therefore be recorded, within both spheres simultaneously. This global apprehension opens the path for a more realistic approach to contemporary economies, together with action by the central banks. In a word, within the famous quantitative equation of money as PV = MT, one should at least have a broader definition of V (V').

One must, accordingly, imagine that the two spheres are added together, that they overlap more than they offset or neutralise each other; one must imagine that the links between them are governed by a form of aggregate dynamic. One must, therefore, make room for memory and forgetfulness at the heart of that which actually "prints" the stock of money and grants it life in the form of that which is called liquidity. One must break away from the idea that the financial sphere is not independent and that it is a veil over reality. That which is financial transforms that which is real, as much as the opposite.

PART III

DURATION, MEMORY, FORGETFULNESS AND ASSET PRICES

Essay 9

ANATOMY OF THE STOCK MARKET[9]

Time referential and genomial identities

We have established the essential role of the memory of the conscious Subject and of the temporal referential which is structured by that memory. Events and facts are perceived within this framework. The time-referential is psychological, i.e. made up of the temporal matter which makes consciousness and whose dynamic is based on memory recalls and forgetfulness. Duration, memory and forgetfulness provide the fundamental structure of the time-referential. Duration is the essential matter of economics and finance and is closely linked to the manner in which the Subject perceives the world and projects itself into that world. Economic facts and events only exist for a Subject-consciousness which is there in order to grasp them. Within the referential, there is a profound analogy between memory/forgetfulness and discounting (non-linearity, no segmentation of past-present-future).

The Stock Market is the place of perceptions and is the incarnation and automation of such perceptions.

Stock market time is the time of the Subject and, within the referential, the essential element is that which has taken place, since this is the time-matter which is driven by the process of memory and forgetfulness.

The stock market dynamic is independent of immediate facts and events, except insofar as the latter bring up to date something which may significantly modify time-matter, the stock of the past, by recalling an element which has been forgotten or by deleting another.

[9] This work restates certain theories advanced in *La dynamique boursière*; *Théorie globale de l'intérêt, du cycle et de la mémoire*; *Money, Memory and Asset Prices*. The reader can refer back to those works.

The value of a share lies in the stock of time-matter and the dynamic is provided by the time differential within the referential of duration, memory and forgetfulness. It is a space of discontinuities, contractions and dilations with threshold effects and switches from one regime to another.

The dynamic of the absolute and relative equilibria is provided by the value given to time, which governs the preferences and the arbitrages.

The intensities of the price variations, i.e. the energy in the Stock Market dynamic, are produced by the recalls of memory and the acts of forgetfulness. There is an analogy: energy diffuses heat within a substance in the same way that the movement in price of the financial asset is driven. Temporal intensities are spatio-temporal: one moves more quickly within the stock market time-referential in accordance with how intensely one remembers or forgets.

Psychological is understood to mean that "which forms part of the consciousness' way of working". The encounter of the consciousness (economic Subject) and the world structures the economic and financial facts and events. The comprehension of the world by the consciousness and the time-referential, which we have described, form one and the same, and time measured by clocks is foreign to stock market time.

The price of a stock market asset expresses, at any given time, a certain value given to time, that of the expectation of what is to come and *therefore* that of the memory of that which comes to the Subject from the past.

The speed of movement within the time-referential is a function of the intensity of memory and forgetfulness.

The first (ontological), temporal stratum is that of duration, which pre-exists the structure of the consciousness. Duration is both matter and the passage of time. The passage of time is the perceived stock market time, the general regime of economic and financial temporality, of which time measured by clocks is only one particular instance, effected in certain circumstances.

Energy, on a financial market, lies within duration. The driving force is this time which persists. The concentration and distribution of the price variations, as well as their direction, are characterised by the phenomena of persistence, which represent a distortion of the time-referential: the more intense the price variations and the more stock market prices rise or fall in persistent trends, the more the timescale stretches (a high increasing number of price variations or upward/downward trends per unit of time as measured by clocks). There is a correlation between such distortions and those of the time-matter (duration) which receives energy from memory and forgetfulness. Memory recall is an emission of energy which produces a force of attraction and reduces the distance, within the referential, between various objects/events, facts, prices ...) - between them and by comparison with the Subject -, a distance from the point of view of time measured by clocks. The dilation of the reference time is a compression of distances and everything circulates more quickly (this same word that we will encounter when analysing the circulation of money, since it concerns the same phenomenon). The force of attraction between two prices, but also between a price and a real fact, will depend upon their time-distances, a function of memory and forgetfulness. It should be noted that asymmetries may exist between memory and forgetfulness (Does one forget in the same way that one remembers? Does one forget more quickly than one remembers?)

That which is relevant on a financial market cannot be seen (the non-cyclical, non-instantaneous components).

The past-present-future tripartition is of little relevance. Expectation is equivalent to the manner in which the past makes itself present. The only past is that which makes itself present. The more that duration (that which lasts) makes itself present, the more persistence there is, the more stretching of the *continuum* of the matter of duration, resulting in the dilation of the referential.

The extreme values sustain themselves, as if in an apprenticeship process, through memory (and forgetfulness), where nothing is really learnt but rather recalled: the mandatory corrections do not take place because there is an established risk of inflation but because it has taken place and is therefore expected.

Everything seems to take place as if, like torches planted in the night, the memory of multiple variables traced a frail path. One by one, the trembling torches of memory are extinguished as the passer-by comes through, whilst others are instantly lit.

The memory of a real or mental object includes a rate of forgetfulness: memory and forgetfulness form one unitary concept.

The persistence which is at work in Stock Market prices is the persistence of a relationship between the price and the blocks of the past, which are cut as if in stone. Each new price is added, drop by drop, until it modifies the shape of the stone. One price may prove so exceptional that it causes the stone to explode, thus hastening a reconstruction. The immediate moment, the present or even that which is cyclical do not seem to have the power to modify the block of the past, with certain exceptions. The present is determined by the past and the relevant information is, always and throughout, already known (duration persists, at varying degrees), even if it is not necessarily visible, insofar as one tries to find it. The instant price has no substance. That which comes (which may adopt a future meaning) is that which comes from that which has been, that which persists when faced with the erosive forces of forgetfulness. The untenable, immediate point of the present must be seen as the distant light produced by a star, which has occasionally travelled for such a long time that the light which is seen is nothing more than the reflection of a star which is already dead. Memory and forgetfulness determine the distance, energy and speed. It is suggested that the series of immediate prices come from galaxies which are *a priori* far away (the distance may be reduced within the referential) – *a priori* since it is assumed that there is, at the start of the process, a stock of past which is in some way inert and lacking in energy – and move as if drawn by equilibrium values which express a state of memory (and forgetfulness), i.e. a spatio-temporal state within the referential which incorporates everything which may be relevant within the determination of the stock market equilibrium price.

The DNA of a stock market value or of the Stock Market as a whole includes a core, which incorporates sequences or slices of past time for certain facts and events, which are as it were fundamental, together with bits of sequences which are more remote or closer. The whole is driven by a dynamic.

Economic time is matter which melts like wax in a flame or hardens under the effect of memory and forgetfulness; which like the wind rose collects sand or is reduced, always under the same effects of time, duration, memory and forgetfulness.

Past sequences, which are relevant for the market, when they form a stable memory, provide a fixed point, a reference to which the market will return and an expression of a regime which will undoubtedly experience evolutions and may even disappear. The core of DNA may change, other sequences may be recalled and others put to sleep. A change of regime. Such processes may be endogenous but maintain a link with a series of facts and events which, due to their importance, will eventually trigger a transformation. The fixed points (regimes) are moving and the regimes are galaxies which form parallel worlds. We assume their existence, we do not see them, their light comes to us. In these parallel worlds, the financial objects travel with stock market time which may compress the distances.

These considerations all have practical consequences. The industry of finance devotes considerable resources and time to analysing the immediate information. However, as we have seen, this information, although not useless, is not essential to the understanding of what is at stake. The fixed points are much more important, even if the immediate information may, with regard to certain facts and events, exceptionally modify fixed points and regimes. Finally, the current price is always the light of a star which is more or less remote and which has travelled for a greater or lesser distance within the space-time of the financial referential. The priorities are the understanding of the regimes and their characterisation, and the identification of the memorised sequences of past time (the segments of DNA). The present does not deserve to be analysed for itself but rather in the context of a *memory plane* (for any direct or indirect relevant variable for a company in the case of a share).

When analysing blocks of the past, sequences/segments of DNA which may be recalled (or forgotten), elements other than the mere earnings of a company listed on the Stock Market may prove to be relevant. There is a whole context, environment, an ecosystem of facts and events, well beyond that which seems directly attached to the subject under analysis, which needs to be understood. The price of a share tells us much more than merely the earnings of the company in question.

The immediate moment, fact or event, literally causes sequences or bits of sequences (memory recall or forgetfulness) to travel, such sequences must be seen as financial *objects* which inhabit the psychological-style referential which has been described. The fixed points discussed above are such financial objects.

The velocity of money, its capacity to produce inflation of the price of financial assets, when it unfolds within the financial sphere, may be understood on the basis of the displacement of financial objects within the referential. The amount of financial transactions realised per monetary unit experiences contractions and dilations, where appetite (and aversion) for risk play a significant role, similar to that which Keynes calls a preference for liquidity. Money is informed/driven by the dynamic of memory recalls and acts of forgetfulness, which makes the financial objects travel and produces speed (deceleration) and abolitions/compressions (extensions) of distance. The acceleration of the velocity of money, as such, creates money (or, in other words, it is not the monetary stock which increases but its speed of circulation and the motivation for such speed lies in the dynamic of the referential discussed above.)

Rises, falls and speed

Similarly, one can in this way obtain a better understanding of the phenomena of asymmetry between the rise and fall of certain asset prices. We have shown that thick and asymmetrical distribution tails existed. Accordingly, interest rates seem to have risen more quickly than they fell since the 1970's (cf. P. Blanqué, "*Asset Prices: Fall Faster than Rise?*" Economic Research Paper, Paribas, 20 April 1998), with a concentration of increases in the temporal sequences which were collected and, for their part, shares seem to have risen faster than they fell. It is relevant to note that these results were obtained at the end of the 1990's, at the time of these initial works, in a context which constituted a regime (downward trend in interest rates and increase in share prices), since the disinflationary disruption at the start of the 1980's and before the deflationary breach of the decade starting in 2000. This means that the results may evolve but will not modify the essential element, the means of understanding such results.

This accordingly describes, in the case of interest rates, such a phenomenon of asymmetries and non-linearities (asymmetrical distributions: thick tails on the right-hand side, this rises more quickly; increases which are concentrated within time). There is a time-referential of memory which sets in motion a sequential slice of the rich past (the struggle against inflation), which sustains the self-regulation of the bond market (the fear of inflation makes the emergence of inflation improbable). Any published inflation figure, which seems more worrying, triggers, within the referential, a journey of financial objects which contain the memory of inflation and of the action taken to prevent it. Such objects are gathered together (compression of the time-distance) within the psychological referential. Speed and energy are released within the acceleration (rise in rates which takes place rapidly). This is a description of a stable regime (1980-2000), characterised by stable fixed points, which help facilitate interpretation (again one can see that one of the principal questions for an investor is: what regime am I in? What are the fixed points? What is the direction of the regime?) This is because all regimes will ultimately produce the forces for their own recovery (this is true of the paradox of tranquillity which causes the threat of inflation to be forgotten), as familiarisation and forgetfulness modify the original sequential slices. Accordingly, the retreat and later good behaviour of inflation ultimately renders expectations dormant (because, at a certain moment in time, memory only retains the drops in inflation or at least only reasonable prices.) The regime may remain there for some time or start to incorporate a new deflation sequence. Such evolutions are obviously relevant for the risk premia of financial assets. Rendering the inflationary genome dormant does not mean that it disappears. Like a flash of lightning in a clear-blue sky, the fear of inflation may return, suddenly recalled to memory from considerable distances which are then compressed. The financial object "inflation" starts to travel rapidly within the referential, bringing to the present a DNA sequence which will structure the expectation. The *memory planes* must be seen as infinite parallel worlds, which ultimately intersect within the dynamic of the psychological referential.

The example of inflation and interest rates between 1980 and 2000 is that of a stable time-referential in which the memory of inflation *and* of the action taken against inflation was predominant. The entrenchment of disinflation and then the increased risk of deflation modify the regime with an increase in the rate of forgetfulness (of inflation) within the psychological space-time referential and in the memory (of deflation) - where the unitary nature of memory and forgetfulness can be seen once again, since to state what one remembers is also to state simultaneously what is forgotten; or, in other words, at the height of a bubble, one only remembers the increases and one has therefore forgotten that which might encourage a greater degree of prudence: the situation may still be described in terms of memory or forgetfulness.

In the same way, unsurprisingly, shares tend to rise more quickly than they fall in a regime of disinflation and therefore a regime with a downward trend of nominal and later real interest rates (and therefore, once again, a regime with a stable, negative correlation between nominal bond yield and share price: the two assets are interchangeable, shares being the most attractive bonds and the "liquidity" component – with velocity of money and appetite for risk dominating the "earnings" component). The decade starting in 2000 and the occurrence of crises and crashes led to a change in regime. The "liquidity" component plays all the more important a role, since the structure of the time-referential includes more financial *objects*, which are directly relevant for interest rates, such as inflation. As we have said, there is a profound analogy and correlation between the financial objects which circulate within the psychological referential and the money which circulates within the real and/or financial spheres. The forms of dilation and/or contraction of the referential's time-matter, the stock of money and the share prices form part of the same structure. Money circulates on the markets in the same way that memorised, mental, financial objects circulate within the psychological referential and in the same way that share prices rise or fall.

Observation also suggests that a *reactivity* function exists, with an opposite correction of a rise or fall, each regime being characterised by a certain speed of correction, by comparison with the speed of the first movement – is the corrective movement faster or slower and are there any asymmetries between the rises and falls?

Hereditary macro-financial regimes

A memory, or time-referential, is linked to each macro-financial *regime*, which stems as much from the remembering of essential elements (such as macro-economic elements which are likely to "polarise" the various segments of a portfolio, as we stated above, during our examination of the role played by macro-factors in the construction of allocation) as from forgetfulness (which dominated the previous regime) – memory and forgetfulness being two sides of one and the same phenomenon. It should be noted that the task of identifying the sensitivity of the financial assets to the macro-factors, of the polarisation of such assets through possible macro-scenarii, of the polarity of the asset itself (the financial asset is defined as containing a macro-economic DNA, i.e. a bearer of original, memorised sequences which involve macro-factors) seems promising. Accordingly, an appreciation and understanding of the genetic macro-factorial (in the sense of macro-economic) heritage of each asset is required, when approaching the portfolio through macro-factorial sequences. This can only be effected as part of a close analysis of the time referential which has been described. In particular, a consideration of duration, memory and forgetfulness enables the investor to identify the regimes and, even better, the transformation dynamic.

There is much at stake for the investor in correctly identifying the current, and even more so the future, regime. Estimations of the portfolio's macro-economic polarisation must be placed in this context – locating points of attachment or adherence for memory, events or wider sequences. Consequently, appropriate attention must be paid to the typology of macro-economic regimes (accordingly, and without limitation, (i) growth without inflation, (ii) inflation, (iii) deflation) and regimes with attached risk premia. We saw that the period 1970/2000 was dominated by the theme of inflation (inflation and then disinflation), inflationary fears (some of which are immersed in blocks of the more distant past, the 1930's in Germany and some references lie even further in the past) *and* action taken to fight against inflation (Volcker and, together with him, a certain central bank model). This period is exceptional in many respects, by comparison with the reality of the long period (a regime of growth without inflation and inflation with low volatility), while containing, at the end of disinflation, the risk of a deflation regime which would set in motion a sequence of memory which is itself vast (the 1930's in the USA, Japan in the 1990's). The regimes of correlation between interest rates (let us say 10-year government bond yields) and share prices vary sharply from one regime to another, for the three regimes which have been briefly discussed (*a fortiori* when the possibility of a public debt crisis is enshrined in the regime, such as the deflationary situation which occurred in the decade starting in 2000 in Western economies, where such a risk actually exists). The nature, sign and stability of the relationship between the said government interest rate and the price of risky assets (shares here) is important because – as discussed above – the reference structure for allocations linked these two assets and because the government asset has been deemed to be risk-free. The onset of crises in the decade starting in 2000 literally set in motion, within the referential, while bringing them closer, deflationary referential items whose force of attraction started to modify the stock market regime and the relations between variables. These forces of attraction between *objects* (it should be noted that by such objects we mean memorised facts, events or any other piece/sequence of DNA) cause the *circulation* within the psychological space-time referential, which is a distortion of the primary temporal material (duration).

Economics and finance are defined by hereditary, proprietary and generic phenomena which form a structure. Each asset, class of assets or market segment contains an identity which defines it. The identity card includes genomes, i.e. bits of DNA which are stored and memorised/forgotten. The identity dominates that what is cyclical and also the current economic situation and immediate moment in time. The means of formation of the contents of the Stock Market time-referential and its operation, are specific and identifying. Where there is a phenomenon of identity, there is persistence. The name "Stock Market" is the name for a certain genomial identity for a certain space-time referential, which is in a certain type of relationship with the world.

Time, money and the equity risk premium

The Stock Market gathers together all the elements which relate to the future. In particular, because it incorporates expectations of growth, it contains a form of future consumption and investment function. It accordingly relinquishes part of immediate consumption for an expectation of deferred consumption or investment. In a regime of debt and/or growth, which can be described as hereditary, there is a simultaneous fall in the rate of savings, a rise in the price of financial assets and of immediate consumption (or investment). Immediate and future prospects are assessed together, simultaneously. The intertemporal mismatch of preferences leads to an inordinately large inflation of supply for a future demand, which will not be able to satisfy it unless the debt is maintained, since in the meantime savings have been made once again. The risk premium is the junction between the various temporal sequences of preferences. It can be understood, in passing, that, in a normal context (without debt or immediate wealth effects), the Stock Market will rise at the bottom of the business cycle or that the rise may at least logically coincide with a neutral function of consumption and investment (there is a neutrality of the Stock Market increase with regard to the function).

In reality, the share risk premium is exposed to interference by money to such an extent that its very nature depends upon monetary phenomena. There is, in particular, a link between the phenomenon of liquidity and the risk premium, the latter being weaker, the higher the speed of monetary circulation within the Stock Market for the purposes of financial transactions. This circulation may include *ex nihilo* monetary creation, if credit prevents the progression of transactions in the financial sphere leading to a reduction of transactions in the real sphere (neutrality would require a mere transfer of means of payment from one to the other). The temporal planes are then inconsistent. The monetary nature of the risk premium is generally underestimated, which makes it even more enigmatic.

The Stock Market, over and beyond the companies which make it up and give it its immediate appearance, must be seen as a global, institutional form of the economic Subject's relationship with the world, a complete form of intermediation of projects, risks, facts and events. In contemporary forms of capitalism, the Stock Market plays the role of complete consciousness, by means of which the world appears to itself. This form is very autonomous. Consequently, the risk premium must certainly be seen as including a risk premium which is specific to the companies which make up the Stock Market (this premium is commented upon) *and* a *global* risk premium, which reflects the fact that the Stock Market is the most complete and total approximation of future reality. The Stock Market thus incorporates a complete representation of the world and the risks, which clearly go well beyond simply those risks which affect companies directly, as it were. One may consider that this is so because numerous risks are not, or not yet, financialised, i.e. represented by a market segment and incorporated in the Stock Market. The total risk premium would accordingly be even higher. Ultimately, the Stock Market risk premium can be expressed as Rp = Rp (equity) + g, where the factor g represents the *other* overall risks, those located beyond the factors which are most direct and visible for companies, factors which are potentially infinite and which are barely integrated at all within the Stock Market structure (a form of market inefficiency). This space is not considered or researched as it should be, whilst the essential share of resources is directed at more immediate, more visible and more direct issues.

Since the long-term ownership horizon leads to an expectation which is itself long-term, it is relevant to take account of a long period of time which has elapsed and is memorised, even if partly forgotten. The consideration of the phenomenon of persistence forces one to align consistently, within the time-referential, the temporality of the project, that of the ownership of the financial asset and, finally, that of the expectation and memory, which are analogous.

Anything which has the capacity to modify or break a given memory regime of facts, events and data, which constitute, whether directly or indirectly, the approach adopted in respect of the object analysed in the Stock Market (e.g. a company, for the purposes of the equity market) or its environment in the widest sense of the word, whether real or potential, together with its associated risks, is called a *fundamental* element in the approach to the Stock Market (and over and beyond the financial markets as a whole). A given memory regime is understood to be that which provides the most acceptable approximation of the equilibrium of the object under analysis, the value and condition, from which the price of the object under analysis cannot be distanced definitively.

The memorised matter (therefore that part of the total, relevant matter which has not been forgotten), i.e. the time-matter, is (in)formed (distorted) by the energy produced by the memory recall and/or the act of forgetting, which determines a dynamic and a speed of movement of the memorised or forgotten objects within the psychological space-time referential, together with the relevant asset prices. The dynamic which results from the memory recall and/or the act of forgetting is itself determined by the movement of preferences, which is governed by the value given to time by the economic Subject, whether the latter is an individual or a collective body (institution). *As part of this analysis, it is assumed that an analogy exists between, first, the value given to time and, second, the preference for liquidity (or lack of liquidity) and risk aversion (or appetite).* It is noted that the value given to time and the movement of that which persists from the past within the present (that which literally makes itself present) provide themselves, as concepts, a profound and broad analogy. The complete memory of that which is completely relevant for the object under analysis refers to an absolute equilibrium (which is undoubtedly unattainable, since, once attained, it would be a fixed point removing temporality and the dynamic from the states of memory and forgetfulness). Real life shows relative equilibria (imbalances), the complete memory of which is a rather theoretical, special situation.

The function of preference for the Stock Market

The preference for the Stock Market (or its absence), the preference for liquidity (or lack of liquidity) and the appetite for (or aversion to) risk constitute three analogous concepts. In particular, the concept of a preference for the Stock Market contains that of a preference between the Stock Market (let us say shares) and *something else*, between the Stock Market and *everything else*. There is a good deal at play within the terms "something else" and "everything else". On first analysis, it is a form of proxy for a competing asset within the portfolio or the investment universe (a government bond or corporate bond or any other long-term asset). It is also *everything else*, which explains the presence of a *global* risk premium. As seen above, the first dimension (a preference between shares and another competing asset class) could be reduced to a simple equation: the preference between the Stock Market and the risk-free asset is equal to the preference between shares and any other competing long-term asset class to which is added the "absolute" value of the competing asset (in the sense of the relative equilibrium discussed above). In passing, one can see and assume the proximity and analogy between the appetite for (aversion to) risk and the preference for the Stock Market (or lack of) – provided that the competing asset is a low-risk asset (government bonds were deemed for a long time to be a good proxy for risk-free assets), which cannot be the general rule but a special situation for a competing asset. The second dimension (a preference between the Stock Market and *everything else*) cannot be easily approached other than through a risk premium.

If one returns to the preference for the Stock Market, in the sense of a preference between the Stock Market and *something else*, one can see that it may be equivalent to the function of liquidity (and of a preference for liquidity) in proportion to the animation of the stock of money (concepts of information/distortion of money by the processes of memory and forgetfulness, of monetary circulation and exchange – liquidity incorporates the other within that which becomes liquid through this exchange connection). The narrowest definition of a preference for the Stock Market, i.e. of a preference between the Stock Market and *something else*, as stated, is established within the preference and the arbitrage between the equity asset class and theoretically any other asset class; the second definition is provided, in our approach, by means of a global risk premium, taking into account the fact that the Stock Market incorporates facts, events, risks and projects well beyond the mere companies which make it up (in fact, if one takes this approach one step further, it can be assumed that the Stock Market is an empowered consciousness of the world, the impersonal, collective Subject (*The* market says, thinks...)

The interest rate is the price for such preferences, arbitrages and substitutions. It is also the price for the preference for liquidity, since the preference for the Stock Market and the preference for liquidity are linked by a strong analogy. Given that such preferences are the result of a monetary dynamic, which is determined and driven by the processes of memory and forgetfulness, within a psychological space-time referential which is specific to the economic Subject, one is led to assume a definition of the interest rate which incorporates such a referential component of time, duration, memory and forgetfulness, a psychological component of the interest rate in the sense in which we have defined it (see *Théorie globale de l'intérêt, du cycle et de la mémoire*; *Money, Memory and Asset Prices*).

It can be argued that the dynamic of preferences, which broadly results from monetary factors, is dominant in the short-term and that in the long-term "real" factors are imposed, whether factors of earnings or other variables, whether direct or indirect, with regard to their component of persistence, i.e. the density of duration as discussed above.

One may express this as: Pm = f (Pf, SM/F, rp),

Where:

Pm = market price

Pf = preference

SM/F = memory and forgetfulness of that which is specific to the company listed on the Stock Market (stock, memory, forgetfulness)

rp = risk premium

Such an equation allows one to incorporate several dimensions and planes which are often separated. First, one assumes that the Stock Market moves, over the long-term (using the definition of long-term which we have adopted, over and beyond a mere succession of short-terms which is not the long-term) towards a *value*, an equilibrium (absolute version) which is untenable/unattainable (relative version), which fluctuates around a *line of value* provided by the density of duration and the persistence which merges with the expectation for the whole of the relevant data and elements for the stock market trajectory. A profound analogy is assumed between expectation and memory/forgetfulness and a function of long memory is defined, i.e. of persistence, together with a factor of forgetfulness. From a methodological point of view, the task of identifying and dissecting the matter of memory and duration for the relevant sequences and data is an essential one. The idea of an absolute value is maintained, as a premise which holds the whole of the system, and on which the absolute concept of equilibrium is based, a total density of duration which, because it removes temporality at the maximum point of density (the absolute intensity of that which persists no longer lasts, removing temporality) acquires a status of being and of substance. The idea of substance is maintained/saved, together with this idea, for a concept of value around which fluctuate the observable variables, which return to it sooner or later by means of *magnetisation*.

Second, and this approach is often separate, one assumes that the essential element lies within the function of preference for the Stock Market, i.e. a preference between the Stock Market *and something else*, which can itself be broken down into two dimensions of arbitrage: Stock Market shares as compared to other asset classes; Stock Market shares as compared to *everything else* (which is expressed in our approach by a *global risk premium*). Regarding the first dimension, the arbitrage function between yields of relevant asset classes is enriched with a function of persistence (memory and forgetfulness):

Pf = [ey – (ay’, by” ...)] M/F

Where:

ey = Stock Market yield (earning yield)

ay' = yield of another asset class, of any other asset class for which the preference for the Stock Market is expressed (as between the Stock Market *and something else*)

by" = the Stock Market may be preferred to an infinite number of other assets.

By incorporating the two dimensions, one assumes that, *in the best case scenario*, value is defined as the sum of a function of preferences, arbitrages and substitutions (here, memory and forgetfulness provide the dynamic for driving the money) and of an absolute function of determining value (here, duration and persistence). Faced with the difficulties linked to the function of determining absolute value, it is still possible to return to a compromise by means of preferences, the idea that the Stock Market may be known in a relative manner. An "absolute" version, impaired by the function of preference and arbitrage, requires one to add to the comparison of instantaneous yields from competing asset classes an absolute consideration of one or other asset classes. The complete, "absolute" version will incorporate a global risk premium. This definition remains the most practicable circumvention, an alternative to a direct approach to the absolute value of the Stock Market, the North face of a mountain which is still inaccessible – one of the principal obstacles continuing to be that the absolute approach rapidly removes *temporality*.

The Stock Market price is the result of a preference for the Stock Market (external choice), a projection of value regarding the *specific elements* of the Stock Market (linked to the companies), and a *global risk premium*.

There is an absolute (in-itself) value plane and there is a preference plane (i.e. between the Stock Market and *everything else*). The stock market dynamic incorporates both planes, the absolute value becoming value for an economic Subject (e.g. the investor, i.e. for-oneself and for-others, since this involves an exchange, which will make the asset liquid). The absolute "in-itself" value is a slice of a block of time-matter (the past). This absolute value becomes "for-oneself" once it is the subject of a preference, i.e. of a design by the economic Subject. The function of preference is an act of remembering and/or of forgetting, which drives the absolute time-matter made up of duration. The time-matter comes to life *for someone* and is made visible. Moreover, this preference function sustains its dynamic of arbitrages with *everything else* which is not directly the Stock Market (a comparison with other asset classes, more global factors). There is not, on the one hand, a function of preference which sustains the short-term noise of the market and, on the other, an inaccessible plane of absolute value: the noise is the sign of the dynamic management of the stock of time-matter (memory-matter, duration); the driving force lies within the concept of circulation (cf. the circulation of money); circulation and liquidity provide meaningful analogies, insofar as they both imply an exchange with others.

We emphasise the unitary nature of the integration of both planes. There is a great temptation to abandon the absolute value plane (and therefore the very idea of substance) (non-observable, inexistent), handing the stock market dynamic over to erratic and irrational forces (i.e. a function of preference governed by animal spirits). The absolute value plane makes itself present and visible through the setting in motion of the preference function, which is determined by the designs of the Subject as consciousness, i.e. time and the forces of memory and forgetfulness.

Two areas of work result from this: to standardise, identify and clarify the sections of the block of time-matter which form the approximation (proxy) of absolute value (the background); to understand the preferences and arbitrages, since the Stock Market dynamic ultimately relates less to that which directly makes it up than to *that which is not the Stock Market (everything else)*. There is a significant lack of more extensive and more reliable indicators for the functions of preference and arbitrage.

There is no stock market present: that which is present is a presence of that which lasts, in the form of persistence at odds with forgetfulness. The present has no specific substance: it is in a state of non-being, torn away from itself within the expectation and the projection. All that remains is the presence of a duration and a memory which merges past and future within the same temporal regime (which we have called a *referential*). Being non-observable, absolute value holds itself in retreat and makes itself present through and within the expression of preferences. Stock market equilibria are relative. The stock market dynamic depends on that which makes up the Stock Market (the absolute component) but above all on that which does not make it up (preferences, arbitrages and substitutions).

In the analysis of preferences, all the direct or indirect elements which are involved in the formation of arbitrages and substitutions, even when they may appear to be short-term, must be understood within a dimension of duration, memory and forgetfulness (an arbitrage of the one-year yield between shares and another asset class must accordingly incorporate a memory of that differential).

The immediate moment merely slides like a drop of water down a pane of glass.

The Stock Market is dominated by a global risk premium (the preference between the Stock Market *and everything else*) which incorporates the phenomena of persistence and is governed within the psychological referential by the functions of duration, memory and forgetfulness. The very limited usual estimates of the risk premium for shares alone (i.e. in relation to earnings or competing asset classes) only relate to one specific case of the global premium (i.e. one of its segments, which is the only one, when all other factors are invalid or neutralised).

The risk premium expresses a value given to time. The higher the value given to time, the lower the premium. The value given to time is itself a function of memory and forgetfulness within the Subject's psychological referential which we have described above. This value relates to a very broad set of elements which may or *may not* relate *directly* to the Stock Market, since the latter contains a global representation of the world for the economic Subject. The premium is an inverse function of the accessible information. A preference for the present will increase the premium, a preference for the future will lower it. The premium establishes a link with (i) that which is to come, merging past and future in their analogy, (ii) that which is other, i.e. everything which is not the Stock Market (*everything else*) and *the others*, those through which exchange and liquidity will be possible. These two links structure the interplay of preferences and substitutions.

The value given to time depends upon the greater or lesser density of duration (memory). The preference is both a preference for a certain regime of temporality (the value given to time) and a preference for the Stock Market, i.e. between the Stock Market and *everything else*. The assessment of the risk depends upon the manner in which one remembers and forgets.

Preferences and the future performance of the Stock Market

The expected return on risk and the value given to time are two sides of the same mirror. The memorised function of the excess return (of the Stock Market as compared to the risk-free asset) may be a proxy for the risk premium with a certain predictive capacity. It is assumed that the risk premium is equal to the *expected* surplus return on shares by comparison with cash and that the memorisation of the surplus is an acceptable approximation for the expectation (with a factor of forgetfulness). Since cash alone provides a limited arbitrage, other elements of preference may be sought over and beyond what we call "the simple preferences" (as between shares and bond assets). Finally, any investigations used will encounter serious limitations: such investigations state the near future as a direct function of the recent past, the pervasiveness of the most recent past within memory. We have thus distinguished three dimensions and their limitations.

We are trying, in particular when determining the functions of preference and arbitrage, to identify and standardise the *regularity* of the conduct of the economic Subject (e.g. concerning the substitution between asset classes or preferences), such regularities incorporating an adaptive function (adaptive memory/expectation).

The future performance of the Stock Market (shares/cash) may be considered: as a preference between shares/bonds (a memorised function of the instant return differential) and a preference between bonds/cash (a memorised function of the risk of inflation and growth); as a preference between shares/cash with a memorised function of relevant series linked to earnings or dividends (dividend yield, earning yield); as a composition of the Stock Market value (a memorised function of series of earnings, dividends etc...) and of the shares/bonds preference (see above).

The risk premium remunerates the risk taken in excess of the pure time-value of money. The question of the (expected) excess return on shares is a question of the scale of values given to time (*simple* preferences between assets; arbitrage between the Stock Market and *everything else*). Each object of a potential preference, as compared to the Stock Market, is allocated a value given to time by the economic Subject. Pairings are formed which show a strong analogy to the risk/return pairings.

Money is a form of cold wax which is warmed up by the processes of memory and forgetfulness within the Subject's space-time referential. The resulting dynamic leads to a circulatory definition of money for an economic Subject which expresses preferences. The pure time-value allocated to money and the expression of the expected yield of the risk-free asset provide an analogy.

The expected relative returns may be approached through the memorised function of such returns.

It is stated that the preference for the Stock Market (one of the determining factors of the excess return on shares as compared to cash) is a composition of the functions of shares/bonds and bonds/cash or shares/bonds and shares/cash.

Eq preference = f [(Eq/Bd) preference, Bd preference]

One refers to the "value" of the various asset classes for the purposes of an *expected* relative return, the memory of which is enough to define the expectation.

The expected (memorized) yield differential pre-empts the shares/bonds performance, which pre-empts the economic cycle because it incorporates expectations in respect of the said cycle.

The *global risk premium* incorporates everything which may divert the investor Subject from the Stock Market, whether insurable elements (or elements which will become insurable – the premium will then decrease proportionately) or non-insurable elements. This premium is no doubt contained in the expected excess return as between the Stock Market and the risk-free or low-risk asset. The investor expects to be remunerated on the Stock Market in excess of the specific risk of the immediate Stock Market components. It follows that the expected yield differential as between the Stock Market and the risk-free (or low-risk) asset may be expressed as a function of a *specific risk premium* and a more *global premium.*

Pref Eq/cash = f (Rps, Rpg)

The concepts of stock market value and preference form one unit. The preference lies at the origin of the dynamic energy which sets one on the path towards value. Value attracts the preference. In modern economics and finance, the powerful role played by the Subject (here the investor) with regard to its appropriation of the world brings the concepts of value and preference together and causes them to merge, to the extent that value is progressively internalised (that which is established by the Subject and no longer that towards which the preference is directed). It is more difficult to distinguish between three possible propositions regarding the concepts of value and preference: (i) the preference is directed towards value; (ii) the preference establishes the value; and (iii) the value makes itself present to the Subject by means of the preference.

The Stock Market premium, because it is a summary of a global relationship of the Subject within the world, remunerates risk *and something else*. ERP = f (R, α) and

$$ERP = f(Rs, RG, \alpha)$$

Arguably two forms of risk premium exist. One is observable, it is the subject of traditional debates and well-known problems. The other is not observable and is specific to the stock market referential: it is "*real*" in the same way that one speaks of a real, unobservable interest rate, since, if one takes the usual strict definition as a starting point, the share premium is equal to the *expected* yield of the stock market asset less the *expected* yield of the risk-free asset. The word "expected" refers to a *real* notion, the solution for which can in our view be found in the analogy between expectation and memory.

$$(ERPM/F = Aer - rf\, Aer)$$

Where Aer = expected asset return and rf Aer = expected risk-free asset.

Observation shows an excess real return on the Stock Market by comparison with that on the so-called risk-free asset (T-bill) to such an extent (6.4 over a century) that one may wonder whether the data or the calibration thereof is correct and/or whether this premium incorporates elements over and beyond those which are usually stated as specific risks, and/or whether the approximation of a risk-free rate provided by the T-bill is acceptable for the determination of the function of intertemporal substitution of preferences.

Intertemporal substitutions are probably not linear and nor is the trajectory of the risk premium (and consequently an average premium has little meaning within a psychological space-time referential, where the movements may be surprising). Moreover, the magnitude of the risk captured by the *real* premium is considerable, much greater than the specific premium which is traditionally discussed. Similarly, the concept of *consumption* must be expanded to include the more global relationship of the economic Subject with the world which is reflected and expressed by the Stock Market, the functions of utility and *consumption*, thus defined, are determined by factors of heredity, persistence and memory and the elasticities of the preferences, choices and intertemporal substitutions are themselves non-linear.

As part of this analysis, it is established that:

(1) Risk is a section of duration affected by factors of memory and forgetfulness, the movement within the referential of the energy generated by the forces of the acts of remembering and forgetting. Risk is not external to the Stock Market, it is the internal element of the referential.

(2) The space-time referential cannot be the same as time measured by clocks or the space of sports fields.

(3) Many risks which are relevant for the Stock Market (i) are neither identified nor known, (ii) are not insured against, will become insurable (reduction of the global risk premium) or not, (iii) will produce an upward pressure on the premium without anyone being able to identify what it relates to.
The utility functions which are based on the intertemporal choices and which determine the preference regimes are only useful for much broader concepts of *consumption* (the concept of consumption/investment is equivalent to that of the relationship with the world).

(4) Within the referential which we have intentionally described as psychological, the principal force and energy come from the memory, understood as matter, and from the processes of recalling and forgetting. Memory and forgetfulness are the dominant psychological forms (in fact we give duration an

ontological status, that which is "in-itself", and we give memory the essential role in the economic Subject's operating mode which is defined as consciousness). Such forms dominate other psychological forms, such as those of vexation, remorse, regret and many others which are identified as cognitive biases of the human being or animal spirits (such as optimism, imitation etc...).

The imaginary nature of the Stock Market

The Stock Market organises the exchange and trade of images. Such images are produced by the expectation and projection of a Subject-investor. Finance, unlike most other sciences, is based on projects (that which is in a state of non-being) and not on things, facts or events. Finance obliterates the latter by projecting them. This is the profound meaning of the Stock Market. The Stock Market organises the presence of that which is to come. *Negativity* thus constitutes the principal matter of the space-time of finance and economics. This negativity inhabits the objects which are projected (expected) by a Subject defined as consciousness. This consciousness is the force and energy of an obliterating projection. This force provides a narrow definition of the project, expectation and action. On the Stock Market, an object is never that which it appears to be, always being projected beyond, outside itself, like a reflection or an extension of the projection of the Subject beyond itself within the action. Economic and financial facts are in this sense facts of consciousness.

There exists a profound analogy between the trade of images and that of promises and credit. Stock market space-time is anti-matter, an imaginary world. The Stock Market is inhabited by nothingness, there is always a concern of what is to come, to be done, a perfect symmetrical reflection of the acting Subject's consciousness. The Stock Market does not contain real objects but images, which correspond to real future images which literally will or will not occur. The Subject's acts of consciousness aimed at the world are imaginary objects which float within the stock market referential. Such objects are not virtual: they may possibly come into existence and, as such, may modify reality or remain as illusions. There is no economic action without the assumption of an imaginary universe of the Subject, the practical form of which is the Stock Market.

The matter (anti-matter) of the financial object within the imaginary universe is made up of duration and memory. The financial object must be seen as being in a permanent motion of incompleteness, without any prospect of ever being compatible with itself.

The Subject is defined as acting consciousness, which only exists by coming out of itself and by manufacturing imaginary objects. This space-time which is placed between the world and us, once the action plans appear, is that of economics and finance. The financial object is an analogon, a mental image which maintains an anti-material link with the real object, while still having the power to transform it.

The economic Subject which acts takes possession of the world and of its real objects by surpassing them, i.e. by making them absent, by *imagining* them.

To act is to project oneself and to anticipate. To anticipate is to imagine and one imagines in the same way that one forgets and one remembers. Such analogous forms are essential to the understanding of economic and financial phenomena. That which lasts provides *continuum* and the raw matter for such processes.

The stock market object as a financial image is one and fixed, one undivided whole with distinct properties. This image-object presents itself to the economic Subject as an undivided package, saturated with the knowledge injected into it by the consciousness, archaeological layers of duration and memory, strata of knowledge. The dynamic of mental images will exert its influence on this knowledge.

One imagines in the same way that one remembers. The process of surpassing reality and of converting such reality into an image, this process of distancing, making absent and of projection is of the same type as that which involves remembering. The image is a total object sustained by memory and duration. There is a fundamental identity between memory (and therefore forgetfulness) and imagination from the point of view of the nature of the mechanisms of imaginary projection-creation.

The Stock Market is a financial space-time referential of an imaginary nature, populated by image-objects, produced by the projection of the Subject's consciousness and elements of the mental or psychological referential. Such objects exist in their own right and also form part of an individual or more collective dynamic. Since the phenomena of the projection of the consciousness are central to the understanding of finance and the Stock Market, what is described here constitutes a theory of the economic and financial Subject.

The images which have already been produced continue to exist within the referential. The mental world of finance and its imaginary objects must be thought of as an expanding universe.

The financial image-object is in a state of non-being and negativity is its mode of being.

The Stock Market, finance and economics develop within a field of *unrealities*. Since the (economic) Subject is condemned to remain at a permanent distance from reality, the financial "sciences" will only ever deal with reality behind the window of the image. The image imposes a distance on reality which cannot be abolished. It is these images which, in various forms (analyses, predictions, expectations of earnings, professional strategies, macro-economic and sector-specific theories, risk scenarii ...) constitute what is called *the market*. The market is the place of confrontation and exchange of all forms of unreality; it is made up of unrealities (images) and its fundamental energy is negativity (the projection-creation of that which looks towards a future, another reality). The process of constituting images is closely linked to *time*. Time and space cannot have the same nature or substance within an image-making referential which is made up of image-objects.

Each act of thinking by the Subject (each design of the consciousness, which also includes more unconscious strata) which produces an image-object *is* an image-object. The image-object is made up of time, sections of time and its structure is an intertemporal summary of sequences, of special cuts (sections) of time-matter. Accordingly, each image-object has a DNA. These unitary elements can be linked within more complex structures. The DNA of the image-objects, e.g. an expectation of company earnings/profits contains a specific texture of duration and memory and its structure contains an intertemporal summary of facts and events. The capture by the economic Subject of this image-object will both create the image and project it into a dynamic which in our view is largely provided by the force and energy of the act of remembering and forgetting.

Saturated with anti-matter, the financial or stock market image-object is a strange anti-world by means of which, paradoxically, the world appears to itself and ultimately exists for the Subject.

The act of consciousness which gives rise to the image-object constitutes the object by transferring knowledge to it. The object is supported by the reality which it aims to transform. It may also be a mere illusion.

Economics and finance are structured like imaginary worlds. There is a fundamental analogy between memory and imagination. One remembers or forgets in the same way that one anticipates or imagines. These are our main propositions.

One only finds within the financial/stock market image-object what the Subject has placed there and the Subject only imagines as an image-object that which it knows in one way or another, which it has perhaps forgotten or repressed (dimension of the unconscious).

Economics and finance (the Stock Market, the financial markets) are structured as imaginary worlds and populated by image-objects, which are produced by the consciousness of the acting Subject. The financial market is the contemporary form of the place of circulation, exchange, confrontation, creation and destruction of image-objects. As such, the market has a function and constitutes the form of a collective consciousness (it is often said that *the* market thinks this or that), which aggregates and summarises. Since economics and finance are traversed by negativity, i.e. the projection towards that which is not yet (project, action, calculating and imagining expectation), the two disciplines express a relationship with the world; which passes through the image-object which is in a state of non-being. All of this implies a close relationship with time, specifically within the negativity discussed above and which creates the project, the action and the expectation. Economics and finance are traversed by absence, inexistence, that which is not yet or is not, will perhaps never be, that which is promised (confidence, credit), predicted, projected, expected or agreed (contract) for the future. Within the field of economics and finance, there is a symmetry and indeed an identity between the creative act of consciousness which produces the image-object and what is called *action*.

The financial markets in their contemporary form are machines for dreaming, imagining, creating and destroying images, a physical form and place of a collective consciousness which is total and totalising. Everyday language is not mistaken when it refers to the Market as a person, the collective extension of the individual economic Subject.

The image of the object which is targeted by the consciousness of the Subject (investor, consumer...) is not the real object, either because the real object exists but is kept at a distance by the act of consciousness, or because this real object is intended to be transformed – it is to come and is therefore absent – or, finally, because the object is inexistent and will remain so, an illusion haunting the universe of financial images. The object of the image is different from the real object targeted by the act of consciousness. It has its own substance and special parameters within space and time. Within the referential, where it is located, one moves more or less quickly the more or less strongly one remembers or forgets. However, the object of the image always takes with it a trace of its origin and of the past, duration and memory.

The image-objects which are exchanged and which circulate on the markets contain variable degrees and densities of time-matter, linking them through duration and memory to real objects from today and/or from the past (only pure illusion pushes unreality and the absence within negativity, which characterises any image-object, to the extreme). The density of the time-matter and its variations play a significant role in establishing value and prices.

The constitution of the image-object (whether financial, stock market or economic) presupposes a certain amount of knowledge, since the image-making consciousness of the investor Subject which will produce the financial image-object can only imagine as an image that which it already knows and/or remembers after having perhaps forgotten. This image-making consciousness loads itself with duration and memory, as if with energy matter.

There is a form of internal life of the image within a referential of duration which is stimulated by memory and forgetfulness. The image is a pure, individual unit which may assemble itself in more or less complex chains of image-objects, which form a structure and language and have their own dynamic. The image-objects may be classified as pure, fundamental units and as complex images made up of primary images. Each image-object contains within it, in the form of a cell nucleus, a DNA of duration and memory.

Essay 10

MONEY, MEMORY AND THE INTEREST RATE

When the rationality of an economic action is formed, this rationality includes the effect of memory. A "rational" individual is an individual who determines himself with powerful effects of the past. This means that a rational expectation must include the temporal dimension of memory and that any expectation depends upon what has taken place. This is an imperfect rationality, which is formed from a memorised matter and an adaptive apprenticeship. An act of economic policy may therefore effectively play with effects of memory. A sub-equilibrium is therefore a disruption of time-matter and memory. The very essence of the cycle lies within the time-matter which is accumulated in memory and which is eroded by forgetfulness. A neutral economic policy respects time-matter, memory and forgetfulness. It may, however, become active and activist but this means running the risk of underestimating the fatal character of the nature and movements of this time-matter and therefore exposing oneself to a risk that the action is useless or indeed to the undesired consequences of a change of regime which may result from the action. Similarly, an economic policy action which ignores time-matter, duration, memory and forgetfulness – and their powerful effects – is a mere veil over reality, since (macro-economic) action seeks to modify the relationship maintained by the Subject (whether an individual, i.e. *homo economicus*, or collective body, i.e. an institution or company) with time.

What we have called a "sub-equilibrium" (it could even be characterised as an equilibrium of under-efficiency, e.g. an equilibrium of under-employment) results from the inertia which is specific to the past of an economic fact, event, phenomenon or variable. This past overhangs the variable, in the sense that it always becomes that which it is and it is at any given moment that which it has been. This past is slow to adjust, i.e. slow to be forgotten. Accordingly, there exists a permanent discrepancy between the pure present, the immediate consciousness of the Subject and that which comes from the past and is superimposed. This discrepancy lies at the origin of that which we have called "sub-equilibrium". This discrepancy is natural and, if one tries to eliminate it without precautions, there is a risk of disruption. Frequently, contemporary action will only manage to cut very feebly into the depth of memory (inefficiency), unless it produces a shock (change of regime, which is called a crisis).

At the densest point of time-matter, the efficiency of the economic policy action is zero. In other words, the efficiency of the economic policy action is a decreasing function of memory-time or an increasing function of forgetfulness. A rational expectation is adaptive by nature and is characterised by a time-matter effect. The action comes up not so much against the fact that the agents will know everything in advance but rather the fact that the impact will be limited by what has already occurred, i.e. the fact that the agents expect in the same way that they remember and forget. The interest rate is the name of the Subject's relationship with time-matter.

In the same way that there exists an *immediate interest rate*, which is observable, there also exists a *memorised interest rate*, which is non-observable, which is the name for the link between the Subject and time-matter within a referential of duration, memory and forgetfulness. By placing the immediate interest rate below the memorised interest rate, an action is triggered in respect of time-matter. An economic policy action aims to contract or dilate time-matter through the movement of the immediate interest rate above or below the memorised interest rate. When the immediate interest rate (whose time-matter function, i.e. time-density, is close to zero) is equal to the memorised interest rate (whose time-matter function is positive), everything takes place as if the pure present (of the Subject's immediate consciousness) were determined entirely by the effects of memory and therefore as if the present action (the economic policy) were neutral with regard to the said temporal reference equilibrium. This neutrality of the action allows the fundamental forces of the cycle to unfurl. Neutrality is therefore attained when the immediate interest rate is equal to the memorised interest rate. In a position of neutrality, time-matter plays a full role in the present situation. Finally, there is at least one economic situation where neutrality is attained when forgetfulness is maximal.

When the immediate interest rate is lower than the memorised interest rate, there is an erosion of time-matter and memory and an increase in the rate of forgetfulness. When the immediate interest rate is higher than the memorised interest rate, there is an over-representation of time-matter in the present.

Money maintains a profound link with the time of duration and memory. Value is the value given to such time. At any given moment, for a given stock of money, there exists a *footprint* of a memory of facts, events and variables, which forms a (macro-financial) regime. When the velocity increases (i.e. a greater volume of real or financial transactions per monetary unit for a given stock of money), there is a dilation of the real sphere or the financial sphere. This dilation is an inflationary form of monetary erosion of value. There is an analogy between the monetary erosion and the erosion of time-matter, and therefore forgetfulness. Such phenomena of forgetfulness and erosion are observed in the special case of financial bubbles. The inflation of the price of financial assets represents a withdrawal of memory, of duration and therefore of the depth of economic time, which is diluted and expands. Inflation is admittedly always and throughout a monetary phenomenon. It is always and throughout a loss of memory. The erosion of monetary value is a superior form of forgetfulness and a decline in the value given to time. The monetary function is a function of memory and forgetfulness.

Equilibrium and the memorised interest rate

Many economic relations which should work well and yet do not owe this apparent breach to the fact that time-matter is not adequately taken into account. There is arguably only a rule for a certain function of memory and forgetfulness which defines a regime. A state of equilibrium may be defined as incorporating a function of stable, dense memory, i.e. a low factor of forgetfulness.

Even though many things seem to be determined by present flows and movements of immediate action, it is the distortion of stocks of memory which provides the key to economic phenomena and expectations. The interest rate includes a dimension which is linked to time-matter (the memorised interest rate) and constitutes a function of the memory of the variable. It is, therefore, as such, an act of immediate perception of a reality of duration. Any action which, at best, produces a distortion of the immediate interest rate, without modifying the memorised interest rate, is thus at best neutral. A situation of general equilibrium shows that the functions of memory and forgetfulness are stable and that there is therefore no significant distortion of the memorised time-matter. Equilibrium occurs when memory and forgetfulness are stationary.

The interest rate is defined by the immediate interest rate, the memorised interest rate and a risk premium, which is fairly close to the idea of expectation and represents a memorised function of the variable, together with a factor of forgetfulness (a variable is understood to mean the variable and its environment). The memorised interest rate may be considered as a discrepancy between the nominal interest rate and the memory of the economic and financial variable which is used, a notion which can be compared to that of the real interest rate, although it is different. In the case of the inflation variable, a broad definition of inflation will be used, including the memorised inflation of the price of assets. The incomplete estimate of the real interest rate has undoubtedly led to underestimating the powerful stimulating role played by the price of assets in the macro-financial regime which was implemented with effect from the 1990's. This is true of the constitution phase of a bubble and of the deflationary process when it bursts, and finally of the attempted stabilisation by means of the purchase of assets by the central banks. It will come as no surprise if we treat the velocity of money as a global phenomenon (in the real *and* financial spheres). Consequently, the behaviour of the price of assets, whether natural (i.e. left to market forces) or the result of stimulation by the monetary authorities, whether involuntary or voluntary (indirect through the interest rate or direct through the purchase of assets), plays a decisive role in the search for equilibrium in the real and financial spheres. The inclusion of the price of assets in the objectives, transmission channels for the monetary policy and in the response function and objectives of the central bank proves, from this viewpoint, to be relevant. Accordingly, if the real component of inflation (the price of goods and services) is under pressure from deflationary expectations, it is possible to target the stimulus of the financial component. Such a regime was effectively implemented, following the crisis in 2008, which modifies the regime, with the degree of uncertainty and risk which that entails (accordingly, the financial asset, for example the equity market, is both the product of monetary policy and an element of such policy, a sort of conflict of interest). The concept of a memorised interest rate, as defined, therefore constitutes, through its natural or intended distortions, a significant variable or tool for understanding the distortions of the cycle and the equilibria.

One of the principal consequences is that the intuitions and conclusions of Keynes' *General Theory* arguably only constitute one specific instance of a global theory. Accordingly, it is probable that unemployment is not solely the result of a lack of demand for goods but also of inadequate monetary stimulation of the price of financial assets. Unemployment also results from an imbalance in supply and demand on the stock market. Keynes considered one specific case of monetary stimulation of the economy – the demand for goods, a monetary injection on the market for goods whilst, in contemporary economies, injections take place on the financial markets, where they may remain trapped or join the real sphere by uncertain paths. The stimulation of the demand for money for speculative purposes, if one adopts the Keynesian concept, seems destined to have an increasing role within the regime of economic policy action, the efficiency of which is assumed to be greater than that of the budgetary policy but which is also accompanied by risks.

Velocity of money

The velocity of money is defined as a function made up of circulation within the real sphere (inflation of the price of goods and services) and circulation within the financial sphere (inflation of the price of assets), with transfers from one to the other. The question of the stability of velocity requires (i) such velocity to be broken down into two segments, real and financial, and (ii) the introduction of expectations, i.e. duration, memory and forgetfulness. Transactions evolve in sympathy with the stock of money, when velocity is stable. The distortion of velocity is dependent upon the distortion of the memorised real and/or financial variables. Velocity within the financial sphere depends upon the memory of the demand for cash for speculative purposes. Accordingly, an increase in the stock of money may result in financial transactions which are comparatively weaker, due to the weakness of velocity. Velocity is neutral, i.e. of comparable or proportional evolution to that of the stock of money, when the effects of memory are themselves neutral. It is not inconceivable that the effects of memory may have an asymmetrical impact on the financial assets, depending upon whether one is in a period of increase or decrease. In order to produce stimulation, one must accordingly at least neutralise velocity by means of an increase in the stock of money and/or action with regard to velocity. The opposite is required, when transactions increase more quickly than the stock of money.

A monetary policy is optimal when close to the neutrality of the effects of memory and the neutrality of global velocity (whether real or financial). In a regime driven by wealth effects, where financial assets play a significant role, in particular through wealth effects, the velocity within the financial sphere undoubtedly has a position which is at least equivalent to or greater than that of the velocity recorded in the sphere of goods and services. This *global velocity* is a delayed (memorised) component of the demands for cash for the purposes of transactions in goods or services and transactions for speculative purposes.

Global velocity encompasses two phenomena within the real and financial spheres, which behave like communicating vessels. Financial inflation thus stems from a form of transfer of means of payment from the real sphere to the financial sphere. There are three preference functions connected to a referential of memory and forgetfulness: real transactions (goods and services); stocks and long-term financial assets; liquidity.

A disruption represents an acceleration of forgetfulness and therefore a concentration of the memory-space. The phenomenon called a liquidity trap is a phenomenon of extreme forgetfulness: there is nothing left of a memory of demand for cash for transactions, whether real or financial, but merely a preference for liquidity. Between the two spheres, arbitrage and transfer are determined by a form of struggle and competition between the functions of memory and forgetfulness. There is a switch when a preference function (whether real or financial) eventually prevails, i.e. when the memory of one dominates the other. When a central bank reduces its interest rates, it is at first the effects of resuscitating the memory of comparable past periods which intervene, even before the supposed "real", mechanical effects. All economic and financial functions are determined by the effects of memory and forgetfulness, the coefficient factor of which is unstable. This instability expresses the cycle's dynamic.

Absolute and (limited) relative equilibrium

At *equilibrium*, there is a neutrality of the effects of memory and forgetfulness or, if dynamic, an iso-distortion of the factors of memory and forgetfulness. *Absolute equilibrium* is a static situation, where time is absent, a situation which is not very realistic within the observable world. *Limited relative equilibrium* defines a situation of consistency or stability of the factors of memory and forgetfulness within the Subject's space-time referential. *Relative equilibrium*, which is more dynamic and realistic, includes the fluctuations of the said referential and, therefore, those of the factors of memory and forgetfulness.

This is also true of the example of supposed equality at equilibrium of savings and investment. This is only acceptable for functions of memory and forgetfulness which are neutral (*absolute equilibrium*) or consistent in their effects (*limited relative equilibrium*). The equality discussed above is a specific case of global equilibrium. In observed reality, there is a fluctuation of the factors of memory and forgetfulness and therefore multiple equilibria (*relative equilibrium*) which may appear as sub-equilibria. The relative dynamic of the Subject's spatio-temporal referential is dominant.

An increase in forgetfulness indicates an invasion of the Subject's referential by the present or the most recent past. The phenomena of euphoria or depression stem from such forgetfulness. At the extreme point, a pure present of immediacy takes hold, since there is nothing left in the memory other than facts of the same nature and the same trend which are self-sustaining within an extended persistence.

Within the regime of relative equilibrium, whether or not the regime is limited, the discrepancy between the memorised interest rate and the immediate interest rate contains a good deal of information. This discrepancy determines the cycle's dynamic. The memorised interest rate is determined by the tension between forgetfulness and the recovery of memory. Forgetfulness and memory form one unitary function, two aspects of the same phenomenon which is called memory. In limited relative equilibrium, the memorised interest rate incorporates a stable and constant value for memory and forgetfulness. Accordingly, there exists an equilibrium interest rate which corresponds to such a situation. At absolute equilibrium, there is neutrality of the time of forgetfulness and memory and therefore of the unitary factors. Starting from absolute equilibrium, the cycle's dynamic stems from three types of sequential functions: the accumulation of value-time (the time-matter of memory); the erosion of forgetfulness; the recovery of memory. Monetary accumulation and erosion have a profound analogy with the accumulation and erosion of time within the Subject's referential, as we have defined it, by means of duration, memory and forgetfulness.

By way of example, in a situation of recession/depression, until the immediate interest rate (the market rate) has been established below the memorised interest rate, which incorporates a negative memory of activity, no effective action will be taken in respect of the stock of memory of negative activity which will maintain, in a situation where savings and investment are equivalent, a level of under-employment.

The purpose of the action taken in respect of the immediate interest rate, and by means of that rate, is to modify the memorised interest rate. The memorised interest rate itself takes an absolute interest rate as frame of reference (recalling the concept of a natural rate, while still being different), which defines what we have called absolute equilibrium.

In a regime of relative equilibrium, the distortions of the relative real interest rate are produced by the discrepancy (and any variations thereof) between the immediate interest rate and the memorised interest rate. The cycle results from such distortions (it merges with them). And when one assumes the existence of a transmission link between the real interest rate and the activity, one is in fact stating that any dip in activity is an accumulation of a negative stock of memory which must be reduced by increasing the rate of forgetfulness or recall through positive memory. This is what is indicated by a reduction in the real interest rate.

One can consequently understand why cyclical trends may be self-sustaining. The consolidation of the effects of positive memory up to the point that only positive memory remains has the effect, all other things being equal, of depressing the relative real interest rate. If there is a comparable negative effect, the memorised interest rate is reduced, all other things being equal, and, without any movement on the part of the immediate interest rate, the relative real interest rate increases. A positive, rising, real interest rate indicates a memory which is, mechanically, tightening its grip on the activity.

A real interest rate may be negative due to positive effects of memory and, conversely, positive due to negative effects of memory. The dilation and contraction of the temporal referentials are essential.

The distortions of the relative real interest rate form the cycle, which explains the importance of movements of the immediate and memorised interest rates. Finally, there is the absolute real interest rate, which is the point of reference for the absolute economic regime, i.e. which excludes time. The relative real interest rate fluctuates around the absolute real interest rate, which is defined by memory in the sense of duration, which contrasts with the immediate moment. The relative real rate constitutes a point of reference for the relative equilibrium regime, which itself moves around the absolute equilibrium regime. The absolute regime is defined by a concentration of memory and duration which is so extreme that time seems to have disappeared and to be frozen within a fixed point. That which is steeped in matter and memory, and which adopts the substance of matter, is absolute.

Our reality is dominated by the immediate interest rate, which is the only observable one. There are three planes or sections of reality, represented by three concepts of interest rates: immediate, relative real and absolute real, the latter two incorporating the essential role of the memorised interest rate. The memorised interest rate governs the functions of memory and forgetfulness of the financial markets, which provide the keys to understanding them.

A global approach to inflation and the interest rate

The global approach to the interest rate enables one to grasp the extent to which the equilibrium attained on the market of goods and services may include an imbalance on the stock market: equilibria of under-employment linked to the imbalances on the financial markets may therefore exist. This has consequences for economic policy, in particular monetary policy. The simplest illustration involves starting with the most conventional concept of the real interest rate and thus adopting a global definition of the notion of expected inflation (the price of goods and services *and* the price of financial assets). It follows that in the event of a recession/deflation, even though the price of goods and services is on a downward trend (the majority of commentaries then adopt an upward trend in real rates, the price of goods and services falling faster than the nominal rates *and* the real rate only being defined on the basis of a partial vision of inflation, solely the prices of goods and services), the trajectory of the price of financial assets proves to be a determining factor for a full understanding of the real interest rate. The well-understood aim is to obtain a decrease in the real interest rate, which then undergoes, at least in the short-term, an increase in the financial component (the price of financial assets) of global inflation. This may take place naturally, as it were, by means of the positive impact of a fall in nominal interest rates on the valuation of assets, and/or may result from a voluntary act of monetary policy, whether conventional (official market rates) or less conventional (direct purchases of assets by the central bank). It should be noted at present that the distinction between conventional and unconventional no longer applies once (i) the real interest rate incorporates the global notion of inflation and (ii) the price of financial assets is, accordingly, included in the monetary equation and the central bank's response function. A broad range of tools then exists, of which the official interest rate is only one aspect. The definition and action of monetary policy over the last thirty years constituted, in fact, a rather special situation (a partial definition of inflation reduced solely to the price of goods and services, an official interest rate which is the principal tool of monetary action) of a reality which is much more global. The global transformation which commenced with the crisis in 2008 presents some challenges. The price of financial assets is incorporated in the monetary action and response, even though it is not, up until now, contained in either the central bank's official objectives or its mandate or even in the guidance speech which is supposed to provide the markets with points of reference. The price of assets seems to have come into play even before it became part of the theoretical formalisation of the action and the guidance. It is not unusual for practice to pre-empt theory and theory should follow here, since what will increasingly clearly appear to be a globalisation of monetary policy is not a parenthesis but a turning point, thus ending the decades of the Volcker revolution. Challenges will ensue, in particular because the price of financial assets is henceforth both the result of monetary policy action and an element in its own right of the definition of monetary policy action and response. A circle of actions and retroactive effects then ensues between the central bank and the financial markets, which renders obsolete the idea that the central bank steers the markets.

It is more a shared process of apprenticeship, in which there is no obvious answer to the question "Who is driving whom?"

The integration of a global notion of inflation should ultimately lead to the tempering of any alarmism which is based solely on the consideration of the price of goods and services when, in fact, whether naturally or intentionally, the price of financial assets is supported in a context of recession/deflation. The true real interest rate may consequently be lower than many commentaries would imply in a depressed economic climate. If no explanation is provided for this global concept of the real interest rate, the authorities in contemporary economies systematically run the risk of *underestimating* the degree of stimulation at the bottom of the cycle, which contains within it the seeds for future imbalances and bubbles. This only serves to increase the asymmetrical challenge for the monetary authorities with regard to the price of financial assets, such authorities being more willing to provide support when the price of financial assets is falling than to act or prevent when an increase is pronounced. However, the need to take responsibility for the global management of inflation and therefore for stabilising relative prices (which is already, at least in spirit, clearly understood to be a central bank's objective) requires a departure from such asymmetry.

The clearly understood globalisation of the notion of inflation applies to its *expected* component. This means, in the economic context of deflation/recession, which has been taken as an example, that a decrease in the real interest rate must be obtained by an upward stimulation of the two principal components of *expectations* of price, goods and services and financial assets. Since the transmission effects of monetary policy (whether conventional or not) on the price of goods and services are not direct, *a fortiori* in a context of deflationary pressures and a seizing-up of the banking and financial credit channels, the stimulation of the price of financial assets is presented, in the order of temporal sequences and direct impacts (the act of injecting liquidity and/or of purchasing stocks by the monetary authority is effected on the financial markets), as *a priori* the most effective, or at least the most tempting. It is then, in theory, simple to assume a temporal sequencing of the transmission effects, from the financial markets up to the real economy, via the intermediate channels and effects (wealth effects and real cash balance effects, banks and credit, confidence and expectations

...), although it is known that this stimulation may remain, in a way, blocked on the financial markets.

Consequently, three consequences ensue: (i) since the two components of expected inflation are a function of memory and forgetfulness, it is a question of stimulating the positive effects of memory (upward effects on prices) and/or the effects of forgetfulness of downward sequences; (ii) since the adjustment to (decrease in) the real interest rate is effected through the reduction (elimination, reversal) of the discrepancy between the immediate interest rate and the memorised interest rate (decrease of the former and/or increase of the latter), the memorised interest rate which applies to global inflation is decisive; (iii) by assuming a sequencing in which the price of goods and services is more rigid, as it rises, than that of financial assets, action will essentially have to be taken with regard to the memorised interest rate as it applies to the price of financial assets. Since this action can only bear fruit within a certain period, during which expectations are anchored, it follows that (i) the premature suspension or reversal of the action, and especially any suspension or reversal which is *considered* to be premature, will be counter-productive, *a fortiori* if the objective is to do more than offset the negative effects of a continued depression in the price of goods and services: the asymmetrical nature of the action taken with regard to the price of assets imposes a requirement; (ii) the action takes the *assumed* risk that it may lead to a situation of strained valuations (bubble). Since this final configuration of a "bubble" proves to be necessary, it assumes the appearance of a *rational bubble* (it is rational for an investor to purchase that which the purchaser of last resort purchases, provided that there is an expectation that the latter will continue to do so and, at least, will not create any surprises linked to a disorderly withdrawal). It should be noted that the reasoning concerning the components of global inflation can be applied to the components of the activity.

Such developments have an impact for the investor and contain their share of challenges. The legitimate attention paid to the creation of bubbles, on the basis of historic valuation metrics and a return to equilibrium (a normalisation which reveals the artificial nature of the original increase – fake alpha, where the profit is obtained through a position on the future risk fat-tail-,) must deal with the reality of a change in the macro-financial regime, where (i) the *duration* of the phenomena for the stimulation of the financial asset price is *necessarily* extended, at the intentional initiative of the monetary authority, since time is required in order to anchor the expectations, for the reasons we have just discussed, (ii) the equilibrium value matrices must incorporate this dilation of the unit of time for normalisation and also incorporate the transformation thereof. Accordingly, with regard to bond investments in a climate of recession/deflation, normalisation is systematically postulated too early (if it eventually arrives, and for equilibrium levels which are themselves postulated), since the discrepancy between the immediate interest rate and the memorised interest rate is underestimated (even if the immediate rate falls, it is not necessarily equal to or less than the memorised rate, even though, in a situation of a pronounced imbalance, it should be and *over the long-term.*) Investors must undoubtedly (i) pay more attention to the effects of memory and forgetfulness and try to formalise them in their approach to value, (ii) not underestimate the opportunity cost of failing to invest in what we have described as a rational bubble, which is accompanied by a change in the macro-financial regime, insofar as it is effected in an appropriate context; and (iii) treat as such, by isolating them, those assets which are likely to be subject to such a configuration; thus, in such a regime of asset-targeting by the monetary authority, the target equilibrium value for the asset is higher than that which would result from a "normal" calculation, since it involves the production of stimulation effects: the estimation of such an equilibrium value reveals the opportunities and indications for the investor, at least for its tactical arbitrages; in other words, the erosion/lack of "traditional" risk premium, due to the authority's action, conceals a more comfortable premium and, accordingly, the equilibrium value is increased by the differential between the immediate and memorised values (immediate interest rate and memorised interest rate); the investor then takes a long position on a risk premium with regard to the monetary authority's action, which is neither unlimited nor risk-free but which exists.

Accordingly, there exists a memorised interest rate, which establishes an equilibrium on both markets (goods and services, financial assets) and, consequently, an immediate interest rate and a real rate. Consequently, a *natural* interest rate can be defined (that which has not been affected by an economic policy action is natural, that which assumes the existence of a *natural* function of memory and forgetfulness and, consequently, that of a memorised interest rate). The regime of relative equilibrium (i.e. reality) is established in connection with the reference point which is constituted by the natural function of memory and forgetfulness.

The natural interest rate

The dynamic of the financial markets is a process of stocks and flows, within which the price is an element which results in one not wanting a certain stock (at a certain price). The process is as follows: is the price such that I wish to modify the stock (if so, there is a flow). This modification of the stock is similar to the process of erosion of memory. There is an analogy.

The interest rate is the price at which the economic agents will decide to modify their stock of memory-matter. What we call a "flow" represents a movement of a stock of memory at a given interest rate (and therefore a certain rate of memory and forgetfulness, as we have stated). The phenomenon of interest is therefore a discounting/depreciation of a stock of memory (that which is literally stored in the memory and which incorporates a certain rate of forgetfulness or (reminder) memory.)

The natural interest rate is neutral, in the sense that it indicates a situation in which economic policy action does not cause a disruption (or is absent). Neutrality is left behind, when the memorised interest rate diverges from the natural rate. Such situations are characteristics of equilibrium and imbalance. The action on the immediate interest rate moves the cursor between the memorised rate and the natural memorised rate, i.e. the immediate interest rate modifies the memorised interest rate through the intermediary of the natural memorised rate.

A link exists between the fall in the immediate interest rate and the price of memorised value (what we have called the memorised interest rate). The instability of the factors of memory and forgetfulness creates the imbalance. Accordingly, the relationship between (un)employment and inflation only exists if the immediate rates of inflation and (un)employment are able to modify the memorised values of inflation and activity (un)employment. A relationship exists between the immediate data and the memorised values, which does not exclude a form of retroactive effect of memory on the immediate moment.

The price of the financial asset is determined by the impact of the movement of the immediate interest rate on the natural memorised interest rate. On the equity market, the memorised interest rate is defined by the memorised value of the equity yield, the value of which fluctuates around a "natural" value, which defines equilibrium within a regime (notion of the natural rate), the fluctuation resulting from the instability of the function of forgetfulness.

The risk premium (shares) may be understood as the differential between the immediate interest rate and the memorised interest rate (i.e. memorised/forgotten value of the (expected) return on a stock market investment). A strong relationship between the immediate (nominal) rate and the price of shares indicates a situation where the equivalence between memory and expectation of the stock market return dominates the direction of the market. The risk premium is zero, if the immediate rate and memorised rate are completely equal. When the premium is negative, there is a preference for the present and forgetfulness is strong, and only the memory of increases remains. The premium acquires a positive value at the bottom of the cycle (the depressed yields dominate memory and expectations); at the top of the cycle, the premium has a negative value (high/rising yields dominate memory; there is an increase in the immediate interest rate/monetary interest rate). At the bottom of the cycle, there is a convergence of a depressed, memorised interest rate and an immediate rate which is still high. A downward action on the immediate rate takes the premium into negative territory, the price of assets starts to rise; this increase eventually leads the memorised rate, which is higher than the immediate rate at the top of the cycle. The latter's upward action (positive premium through a rise in the immediate rate and then a fall in the price of shares) ultimately carries with it that of the memorised rate. One cycle, four configurations, two negative values and two positive values for the premium.

Our approach can be expressed as follows: everything which is *immediate* in the economic world (i.e. which is instantaneous, appears, makes itself present, is observable) is always and throughout a function of that which has been *memorised* (and partly forgotten), i.e. that which is permanent, normal, natural and of a remainder, a differential which is a risk premium.

The cycle as a function of the value given to time

Time may have more or less value and the temporal referential may therefore contract or dilate. Value identifies itself with such distortions by showing them. There is an analogy between value and time. Temporal density is more interesting than the quantity of time and it is linked to memory. The increase in the value of time indicates an increase in the density of time-matter. The cycle is the process of substituting that which does not allocate an important value to time for that which, on the contrary, incorporates a strong time-value, and vice versa. The distortions of the value given to time are those of relative prices, which form the cyclical dynamic. The cycle can be described as the non-linear dilation and contraction process of the "time value". The phenomena of inflation are the result thereof. The paradox of the value given to time takes shape at the extreme point of the infinite number of preferences for that which comes: it is at the point where the value given to time is at its greatest (preferences in the sense of positive expectations) that the turning point is closest. The risk is greatest when it is in the vicinity of certainty, in the sense that, by dint of being given a value, time ends up losing all value. An explanation can be found here for the successive phases of cycle peaks, dissavings, arbitrages in favour of (in respect of) consumption and (over)investment within the real sphere, for the formation of financial bubbles and the manifestation of various forms of demonetisation. This is also true for the bottom of the cycle. The growth phase, more generally the upward phase of the cycle, arguably represents a dilation of the temporal referential (lengthening of the expectations and increasing projection in respect of that which is to come, intensification of expectations with regard to the future, which is expressed by the notion of risk-taking), with a substitution of that which, within the real or financial sphere, contains such lengthening and such projection, for that which only incorporates it in a limited manner. This arbitrage is admittedly that of the financial market as compared to the real sphere but multiple arbitrages exist within each of the two dimensions. The top of the cycle and its excesses therefore includes a regime of projection which is accelerating, accompanied by an increasing forgetfulness of that which preceded this phase and an infinite substitution of that which is to come for that which is. At the peak of the cycle, only increases in memory and infinite projections in duration and in the density of expectations remain. The switch is identified during the gradual return to memory of that which preceded the increase (whether naturally or following action by the authorities). The force of recall of the effects of memory means that the recession is a process of remembering and of memory. This very memory itself will ultimately lead to symmetrical downward excesses (crash, deflation, under-consumption, under-investment...).

The cycle may be described as a process of forgetfulness, i.e. of erosion of time-value, up until recession, which would, on the contrary, mark the return of memory. The erosion of time-value is a depreciation of the value given to time. There is arguably an analogy between forgetfulness and expansion, between (reminder) remembering/memory and the contraction of the (real and financial) activity. Forgetfulness is accompanied by an increasing preference for that which is not yet. The goods, services and financial assets incorporate a more important future value. Accordingly, one may talk about an asset which literally "loses its memory" in the upward phase of the expansion. Memory and forgetfulness govern the substitutions of preferences between goods and assets and thus the rotations of the stock of money. Accordingly, the substitution of long-term financial assets for the monetary base accompanies the increase of forgetfulness within the preference for that which is to come and goes hand in hand with an increase in the price of financial assets. The same process is at work in the real sphere, where there is a substitution of goods incorporating a lower time-value for goods which have a stronger density. There is an acceleration of the rotation of goods (with a unitary reduction of time-value) and of the number of transactions per monetary unit. The origin of the phenomenon of inflation can be found here. There is a conformity between this phenomenon of inflation and the reduction in the value given to time (forgetfulness). Inflation is one of the manifestations of forgetfulness, in the same way that deflation is an extreme manifestation of memory (of a memory recall). Inflation is the product of a quantity of money and effects of substitution (as between goods, services and assets and within each of those groups), which result from distortions in the value given to time, which themselves govern the speed of circulation of money within the real and financial spheres.

Arguably, a link exists between the quantity of money and the value given to time. This does not mean that the quantity of money influences the value given to time (the latter would arguably decrease as the former increases). Instead, one accepts the idea that a modification of the value given to time means that an increase or decrease in the quantity of money has an impact on prices. Therefore, there is not necessarily a link between the quantity of money and inflation. There may be one *if* the movements of money are accompanied by modifications in the value given to time. The quantitative approach must therefore be increased by the value given to time. Economic policy action cannot ignore the value given to time. Accordingly, the so-called situations of a "liquidity trap" and the inefficiency of traditional actions may be understood by including the extreme distortion of the referential of value given to time.

There is, therefore, monetary neutrality, i.e. an increase in the means of payment which are not likely to cause imbalances, including that of inflation, when, for a given growth of the monetary mass, the value given to time (or its distortion) is stable, this value being defined, in one way or another, on the basis of factors of forgetfulness and memory which are attached to real and financial variables within the referential. Monetary neutrality corresponds to a series of pairings, which combine a quantity of money and the value given to time, in level form and/or in variation, each pairing representing a state of the means of payment (or the growth thereof) for a given state of the Subject's psychological referential, which contains the structure of the value given to time. Monetary neutrality is defined in a relative manner within a relativist theory of the quantity of money.

Monetary neutrality remains a creation of the mind. In real life, the exogenous adjustment and management of the quantity of money (which also includes a more endogenous dimension) will have to take account of the greater or lesser stability of the *function of value given to time* and of the possible existence of asymmetries in this function, at the top and bottom of the cycle, in its relationships with money. Finally, although the function of the value given to time has been isolated within the reasoning, one should consider the links of action and retroactive effect which money has with this function, which leaves a window of opportunity for economic policy.

In an economy which has eliminated time, the question of unemployment does not arise. By introducing time, memory and forgetfulness, one understands that effective demand may be established at levels which Keynes identified as sub-equilibria. Reality is made up of relative equilibria. The equilibria of under-employment are determined by memorised relative equilibrium values of economic and financial variables. The purely cyclical action comes up against the rigidity of this time-matter. We are, consequently, left with the possibility of taking patient action with regard to the fundamental components of this matter (which is called "structural reform") or a lack of intervention, since the lapse of time, as such, ultimately modifies time-matter. Cyclical action is disturbing and ineffective, other than in exceptional circumstances. Structural action is more promising, provided that it has identified the relevant, temporal structures. Self-regulation of the temporal referential represents the means for a mere accompaniment of passing time, which is more effective than human action. In any event, to change means to forget. If action must take place, it must aim to change the factors of memory and forgetfulness, which are attached to certain variables, or to stabilise them. This involves the modification or stabilisation of a *structure*. The functions of memory and forgetfulness define a curve of relative equilibria for a given regime or referential. Moreover, they help define the action variables, through, in particular, the interest rate. Economic policy action is a process which inherits temporal functions – which should at the least be incorporated and possibly exploited - and which produces its own temporal functions. Economic policy action is a process of accumulation of time-matter. The memory referential therefore includes (i) raw facts and events; (ii) human behaviour and action; and (iii) economic policy action, strictly speaking.

The concept of global

The concept of global means that there cannot be a separation of what is real and what is monetary. A global theory targets the conceptual incorporation of what is real and financial, absolute and relative, open and closed, rational and irrational, linear and less linear, of memory and forgetfulness and, in general, all conceptual pairings of economic theory which have opposing polarities. A monetary fact has no autonomy and reality does not operate independently. Unitary interpretation provides the key: (i) the first principle of the global theory is that of relativity. The only economic variable is absolute, the only economic dynamic occurs within a relativity, whether limited or complete; (ii) the global theory does not recognise the separation of the real and monetary spheres. Economic reality is unitary. Reality does not give rise to monetary factors any more than monetary factors give rise to reality. The global theory maintains the integrity of the concept of value by recognising and preserving the multiple relative movements. Preferences determine the relative values within reality and monetary factors. Of those preferences, the important one is that, with money, one should be able to buy goods and services but also that, with such goods and services, one should also be able to demand liquidity or take a risk on long-term assets; (iii) the global theory recognises the existence of a spatio-temporal referential which is psychological, broad and discontinuous. Time is that of duration and memory. Space is global, in the sense that it incorporates the physical (a territorial universality) and psychological (space-time) dimensions; (iv) an authentically global theory will only see special situations within the existing theories. In the same way that Keynes treated the classical theory as a particular aspect of a more general theory, Keynesian theory may be seen as the last theory of an economic science which has become a theory of economic policy action, at the cost of a considerable forgetfulness, which is evidenced by the contemporary specialisation of the discipline. Reflation will require a conceptual reunification of the field (history, sociology, psychology, hard sciences, etc...) in order to recapture that which economics has become in the modern era. It is therefore a global project; (v) the global theory accepts that what seems to be a contradiction is often a complementarity. In particular, there are no absolute economic functions in the world of ideas but rather functions of relative preference for a certain value given to time. Accordingly, the functions of consumption, investment, savings or export all say the same thing and they are only distinguished by the value given to time: they constitute differences of degree, degrees of differentiation of the unitary, global concept of absolute time-value; (vi) an authentically global theory cannot be reduced to a theory of the Subject and only to its action in the world. It is possible to postulate that certain principles are universal, provided that the existence of an absolute time-value is assumed. Consequently, the tools of economic policy action are memory and forgetfulness before monetary policy, budgetary policy or any other instrument of action. The global nature of the action modes stems from the unitary time-value which structures them; (vii) the global theory pays particular interest to the issue of confidence. The phenomena of confidence and distrust are distortions of the time-matter within an economic and financial regime. In particular, one trusts and distrusts in the same way that one remembers and forgets. The main interest is a relationship with that which is to come, and therefore that which has been, and this relationship incorporates what is called confidence. To act means to try and modify the parameters of confidence (distrust), i.e. to take into consideration the distortions of time, such confidence being both absolute and relative to the value perceived by the Subject. Confidence and distrust are the principal manifestations of memory and forgetfulness; (viii) the global theory is concerned with totality. The theories of the modern era have established the force of the Subject and its confinement within a unique relationship of creation and destruction with the world, the technical nature of which is so pronounced that it has finally provided a name for the economic Subject's relationship with the world. Keynes has carried the Subject's force through to completion. He puts the finishing touches to the modern movement but does not terminate it.

The global theory puts forward a few elementary propositions: (i) everything which is economic can, always and throughout, be reduced to a time differential; (ii) the cycle develops from the value given to time, which is confused with the concept of value. The functions of preference and substitution are the result thereof; (iii) the equilibrium is determined by time, memory and forgetfulness. The equilibrium is *absolute* (time is absent), *relative in a limited manner* (the stability of the functions and factors of memory and forgetfulness within a referential), *relative* (the instability of the functions and factors which explain the cyclicity); (iv) the economic facts, phenomena and events may, always and throughout, be described in monetary terms. A profound analogy exists between money and time-matter and money is informed and distorted by time in the same way as a piece of wax by fire; (v) economic policy action is relevant and effective, when it takes into consideration the dimensions of memory and forgetfulness, irrespective of its objective. Whether it seeks to base itself on the effects of memory and forgetfulness or to modify them, in the same way that one diverts a river, economic policy action acts on the immediate moment in appearance only, since it always involves moving a more ancient stone and securing a denser temporal dimension.

The monetary dynamics of liquidity

Liquidity is not an object but rather a means of action for an economic Subject which is defined on the basis of a space-time referential structured by duration, memory and forgetfulness and the fundamental otherness of the Subject from which the exchange stems. Observation shows, at the crudest level, the equivalence which is often advanced between money and liquidity. This leads to assumed relationships between some form of definition of the stock of money and liquidity. As if there were an intuition that a link is maintained between the dynamic management of money and the concept of liquidity, a few variants are added to the crude, static approach, which compare the evolution of a real variable with that of the stock of money or seek to identify the relative variations in the components of that stock. One senses here an incomplete intuition that the concept of liquidity is linked to (i) the economic Subject's action; and (ii) the distortion of the function of money. The Keynesian concept of a preference for liquidity adds a further trail: (i) liquidity is linked to the value given to time by the Subject within its space-time referential; (ii) liquidity forms a certain relationship with the other in the nature of the exchange. An observation of crises allows one to identify liquidity a bit more clearly by means of its disappearance, i.e. by means of the termination of the exchange.

Liquidity expresses a predisposition for exchange and the acceptance thereof. Although the symptoms of liquidity are of a monetary nature – an increase in the number of transactions per unit of the stock of money or a reduction/extinction – its origin lies within the Subject's referential, which is governed by the value given to time and the relationship with the other. The state of this psychological referential is also that of expectations. Everything takes place as if money were *informed* by the structures of this referential in the same way that fire distorts wax or a seal imprints its mark. Since otherness constitutes a fundamental structure of the Subject's referential (the economic Subject is for-others), liquidity is a direct marker of the distortions of this special structure which is the other: that which evidences an otherness, which is favourable to exchange, is liquid. Liquidity indicates, at any given time, a certain state of the Subject's predisposition to others. Liquidity crises demonstrate an alteration of the Subject's for-others structure. Liquidity cannot therefore be understood without returning to the definition of the Subject as an acting consciousness which projects itself, through the action, into the world and into the middle of other consciousnesses, a consciousness which is structured by the space-time referential discussed above and which is fundamentally open to that which is to come and to others. The two essential structures of the Subject are therefore time (the projection is in a state of non-being, of that which is to be done, to come) and the other. The temporal structure, the expectations of which constitute the aspect which is most commented upon, refers to a more complex universe of duration and memory. The other is the person under whose watchful eye or under whose action the projection will take place.

A portfolio is made up of liquid and illiquid assets. This means that, at equilibrium, or one might say in a "normal" situation, such assets are *deemed* to be liquid or illiquid, which represents a certain state of the Subject's referential described from the point of view, first, of the value given to time and, second, of the relationship to others in the exchange. Illiquidity here is not a state of crisis but merely a state of the referential which *accepts* a certain state of the relationship with time and with others. Equally, those assets which are deemed to be liquid themselves fall within a certain state of time and of otherness within the referential. The distortions of the two structures (and also one as compared with the other – the modification of the value given to time distorts the relationship with others in the same way that the alteration of otherness modifies the relationship with time) create the dilation dynamic (in the extreme, the inflation phenomena merge with the increase in liquidity) and contraction dynamic (the disappearance and extinction of the exchange). Price structures reflect such movements and the existence of the price will itself depend upon that of liquidity (liquidity crises are periods when there are "no more prices"). Such dilations and contractions are those of the Subject's referential and they *imprint* the stock of money, which is distorted in accordance with the value given to time and the state of the relationship with others within the exchange. The Keynesian concept of a "preference for liquidity" is, therefore, merely one, specific case of a more global function of liquidity.

The investor, who is characterised by an individual function of liquidity dictated by the characteristics of its referential, of which it must try to obtain as clear an understanding as possible, will be best advised to establish a policy and a governance of the concept of liquidity, when constructing and managing its portfolio. L = f (Li, Lg), where Li = the individual function of liquidity and Lg = the global function of liquidity. A portfolio will indicate, at any given time, a certain value given to time and a certain attitude with regard to the exchange, the composition of an individual function linked to the specific referential of the investor, which owns the portfolio, and a more global function. The whole constitutes what is, strictly speaking, called the portfolio liquidity function.

With money, one can purchase goods and, also, stocks or, to be more precise, with goods one can, also, ultimately purchase money. By turning on its head the fundamental proposition which establishes the development of causality from money towards goods, one reveals the role of the stock market and the phenomena of interaction and retroactive effect between reality and the money market. Money summons goods to it, as it were, through the route of financial assets.

The circulation of the stock of money within the real and financial spheres sustains, through its acceleration, the phenomena of classic inflation (goods and services) and financial inflation. An increase in transactions in one sphere must, *in theory*, be accompanied by a deceleration in the other. There is, at equilibrium, a distortion of relative prices, although the general level of prices remains the same. In an open economy, e.g. that of the USA, which is characterised by a current account deficit, a rise in the dollar balances held by non-resident investors should result in a corresponding decrease, within the USA, in the circulation of the monetary stock within the real sphere, in particular for the purposes of consumption. Since this is not the case, there is *ex nihilo* monetary creation at both ends of the chain.

In theory, there is, accordingly, a given stock of money which turns, like a hamster in its cage, on two wheels, which here represent the real and financial spheres. A unique monetary stock is set in motion in two asynchronous, or at the very least desynchronised, spheres for one sole phenomenon of global inflation, which incorporates two states, one real and the other financial. There is a transfer from one sphere to the other, without any *ex nihilo* monetary creation (the stock of money is stable). This is a situation of equilibrium, in the sense that the general level of prices does not vary: only the relative prices are distorted. The price moderation for goods and services may be accompanied by an inflation of the price of assets (as in the 1990's); the inflation of the price of goods may go hand in hand with a depression in the price of assets (as in the 1970's). In this approach, a rise in the interest rate, against a background of inflation of the price of goods, will cause a form of asphyxia in the financial sphere, where significant quantities of money were originally transferred. The interest rate ensures the regulation of transfers. A rise or drop in the said rate will have opposite, symmetrical and simultaneous contraction and dilation effects within both the real and financial spheres. A depression in the real sphere justifies a lower interest rate; there is then a transfer, as it were, of means of payment to the financial sphere (there is, in fact, an acceleration in the number of financial transactions per monetary unit); a rise in expectations of activity and inflation steers the interest rate upwards, which literally drains the financial sphere. The constitution of a financial bubble requires transfers of means of payment from the real sphere, which can only take place for so long as the real sphere is able to do so, i.e. for so long as the monetary policy is accommodating. Taking this approach, there is a neutralisation and set-off of the monetary and real effects. Financial imbalances are described as residue, extensions of the real developments, without any great degree of autonomy. The system formed by the two spheres is, ultimately, regulated, which leaves the general level of prices unchanged. However, observation shows, on the contrary, a more independent financial sphere; the financial world's retroactive effects and effects of causality on reality; the fact that the return to equilibrium is not at all spontaneous, once one of the two spheres is in a position of imbalance.

The approach described above, in addition to the causal effects of the real sphere on the financial sphere and the financial sphere's low level of independence, is essentially *static*, in the context of a general equilibrium of the real and financial spheres and the general level of prices. If one adopts a dynamic approach, by breaking down the general level of prices into two factors (real inflation and financial inflation), one can describe at least six situations, which are distributed around a line of equivalence and which contain the unitary values of the ratio between the two inflations (the same value, positive or negative values of the real and financial inflations). The four zones around the line of equivalence represent a coexistence of different or diverging phenomena within the real and financial spheres; two zones indicate the broader phenomena of inflation or deflation (the general level of prices).

The real and financial spheres and the general level of prices

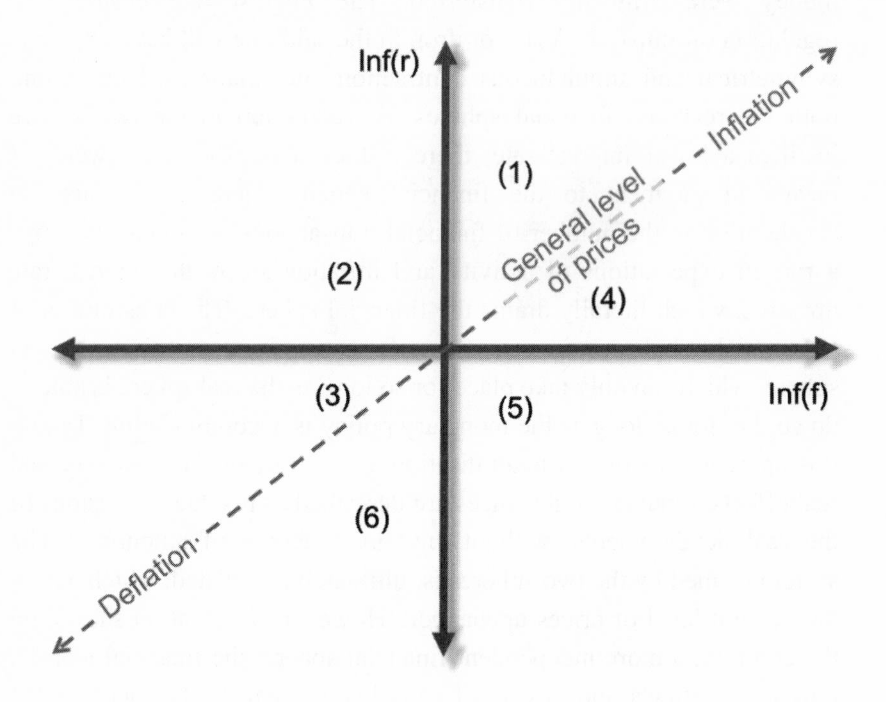

The cycle dynamic steers the rotation from one zone to the other:

(1) if one moves closer to the line of equivalence, one sees a diffusion of inflation from the real to the financial sphere and there is therefore a significant rise in the general level of prices,

(2) a fall in value of the financial assets against a background of inflationary tensions within the real sphere,

(3) a cohabitation of deflation within both the real and financial spheres. A fall in the price of goods paves the way for a fall in the price of stocks, and therefore for a fall in the general level of prices,

(4) the financial sphere benefits from a price moderation within the real sphere. The dynamic may lead to a bubble trajectory,

(5) a low level of inflation of the price of goods combined with inflation of the price of financial assets. This situation exists close to the Inflation (f) axis (an increase in the price of assets, while the price of goods falls deeper into negative territory, is more unlikely),

(6) leads from a dispersion of financial inflation to real prices and then to a bursting of the financial bubble and to deflation, while passing through a fall in the price of goods and services.

This graph requires some clarifications. There is movement from one quadrant to another and also within the same quadrant. There is also a dynamic of situations by comparison with the line of equivalence. To the left of the line of equivalence are situations, where the inflation of the price of goods and services steers the general equation of prices, having a positive or negative effect on the price of assets, particularly if one is located close to the line of equivalence. The opposite direction prevails to the right of the line of equivalence, which is less conventional since, in this situation, the price of assets determines certain evolutions. Movements of the interest rate structure the dynamic from one quadrant to the next and within each quadrant itself. An interest rate exists for each value of the general level of prices, which stabilises the relative prices (real inflation, financial inflation). There are six quadrants and one dynamic, which make the above analyses possible.

The real and financial spheres and the equilibrium interest rate

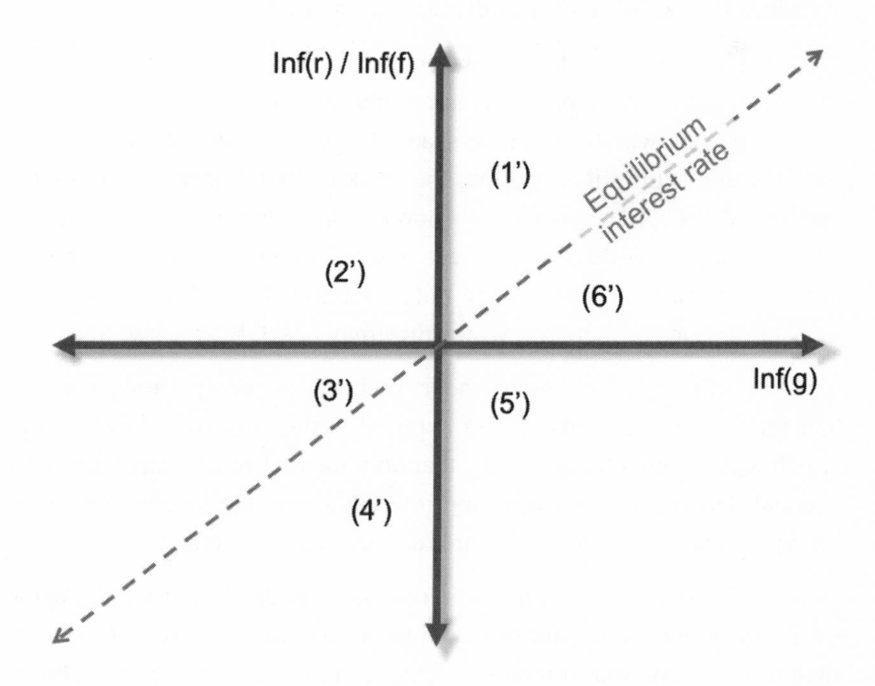

In the original model described above, the stock of money circulates (i) within each of the real and financial spheres, (ii) from one sphere to the other by means of a transfer of means of payment. The stock of money is inert. To take this even further, one must imagine that the two spheres are not governed by a function of set-off (neutralisation – general neutrality of the monetary transfers, adjustment of one of the two spheres in order to re-establish the general equilibrium of the system) and one must substitute liquidity for money as the operational concept for the action. One must imagine that the two spheres overlap and are possibly added together; that the financial sphere is freed from and not an annexe of the real sphere; that the stock of money is set in motion within the movement of the Subject's action which is *liquidity*, which is a movement with/towards/for others; that liquidity as a mode of action imprints the stock of money in the same way that one leaves tracks. The space-time referential (duration, memory and forgetfulness) plays an important role in this imprinting movement.

Liquidity borrows from money as an object and from the Subject's action, under the watchful eye of the other (liquidity is exchange; a liquidity crisis is always and throughout linked to the withdrawal or absence of the other as a counterparty).

There is an analogy between the stock of money and the stock of memory. Monetary phenomena are phenomena of memory imprints. Money is that which remembers and forgets. By driving a stock of memory and setting it in motion, the stock of money becomes liquidity and circulates. All monetary phenomena are determined by links of memory and forgetfulness between the relevant variables. Immediate and contemporary variations are only meaningful for displacements of heavier portions of memory, which they may possibly give rise to.

Velocity, as correctly understood, i.e. as incorporating the real and financial dimensions, is less exposed to the criticism of instability, which was largely due to the fact that only the real sphere was taken into account. However, the space-time referential and the discontinuities of the functions of memory and forgetfulness remain unstable.

The stability of velocity is redefined as the stability of a factor of memory and forgetfulness within a macro-financial regime and therefore a temporal referential. One assumes that there is stability within the regime. This factor may therefore be a target/objective and liquidity, as we have defined it, must evolve in proportion to this factor, in order to ensure relative neutrality within the regime. A change of regime is a change of the relationship with time.

Inflation (the general level of prices) is then defined as a circulation of the stock of money within the real and financial spheres, the intensity of which is a function of the stable, temporal factor within the regime. Equilibrium (neutrality) is attained when liquidity and this temporal factor evolve proportionately. The more or less inflationary nature of a given circulation will depend upon the characteristics of the temporal referential of the regime, by defining the various propensities to inflation.

Monetary circulation will be particularly likely to produce inflation, if there is a significant, engrained memory of inflation and, symmetrically, a forgetfulness of "reasonable" processes which result in a rise in the (general) level of prices; one means by this that the economic Subject is not – at least always – rational, in the sense that a certain theory would like it to be. Accordingly, if the economic Subject were rational – we mean rationality in its strongest form – then the adjustments which prevent inflation from occurring will take place, precisely because the Subject, which is informed of the "reasonable" sequences which may occur – informed by knowledge and even by experience – would implement avoidance strategies. This means that the concept of rationality must be accepted in its realistic and/or positive version: what we tend to call irrationality is part of a realistic concept of rationality, which is closer to the actual behaviour of the economic Subject. Inflation thus returns, not because the Subject is irrational (it should not be lured by the sequences which are at work) but because forgetfulness intervenes, and this very forgetfulness forms part of the positive and realistic definition of the concept of rationality. The economic Subject is rational, in the sense of a concept of rationality understood in its loose form.

Liquidity is introduced in the approach to inflation, as being produced by time from the stock of money, time merging with the action and with a referential of memory and forgetfulness. Accordingly, an increase in the stock of money does not suffice *as such* in order for inflation to appear: that will depend upon the temporal function – memory, duration, forgetfulness – within the regime. Inflation has all the more chance of accelerating, if liquidity, as defined, experiences a higher rate of growth than that of the transactions within the real and financial spheres.

It is not, therefore, the stock of money which sustains the expectations of inflation and inflation itself; as such, the stock of money has no life or action. Inflation as a *dynamic* resides within the transition from money to liquidity. There is a transition, because there is a go-between: time, which *informs* the stock of money on the basis of a referential of memory/forgetfulness of the general variables of activity and price. In this sense, the expectations are *provided*, because they come from far away, i.e. from the past, and have the status of a quasi-external variable.

Accordingly, in real life, the two real and financial spheres are added together and multiply rather than offset each other, the transfers of liquidity from one to the other are not neutral and the cumulative effects of the creation of liquidity concern both spheres at the same time, while increasing the stock of money.

We call all these propositions the *fundamental equation of liquidity*, a reformulation of the quantitative theory of money.

In the traditional approach, imbalances always have a real origin but may be manifested by forms of financial inflation, which may themselves lead to the inflation of the price of goods and services. The financial *sphere* magnifies reality and the only serious, final phenomenon of inflation which is accepted is that of real inflation, since financial inflation is intermediate. We remain within a system of the variation of relative (real, financial) prices and not within a global apprehension of all the factors and transactions within the whole of the two spheres. In the traditional approach, the financial sphere (a concept which is neither that of liquidity nor that of money) is an *effect* produced by reality. On the contrary, there is a multiplication and creation of liquidity within a unitary system, where there is an equivalence which creates two spheres, accompanied by a certain autonomy of each of the spheres, at certain moments in time. This is the theory of creative liquidity, which is dependent upon the two spheres being equivalent. The liquidity dynamic is creative, cumulative and non-linear – discontinuities and dilations – in its expansion phase, destructive, cumulative and non-linear in its contraction phase.

The dynamic process is not that of the allocation of a given stock of money but rather that of the transformation of money on contact with the time of the Subject's action, within the framework of its space-time referential. As such, we cannot "possess" liquidity, since liquidity is itself, always and throughout, a means of possessing the stock of money. Liquidity is possession. Likewise, there cannot be a preference for liquidity, since liquidity is that which appears when a preference is expressed, with regard to money, and a link with the other is established through trade and exchange. Liquidity must be considered as the vast field of money in action. Liquidity is not money. Liquidity is not the risk-free asset but the whole of the structures of relative value of the totality of real and financial assets. The Keynesian grounds for precaution, transaction or speculation define one possible structure for liquidity (risk-free asset) *among others*. The Keynesian analysis remains one specific situation within a more global equation.

Our equation of liquidity suggests that the crisis results not from monetary hypertrophy but from a disruption of liquidity, which is accordingly defined as being produced by time from the stock of money.

The financial veil and reality

Goods are not covered by a financial veil, the financial sphere does not conceal reality and the search for "fundamental" value is not necessarily, always and throughout, an unveiling of the financial sphere. The two spheres form a referential of interdependence. One must, therefore, resist both the (traditional) temptation to place value within reality alone, which is concealed by the financial sphere, and the more recent temptation to place value in the financial sphere alone, which is consequently self-referenced.

The financial sphere discounts and expects in the same way that one/it remembers the past. The financial veil is made up of time-matter and the stock market is a veil of memory and forgetfulness of the real sphere which has a retroactive effect on the real sphere. The stock market preserves the memory of reality. The financial sphere is the necessary veil of reality by means of which reality perpetuates and transforms itself. This veil is powered by liquidity as the temporal differential (memory, forgetfulness) of the stock of money.

Accordingly, one interprets velocity as a function of memory and forgetfulness, a factor which *imprints* money and plays a role in multiplying liquidity and accelerating money. It is a distribution and multiplication factor in respect of the stock of money. One can consequently envisage a simultaneous expansion of the two spheres by means of *ex nihilo* monetary creation. This phenomenon is at work at the turning point of the 21st century on the USA/Asia axis, facilitated by the dollar status.

Essay 11

PSYCHOLOGICAL TIME, VALUE AND LANGUAGE

What is value? Substance, price and exchange[10]

There is a distrust of the very idea of fundamental value. Crises and volatility may explain this. Curiously, proponents of market efficiency and those who cast doubt on fundamental value are united in their decision not to adopt an active strategy with regard to the market, but for different reasons. There is an increasing temptation to abandon *absolute* value (substance) in favour of a unique, relative definition of exchange value. The rescue of absolute value, which constitutes a major benchmark for the (long-term) investor, involves an affirmation of duration as the foundation of value. The essence of value is that which lasts. Value is, moreover, *for* a Subject. Value is given in the same way that one remembers and forgets and value is inhabited by the temporality of that which does not yet exist (action, project). Finally, value is for a Subject in its interrelations with others (exchange).

That which has managed to last (and is, therefore, rare) has value. A fact is a temporary outcome of the action (the substance of value is manifested as a fact through the Subject's action). Value makes itself present in the action (utility), in acting (value-work) and for a Subject which is under the watchful eye of others (exchange). Utility, value-work and exchange are the forms of manifestation of the substance of value. The dimension of otherness is present in the phenomenon of exchange and liquidity, since it is by making themselves liquid for/through the exchange that goods and assets manifest their value. The substance of value is therefore located beyond price, which is

[10] This section restates certain theories discussed in *La Valeur. Substance, échange et prix.*

a manifestation. Price does not extinguish value, which is revealed precisely where there is no price, or no longer any price.

Value as an experience of time

Economic value is an experience of time; it is time incorporated into objects, facts and events. The monetary function links substance and exchange, value and time. There is accordingly no need to oppose substance and economy of relations.

It is important to preserve the substance of value as a concept, in order to preserve the idea of investment and the long-term investor. There can be no long-term projects without long-term investors nor long-term investors without the benchmark or marker of a fundamental value to strive towards or return to (mean-reversion); accordingly an equilibrium value. At a time when distrust is increasing (with regard to the ability to extract this value, to extract it in a volatile economic climate which pollutes it, dilutes it and destroys it; with regard to the very existence of such a value, undermining the very foundations of the idea of active investment over time) and, therefore, also the need to assert investment beliefs in the context of long-term governance, such reminders are undoubtedly not superfluous. Value has two aspects, one which is observable and the other not (substance, the manifestations of substance, in particular during the exchange). When substance is removed, irrationality increases.

In the context of what is more or less observable and of density, value is a result, a process, time. Value is the value given to time, since it is *for* a Subject. Value is thus located beyond any spatialisation of time (it abolishes the tripartition between past, present and future) and cannot be reduced to the point of crystallisation, or the freeze frame, to which it is often reduced, since it is duration, lapse of time, time-process. Value is *continuum* and not a suspension (of time) nor is it a spatial point (of suspension). A *continuum* of duration and not a spatial point.

Value comes to the world for a Subject, through an act of consciousness which is intensely temporal (the value given to time) and under the watchful eye of others. Value is constantly projected beyond the fact and the object where it seems to have come to a stop.

Value manifests itself within the exchange of that which is (objects, realisation, facts ...) but, even more so, in the exchange of that which is not yet, these projects which form the essence of modern economics and finance (which we have called "image-objects" in our work). However, value as substance (time-matter) pre-exists (or prefigures, to be more precise) the exchange.

Value, as we have said, is *a process* by means of which the economic Subject gives value. Although our observation of value originates with objects which are formed in the physical world which is indeed observable, the Subject nonetheless always gives value to an image-object and does so in proportion to a time-matter which is recalled or forgotten. Even after it is incorporated within the object, the fact, *the image* (this negative of the action which is the structure of the project) continues to haunt the thing, a force of recall to consciousness and a summons towards new projections by the acting Subject. The image is the structure which sustains expectations. The images become observable on the financial markets. They are balanced, valued, exchanged or destroyed there. We have distinguished in our previous works between three sequences: (i) the production of images (phase of the imaging consciousness of the economic Subject); (ii) the selection of images (financial market phase) and (iii) the production of the object (impact phase). Economic value is an image governed by memory and forgetfulness, based on an analogy between economic value and the value given to time, which refers to the analogy between the manner in which the Subject projects itself (acts and expects) and the manner in which it remembers and forgets. The most absolute value is a function of the *density* of duration and memory. As such, economic value is a time-value. It is not so much the surface or the weight of the past which are important for value but rather the dynamic density of the concentrations and dilations of the raw material of time as duration. Each spatio-temporal regime defines a sub-set, where value can be defined. This results in dynamics, one of which is specific to the special sub-set and the other that of the sub-sets as between themselves. As such, value is not a static concept (the performance of the action, an eternal in-itself) but rather a dynamic. Any phenomenon of value may be broken down into a static component (the regime's special spatio-temporal identity) and a dynamic component, which is the process by means of which value appears and becomes observable. Without the first identifying component, the second is an incomprehensible and irrational, rudderless boat.

That which is rare is that which lasts and one finds numerous occurrences of a link between that which lasts and that which has value. Rarity states that which has survived, that which has managed to last and which has, therefore, incorporated memory. That which has value and/or, at a given moment in time, "acquires value", always does so from a presence within memory. The acquisition of value *reveals* but does not invent.

Value is located beyond price (it is determined where there is no more price) and beyond the measure of value. At the extreme points, when there is no longer a price, only that which has survived/lasted remains. Duration is concentrated at the highest point. At this extreme point of concentration, value is *almost* static and in-itself but, since it always remains value for a Subject, this point itself is reactivated and is the subject of further projections and actions. Accordingly, value always makes itself present *for a* Subject (relative form) and as such is a measurable phenomenon (value as a measure of value and, therefore, as a price), but its essence is located as close as possible to the concentration of duration and memory.

The monetary function includes, as a sign, the two dimensions of value (value as a measure for a Subject; a concentration of time in duration and, therefore, rarity). A monetary sign is a measure of, and shelter for, rarity. Money contains within it the link to that which lasts and persists and perseveres in its being and, as such, is rare. The monetary function establishes the sign of that which measures and persists, which measures that which persists. Money as a trace of memory, where the precious composition of money (gold, silver ...) is merged with the importance given to time. Any monetary crisis thus expresses a crisis concerning the relationship to time.

Language tends to freeze value (e.g. "that has value", "value is…") and has difficulty expressing (i) the lapse of time which lies at its heart, (ii) the fact that it is *for* an economic Subject and not in the world of ideas. Language provides a spatial expression of time. It is accordingly the source of a good many ambiguities. The profound experience of value merges with that of duration, i.e. that which, from the past, makes itself present as a project.

Value is linked to that which shelters, which sets aside (refuge). Value is shelter, that which will ensure that there will be duration, survival. If value is located close to the concept of a refuge, it is because its essence is connected to a threat.

The concept of value as substance is important for the foundations of investment, since, if it is lacking, concepts such as equilibrium and long-term action are undermined (there will be no anchor in any stable, in-itself value, as shown by observation of prices). The concept of value degenerates into irrationality and paralyses any action, once the being of value (its substance) is denied or fades away. Paradoxically, and from very different starting points, such conclusions, which paralyse long-term action, are consistent with those of the proponents of market efficiency. In both cases, it is recommended to do nothing (in the case of efficiency, a value in-itself exists in some way, which is immanent and the fruit of an invisible hand). Value must be devised beyond these two positions. Deprived of substance, the concept of value will otherwise shift towards the concept of price and will merge with it, a price whose essence is measurement (a modern shift). The link maintained by value with price is accordingly not independent of the place occupied by the form of the market within the economic action process.

Value as a process making substance

Value only exists for a Subject and under the watchful eye of others. It is under this watchful eye that value makes itself present within the exchange by making the economic goods liquid. Value and liquidity therefore maintain a close link with the structure of the Subject and its otherness (others). Accordingly, contrary to the ambiguities of language, which seems to locate value and liquidity within the object itself (value and liquidity are then a quality of the object – do we not say this *has* value, that *is* liquid), it *is* the presence of others within the very definition of the economic Subject which is important. One must go beyond an interpretation from the point of view of things (economic objects), since *it is by making themselves liquid for a Subject under the watchful eye of others that goods manifest their value.*

Accordingly, in the end, the conflict between value and fact is unsatisfactory, in the sense that value arguably refers to that which must be and a fact to that which is. We must look at it the other way around.

We can distinguish between three planes which are all linked: time, the Subject, others; the temporalisation of the project of an acting, economic Subject; the *continuum* of duration against the spatialisation of time (past, present, future).

Value is neither within facts (the action productions) nor in objects. It is not within work, consumption, utility or rarity. However, each of these concepts contains an indelible trace of a more basic substance (time).

Economics and investment can be seen as a normative dynamic (the study of the conditions and processes for transforming the world) and/or as an understanding of the world (the study of the substance(s) which sustain(s) the process of transforming the world). We assert the unitary nature of the discipline and of the two dimensions by giving priority to positive *economics and investment (the understanding of the world).*

Economic grammar[11]

Modern economics and finance are marked by the assertion of the Subject as an acting, temporal structure and of time as duration. All economic concepts, such as consumption or income, which seem to advance within a present of eternity and as grammatical subject of the neutral and absolute economic statement ("consumption *is* this or that thing") are henceforth asserted *for a Subject*, under the watchful eye of others and within the temporality of a *continuum*. In this context, language is both the place of clarification and the place of resistance. The same is true of the past/present/future tripartition, the spatialisation of time, which does not allow one to capture the passage of time and duration. The emergence of the Subject and of time within the discourse of economics therefore creates a tension within language. This results in confusions and misunderstandings, which sustain false, economic problems. This also results in an awareness of more radical limitations which are specific to language: economics is also confronted with what cannot be said in the language where it is located.

Economics as a discourse

Accordingly, economic grammar or the grammar of economics is more than an analysis of economics as a language. It postulates that

[11] For more detailed analyses, refer to *Grammatica economica*.

economics is, in its essence, a discourse, that it is a language. That which forms part of the archaeology of economics as a discourse is an archaeology of philosophical (ontological) and historical forms of language and of that which produces effects/reflections within language. This work must enable one to extricate the *elementary forms* of economic language. The obfuscations of such elementary forms constitute the *economic problem*, strictly speaking. Finally, reality and the word form one whole – the discourse and economics, the effect of language and the effect of reality are one and the same. These four pillars form what we call *economic grammar*.

Language cannot state the continuities, the *effects* of memory and duration. More generally, the manner in which time is stated or shown contributes to the constitution of what we call *economic problems*. How can we state an expectation as accurately as possible? Time is not satisfactorily incorporated into reasoning and language struggles to state time with ease.

The forms of economic discourse are often individual, whilst the Subject is under the watchful eye of others and subject to the action of others. The economic discourse is too often that of a Subject which is alone in the world, of absolute, impersonal forms ("*there is* poverty ..."; "*consumption is* ...").

Economic grammar binds together four propositions. Economics is a discourse, a language. The economic discourse is the whole of the structures and forms which state that which is and that which is to come of the Subject's action. The whole of these forms and structures constitutes reality, i.e. the economic world. The malfunctions and obscurities of all the structures and forms generate what we call economic *problems*, a large part of which stems from the difficulty in stating time. In particular, language speaks in a state of being (this *is* increasing, that *is* the case) without managing to express the state of not-yet-being, that of the projection, the expectation or the action whose design is within this dynamic of that which is in a state of not-yet-being.

We seek to establish time as the Subject's time, this time of the imaging and acting consciousness of the Subject (that which acts, imagines and projects, the action is made up of images); time as matter and a force of obliteration of that which is (the projection, imagination and expectation all *deny* that which is in order to (re)invent it); time as duration, memory and forgetfulness; duration as a series of blocks of temporalities, like a section, a sampling, a survey; memory and forgetfulness as that which drives these blocks of past time, a dynamic of discontinuity; of dilation and contraction. Language experiences great difficulty in stating this.

Within the difficulty of stating time, there is a difficulty in stating that which is in a state of non-being (the projection, the image) – i.e. the fundamental structure of the modern Subject as imaging, and *therefore*, acting consciousness; a difficulty in stating *that which persists*, i.e. duration driven by memory. The expectation is full of time-matter which persists in a non-linear manner. There is, accordingly, no need to separate *past and future*. What we call present has barely any substance, since that which lasts goes beyond the present by merging past and future. It is that which lasts which makes itself *present* to the Subject.

The difficulty of the economic Subject in stating itself within the discourse (which we call the *deletion of the Subject*) and the difficulty in stating time are two aspects of the same reality. Language names the functions of that which is visible and observable (consumption, investment) which represent a simultaneity of the act which is taking place; it does so in the present of impersonality, intemporality and linearity with an individuation of functions (e.g. "*consumption is* ..."). However, economics is the fact of a Subject and its referential – temporal, personal, non-linear and in interaction with others, not in the present but within a duration which mixes past, present and future.

The language of the inner consciousness of economic time

Theoretical statements, by which we mean the structures of the discourse which establish all the economic functions and their arrangement which constitutes the discipline, seem far-removed from *personal* statements, this gap reopening a different awareness of time and the presence of the Subject. *The language of the inner consciousness of economic time* is therefore essential.

The only economic phenomenon is *for a Subject*. Economics is located within the statement of that which lasts. There is no consumption, but rather a consuming Subject, that which is consumed (for a Subject). The act of consuming, which characterises that which is specifically economic, is not consumption. Consumption is not this or that thing but rather a process of the passage of time. "I consume" is closer than "consumption *is*". "I consume" must ideally express that which passes and lasts. We are far from the perpetual present of the function of consumption. Ideally, "there is that which passes, consuming for me and for others". Economic phenomena are not this or that thing. They are temporal processes and not in-itself objects.

That which lasts, i.e. that which is *permanent*, involves a certain state of temporality and, therefore, a certain interpretation of the concept of time. That which takes place within economic language and the specific (psychological), spatio-temporal referential of the Subject – these two structures form one whole – is that which lasts, which passes like a real/psychological *process*. We are desperately short of words to state this.

Economics first and foremost lets itself be *seen* – i.e. be read and understood – as a discourse. Everything starts from this and comes back to this. There is no economic truth beyond the discourse which contains economics. Three sections, three planes can, therefore, be distinguished, which form three orders: the order of discourse, the order of language and the ontological order (the wording, the presence of the statement, that which is and makes itself present within the statement). The original, ontological order is in permanent conflict with the other two orders. There is a good deal at play within the passage from structures, where the economic phenomenon is *grammatical subject* ("*consumption* is increasing") and makes itself present in-itself, to structures where the phenomenon *is for-itself*, i.e. for the Subject and others. Modernity comes from the fact that *the Subject makes itself present* within language and asserts itself grammatically. The order of discourse and statements which constitutes economics has developed within the structures of language, with which it merges and which impose a *reasoning*. The *sequence*, the *apprenticeship* and the *expectation* lay the foundations for a thinking of economics as a process. The modernity lies within the emergence of the *process* as a language within economic thinking. The *economic reasoning* seems to be constructed on the basis of statements which contain predictive propositions and spatio-temporal sequences. The whole forms a reasoning and a grammar. The extreme difficulty in stating time and the lack of thinking of time within the initial, classical thinking are no coincidence. The constitution of a hub of *economic reason* connected to a reasoning and a grammar, at the classical moment in time, constituted a resistance to the thinking of time and the Subject. The rise of modernity is quite complete within the introduction of the two concepts. There are three phases: (i) the absence of time and the in-itself concepts (classical moment in time); (ii) the sudden emergence of time in the wake of the conscious, free and acting Subject (the modern moment in time), the thinking of the *process* is introduced but comes up against a grammar of spatialisation of time and language, a moment in time which is dominated by multiple figures of the Subject and the forms of subjectivity; (iii) the surpassing of the conflict within a statement of *permanence*, of that which lasts and, therefore, of the Subject as pure subjectivity.

There is no other economic thinking than the grammar of language and the order of discourse which circumscribe it.

Three levels can be distinguished within the order of wordings: (i) a *central subjectivity which generates the text*; (ii) a subjectivity of the economic Subject as a principal speaking form ("the Subject consumes") for a *grammar of the Subject*; (iii) an objectivity of the economic fact, object, event or phenomenon as a principal speaking form ("consumption has decreased") for a grammar of the economic fact.

Language constitutes (i) the place where *that which is* (duration) seeks to state itself, (ii) the projection towards that which is not yet (projection, expectation, action), i.e. the negativity which determines the movement – and, in particular, that of language itself as a temporalisation process, (iii) for a Subject which thinks of itself as the other within the action as a process.

Transdisciplinary spaces. Neurology and subjective distortions of temporality

The developments of behavioural economics and some productive parallels between neurological science and the interrogations of economics and finance have both, among others, helped revisit the framework of rationality (e.g. a lack of emotion harms rationality) by incorporating temporality. The notions of immediate or expected emotions, the idea of present moments of the past or of a temporal distortion of memorised emotions (bias) together with peaks of intensity and terminal phases: the referential universe of analysis is expanded (psychological/philosophy, neurology, in particular) and incorporates a new study of time, emotions and preferences.

Studies of neuroscience must gradually be incorporated into the *corpus* of *aggiornamento* of economic "science" in the same way that the rapid expansion in behavioural research contributes, for its part, to that same *corpus*. It is a question of constructing a more realistic and more positive discipline, which involves an understanding of the Subject (*homo economicus*). Initial searches located the function of perception of time within the so-called limbic zone of the brain (which some people call the *insula*, the area of the right anterior insular cortex). Neurosciences thus advance towards a physical identification of that which should be called a subjective consciousness of the self. This is of relevance for the understanding of economic phenomena: the dilation of time, for example, which characterises a number of them, can be argued to be proportional to the emotive intensity. In the same vein, the understanding of neurochemical or pharmacological agents which exert an influence over the perception of time is still in its infancy.

Discounting expected emotions

One of the most promising areas, of those which are close to or intersect with our works, is the idea of a discount rate of expected emotions, higher in the close future and lower over the long-term, which is not so far from that of the discounting of memories in expectation (one expects in the same way that one remembers and one forgets). Also the idea that such discounting functions adopt non-classical forms, i.e. they are not asymptotic functions but rather hyperbolic ones. One finds here certain characteristics of non-linearity and distortions of the psychological space-time of the Subject's referential. Neurology shows, for its part, the link between dopamine activation and asymptotic (exponential) discounting. By placing oneself within the framework of a mechanism of expectations through apprenticeship, one is necessarily tempted by the profound analogy between the expectation model/energy circuit of dopamine *and* the valuation model for option values on an efficient market. Transdisciplinary spaces thus seem to open up, where the brain works like a system of intertemporal arbitrage on a financial market and where crisis phenomena reflect a meandering of the neuro-regulatory systems.

The concepts of "short-term" and "long-term", which are equally intriguing and promising, although difficult to define, might be confirmed and start to be clarified in certain neurological descriptions: accordingly, the pre-frontal and parietal cortices would house those functions which govern the so-called "sophisticated" transactions, a possible but possibly dangerous approximation of the concept of "long-term"; for their part, the limbic regions would house those functions which govern the so-called "immediate" emotions, an approximation of the concept of "short-term". In particular, the function of discounting future emotions which we have discussed above differs from the function of classic discounting due to the existence of a decreasing, multiplying factor, which characterises the activity of the limbic function (a function which, in passing, seems to maintain a link with the phenomena of addiction). The preference for the short-term and the over-activation of the limbic system would maintain links, which are the source of emotions responsible for temporal myopia (short-term). However, at the same time, it is the limbic excitation which will trigger the stimulation of the cerebral cortex, linked here to the concept of "long-term". Such associations attract interest but also raise questions. The concepts of short- and long-term seem to gain very little in terms of understanding or definition, if one removes the short-cuts and tautologies (immediate emotion = short-term; long-term = sophisticated transaction; limbic system = short-term = limbic system). A form of mechanistic determination (neurology) seems to exert its influence over these concepts.

Let us return to the notion of expected emotion. This forms part of a triptych which also includes immediate emotions and the present evocation of past emotions. There is an apparent spatial tripartition of time but attention is drawn here from the *subjective distortions of temporality* which unite with our approach which seeks to describe the Subject's psychological, spatiotemporal referential. Attention is in fact drawn to the discounting of the expected emotions, which encounter the expectations included in the expectations and realisations (the link is not made with the existing analogy between memory/reminder and expectation). The attention drawn to that which from the past makes itself present is just as profuse. The preferences of the theory of choices give way to the agreement/disagreement which will be felt to date in a sort of assessment process of the consequence. We are still in a framework of the emotional perception of time, of distortions and of biases and modularities of the temporal referential. In particular, the discrepancies between expected emotion and immediate emotion, an exponential function, seem to govern the biases. The notion of expected emotion defines that of expectation: an expectation is a projected emotion, together with a discount rate. However, the expected emotion cannot fail to be a certain function of the past (of emotions here). There is a past which makes itself present; a future which is confronted with that which arrives (is immediate). The immediate moment in time continuously assesses expected/anticipated emotions and makes past emotions present.

Definitions of time. Apperception of time and causal asymmetry

Any system is "determined" by the original conditions in which it is formed and emerges. This original bias (limited differences may, however, produce significant effects), and the fact that a certain number of parameters can be measured, because they are statistical, lead to an impression of irreversibility which, however, remains a set of reversible phenomena (and everything will end up joining a set of original conditions, i.e. an original state). This is a set of propositions which we think are at work within economics and finance. The feelings of irreversibility maintained by a statistical system and a mathematical measuring practice (although a very large number of phenomena fall outside this nature), which play their role in the phenomena of extension of trends and continuities, especially in the event of a bubble, of hyperinflation and more generally of distribution fat-tails. The phenomenon of mean reversion is also a reminder of reversibility.]

Fraser's temporal strata include neotemporality (the time of distinction experienced between past, present and future), biotemporality (the time of biological functions), eotemporality (the time of physics, beyond the classical tripartition, a continuous time which does not pass), prototemporality (elementary particles) and atemporality (electromagnetic radiations). The resulting organisation of a certain number of sectors (quantum mechanics, biology etc...) cannot ignore the need to define a referential *for each living being* where intentionality, rationality and emotion etc. are expressed.

Within the referential of economics and finance, there is *apperception of time* and *causal asymmetry* (that which followed cannot have had an influence on that which preceded; the perception of the past is easier and more logical than that of the future; the past, present and the lapse of time seem to be these tangible elements of an asymmetrical perception of time). However, it is within certain analogies (one expects in the same way that one remembers and one forgets) that greater symmetries can be established.

The proposition of absolute time states that time is independent of the space-time relationship which characterises the phenomenon. Space-time *contains* the event and the phenomenon. The relativistic proposition states that space-time is the *content* of the relations between phenomena. Time is absolute (i) with regard to phenomena (events) and (ii) with regard to the Subject. Relative time denies (ii).

The dilation of psychological (economic and financial) time is a function of speed within the Subject's referential, space-time populated with images, and prepares the action.

Habitus, continuum, flat time effects

Memory arguably acts like a clock with an alleviating effect over time (the effect of *habitus*). This position differs from the best known proposition, i.e. the scalar clock, which provides internal time, subjective time, which can be found in the gap with so-called objective time, for a certain number of reasons, including the fact that time acquires even more importance, if it is the object of a design of perception and if this subjective perception of time is generally *a perception of duration* (the gaps between subjective time and objective time are often due to the *apperception of duration*). These phenomena seem to us to be at work within economics and finance.

The effect of emotion on the estimation of time opens up an area of analysis of the adaptive adjustment frameworks in various conditions, situations and contexts. The multiple distortions of the perception of time, the dilations and contractions seem to characterise the workings of the Subject's internal, temporal clock. The perception biases may depend upon multiple factors, the age of the Subject itself being one of them. More generally, the lapse of time and duration are subject to the modulations of perception and absolute duration, in the same way that objective or absolute time gives way to a relative duration (for the Subject) and to the Subject's frameworks for adapting to the modulations of perception (accordingly, a modification of the perceived rhythm of time may lead to a recalibration of memory, in such a way that less beats are associated with a certain duration).

Consciousness plays an essential role in the action, projection, perception and construction of economic and financial facts, events and phenomena. Consciousness is generally a consciousness of time (and consciousness *is* time). In the same way that a succession of musical notes is in fact a passage of the duration of a musical time (that which actually makes the musical act), consciousness is retention (the management of a more or less immediate past, which is more or less intact; certain persons will go so far as to incorporate the recent past in the present) and at the same time projection/expectation (i.e. the construction of that which is in a state of non-being from temporal matter.)

We submit that there is a fundamental analogy between the presence of the past and the expectation/projection of the future within the very structure of the consciousness of the economic Subject and its workings. Duration mixes the past, present and future within a flow of continuities which are more or less long. There is no difference in nature between the perception of music – the musical flow is located beyond the succession of notes alone, which refers to a spatial form of time – and the perception of economic and financial phenomena, between the musical flow and the stock market flow. When I hear a musical note "after" (the term is no doubt inappropriate) the other, the perception is not that of separate fragments but of continuities and fadings which make themselves present and, at the same time, a projection which states both a radical creation where anything may happen and which remains linked to the continuities. The same seems to be true of economic and financial phenomena. The present, which seems not to owe anything to other temporal sequences, remains deeply influenced by the continuities of the past (a paradox of the present, a pure, discrete and autonomous moment *which also* guarantees the unity of time as a flow and as duration). In music, as on the stock market, everything seems to take place according to a temporal *continuum* of memory, the latter merging with the active consciousness of the economic Subject. Music shows us the path of the *continuum* of musical image-objects, i.e. music's interweaving, folds and turning back on itself within a non-linear referential of the elasticity of musical time, which is also that of musical perception.

The time of perception for the economic Subject *is not* a spatialised form of causal successions. Everything seems to take place as if there were no beforehand, no afterwards, nor any now, a *continuum* merging past, present and future and, in particular, as if there were a flattening of the causalities (e.g. by comparison with a past/present/future verticality, a before/after). One speaks of a flat or horizontal causality when, within the Subject's referential, the before and after do not have their traditional meaning. For example, when I remember something, the classic, chronological order of events, as they actually occurred within time measured by clocks, may be reversed. Memory, which is close to the concepts of consciousness and will – whether conscious or unconscious – plays a determining role therein, within a referential of flat causality and, therefore, of chronology *modified* by comparison with the usual points of reference.

CONTENTS

PART II

THE DYNAMICS OF THE FINANCIAL MARKETS

PART III

DURATION, MEMORY, FORGETFULNESS AND ASSET PRICES

Cet ouvrage a été achevé d'imprimer en juin 2014
dans les ateliers de Normandie Roto Impression s.a.s.
61250 Lonrai
N° d'impression : 1402305
Dépôt légal : juin 2014

Imprimé en France